Tomorrow Can Wait
Exploring Europe with Our Autistic Child

Monika Scheele Knight

Edited by Scott Knight

this book is for John,

the boy with a candy agenda
who bites into the garbage can
and plays the guitar as a stand-up bass.
a partisan and a master of pure being.

SCHEELE KNIGHT

CONTENTS

TOMORROW CAN WAIT

Aren't we quite presumptuous,
assuming that, as soon as we first meet,
we should understand each other.
Let's try again.

(Javier Tomeo)

SCHEELE KNIGHT

BEING IN THE WORLD – PROLOGUE

In each illness, two historical events meet:
A person's story, and a story of the society that he or she lives in.
(Maurice Dorès)

Our son John was born in Arlington Heights, Illinois in September of 2000. He was eighteen months old when he suddenly developed seizures and was admitted to a Suburban hospital. His hospital crib was equipped with padded bars surrounding him like a cage. A cord attached to a clamp on his big toe led to a monitor. The display read 126/96 in red digital letters. Our previously happy, strong, and curious child lay in that cage exhausted from pills, examinations, and seizures.

Two weeks before everyone had considered him a normal child. Then one day we noticed a strange jerk in his arms that repeated itself in a more pronounced way four days later, the arms flailing forward, the head nodding towards his chest. We described the event to our pediatrician, who immediately sent us to get an EEG to measure his brain activity. The very same day we received the diagnosis prosaically over the phone: "Your child has epilepsy. He needs to be admitted to the hospital as quickly as possible."

The seizures quickly developed a frightening frequency and we were transferred from the suburban hospital to the Epilepsy Center at the

University of Chicago. A two-year odyssey in the U.S. and Germany followed as countless experts from both continents were stymied. Medications were increased and decreased, combined and discontinued. John was caught up in a relentless cycle of seizures and side-effects of the medications. As a reaction to an anticonvulsant known to affect the skin he developed neurodermatitis that remained indefinitely even after discontinuing the medicine. An aggressive ACTH hormonal therapy was aborted when the cardiologist diagnosed a life-threatening thickening of John's heart muscle. During a genetic screening in which we were primarily looking for the Fragile X syndrome we discovered instead that John had a metabolic disorder called G6-PD-deficiency. We were given an emergency ID and a long list of substances and medications that could be life-threatening for him. For four months, we also tried the ketogenic diet which is a medically observed intervention that had helped some individuals with refractory epilepsy. To no avail. The Epilepsy Center of Bethel in Bielefeld, Germany investigated our final option, brain surgery, but the seizures originated in too many different parts of the brain. The head of the neurosurgery department bade us farewell with the words: "You have to get used to the idea that your son will have seizures every single day and night, as long as he lives."

As if to contradict this careless appraisal, John became seizure-free as mysteriously as the fits had started shortly after our discharge. Nevertheless, even without seizures and medication his development didn't pick up. A psychologist recommended a visit to an autism diagnosis center. Our search that had begun two years earlier in room number 218 of a suburban hospital near Chicago ended after a ferry ride over the Weser river. The autism center of Bremen tested John for two hours and diagnosed him with Early Childhood Autism.

Autism is a pervasive neurodevelopmental disorder with a heterogeneous spectrum of occurrences, in which social interaction, perception and communication can be affected in varying degrees. The observations that eventually led to autism being perceived as a syndrome can be traced back to the nineteenth century to German psychiatrists Karl Ludwig Kahlbaum and Emil Kraepelin. However, it wasn't until Swiss psychiatrist Eugen Bleuler used the term autistic as a symptom in connection with schizophrenic patients at the beginning of the twentieth century that the history of autism took a decisive turn.

As an independent syndrome autism has first been publicly referred to by Austrian pediatrician Hans Asperger in 1938 in a lecture called *'Autistic Psychopathy' in Childhood,* and by Austrian psychiatrist Leo Kanner in 1943 in an article called *Autistic Disturbances of Affective Contact.* Though both men were Austrian, Asperger lived in Vienna and published in German while Kanner published in English and lived in the U.S., where he founded the first Child Psychiatry Research Center at Johns Hopkins University. Communication between the U.S. and Austria was disrupted in World War II, but it's probable that both men had read Bleuler and they certainly shared the same intellectual background, so the coincidence isn't entirely surprising. Other scenarios were speculated upon, though. For example, Leo Kanner could've also heard of Asperger's term from Jewish researchers who had fled Nazi Germany. Kanner helped refugee scientists establish themselves in the U.S. and Hans Asperger had suggested as early as 1934 in a letter to several colleagues that autism might be a useful diagnostic term. At any rate, it is certain that Asperger and Kanner weren't in direct contact and that the children they applied the term autism to were different from one another. Hans Asperger described children who spoke but had social difficulties, obsessions and special interests. Leo Kanner, on the other hand, dealt with children who were more severely affected, i.e. who either spoke noncommunicatively or not at all, and who were prone to repetitive behavior. The broad spectrum that we perceive today as autism can be traced all the way back to the term's double-origin.

John was on Kanner's low-functioning end.

We settled in Berlin. I had left my American employment when John had first been admitted to the hospital and I hadn't returned after the three months allowed for by the Family Medical Leave Act, since we had spent almost two years in and out of hospitals. Once John was seizure-free and attending a special-ed preschool for autistic children I started to work as a freelance translator and program coordinator for North American travel groups. Scott continued his American employment at first, but eventually also relocated. He took German language courses and started to work as a freelancer as well, to give us even more flexibility for John's care.

Germany has universal healthcare. In 1995, a Caretaking Act introduced benefits to acknowledge and encourage caretaking at home. Since then, every family receives benefits from their health insurance once a child is diagnosed and evaluated, regardless of family income. There are three levels of care, ranging from $300 to $900 per month. The Caretaking Act also provides other benefits, for example assistive technology, short-term care, convalescent care in specialized centers, as well as respite benefits. All of the services aim at enabling a family life beyond institutionalization.

With John's multiple conditions he was put into the highest level of care, and therefore into the highest bracket of benefits. We were able to build a good support system. With the respite benefits, a couple of caretakers occasionally came to our house in the evenings or during the weekend. It gave us the chance to go out to dinner, the movies, attend readings and concerts, and spend time as a couple. A social worker was approved to work with John in the afternoons after preschool. Our caretakers were all educated and well-trained in autism. John appreciated them, and they in turn showed affection for him. It felt good that John learned early on to let other people into his life. We greatly appreciated the services put in place to help us.

I had started to attend parent meetings inside the hospitals and had continued to do so following John's discharge. His preschool offered regular meetings as well. The stories I heard were discouraging at times: Tales of struggle and isolation. We knew we were inevitably in for a struggle. Life with multiple disabilities wasn't easy, no need or use denying that, but surely there must be something we could do to counter isolation, we thought.

During one meeting, a sixty-year-old mother talked about life with her thirty-year- old son. From Monday through Friday from 8 a.m. to 3 p.m. he attended a workshop for persons with disabilities. Apart from that he was unwilling to leave the house or interact with others. The mother spent the afternoons and evenings alone with him in the house, as well as weekends, during which he refused to put on anything other than his pyjamas. They ensured that he didn't have to go out. Then there were the holidays when the workshop was closed, sometimes for several weeks at a time. The mother talked about her isolation. Her husband had left several years before. Apparently it had been too difficult for him. She said that she understood his decision. Unfortunately, it didn't leave her with many options for herself. She didn't want to place her son in a residential institution, and at her own house she wasn't able to enforce necessary changes in her son's routines.

She spoke to me intensely and sincerely: "Your son is still small. Train him early on to be part of normal activities, to be in the world. That's why I come to these meetings. I hope that young parents can learn from me. My son and I live in our house as if it were a desert island, completely isolated. Don't let it get that far." John was only three-and-a-half years old, but maybe it was already time to craft a plan to be in the world, as she had put it.

Studies of emotions have shown that the areas in which autistic children differ most from neurotypical children are feelings of shame, compassion, guilt, and the consideration of other individual's feelings. The deficits are in areas that require an awareness of someone else's self being different from that of your own. However, studies have also shown that autistic children can hardly be distinguished from neurotypicals in other emotional aspects. They can be influenced by moods around them. They can feel proud, shy, or jealous. These are feelings experienced on your own; they don't require a sense of someone else's self. Having problems understanding other people's feelings doesn't infer the reverse assumption that autistics themselves don't have feelings. They aren't numb or insensitive as has sometimes been described in the past. Quite to the contrary, their inner life seems to be rich and closely connected to the outside world.

Dawn Eddings Prince, an autistic woman, wrote powerfully about her feelings of connectedness: "Since I remember – and that is from my own beginning – I have been pierced and pained by the intensity of life. I knew from my earliest years that I lived in a culture that trains disconnectedness. Even still, though, as an ageing woman, everything – from blackberry leaves to bends in the stream – has a personality to me, a kind of resonance that is an extended reflection of myself inviting friendly familiarity. My world is a place where people are too beautiful and too terrible to look at, where their mouths speak words that sometimes fall silent on my ears while their hearts break audibly. I wonder how the world avoids going deaf from the din of breaking and thrilling hearts and the roar of unshed tears and uncried joy. I don't have a good sense of where I start and end and where the things around me have boundaries. I am always a living part of a living world."

These anthropomorphic descriptions struck a cord. Scott and I had similar impressions regarding John. From a very early age, he saw things that we didn't see and heard noises that we didn't hear. When John had been three years old, a brainstem audiometry had revealed that his brain received a vast multitude of sounds, above and beyond average for his age. His brain didn't filter and prioritize sounds appropriately. Simply by trying to follow his lead we occasionally discovered what moved him. One evening, for example, John laid on the floor in our living room, underneath the window and a pulled curtain. He giggled and seemed utterly happy, but we couldn't understand it until I laid next to him, looked up as he did, and discovered that the curtain's grey-and-white pattern swayed in the warm air streaming out of the heater, and the pattern's movement between the clear light inside and the descending twilight from outside created light effects that were constantly changing and amazing to look at.

  A common, yet misleading, catchphrase for autistics is that they live in their own world. According to our experiences with John, an autistic person rather experiences the same world in a different, yet also powerful way. Like Dawn Eddings Prince described, John also sometimes seemed to coalesce with the world around him in a way that left him unprotected against its force, and thereby unable to distance himself enough to grasp a bigger picture.

I had worked in travel for many years, and we had always traveled a lot. Considering the depths of autistic perception and feeling, we thought that the experience of new surroundings could possibly be joyful for John as long as we could prevent sensory overload and be sure that John's special needs were met on the road. By seeing new places we could perhaps offer him new opportunities to experience his special connection, and while doing so he might learn that stepping out of one's routine wasn't only an inevitable part of life, but could even be positive. Why not try travel as a means to *be in the world*?

There was also an egotistical aspect to the idea, though. It would be something that we as parents would enjoy. In general, obviously, your own interests don't just disappear when you become a parent, and a child with a disability is also part of a family: A number of people who live together but who also still have individual wishes, dreams and interests. Dealing with a chronic illness like epilepsy or a lifelong disability like severe autism would probably bring with it setbacks and require more compromises than a family without these conditions would likely have to face. Nevertheless, we hoped that the pendulum wouldn't necessarily have to swing into full-force sacrifice. If we wanted to live together, everyone would need space. How could you otherwise be resilient in the long run? If traveling proved to be a horrible and overwhelming experience for John we couldn't continue with it, but if it worked it would be a great common denominator.

Emily Perl Kingsley wrote a parable in 1987 about the experience of having a disabled child. "Welcome to Holland" became widely popular. The parable compares expecting a child to planning a trip to Italy. After months of preparation, the suitcases are packed and you get on a plane. A few hours later, it lands and the flight attendant announces: "Welcome to Holland!" You intended to go to Italy, but you're stranded in the Netherlands instead. Life there is slower and not as thrilling as what you heard of Italy, but after a while you realize that there are windmills and tulips, and there's even

Rembrandt. The text draws the conclusion that you could mourn the loss of Italy for the rest of your life, but then you'd never be free to cherish all that's special about Holland.

On the surface, the parable is conciliatory. It does, after all, acknowledge the beauty of both countries. It still also establishes a clear dichotomy, though. Here Italy, there the Netherlands. The family with a disabled child is restricted to living in a different country. There's a critical response online called "Farewell to Holland." It points out that being stuck in the Netherlands really means that the family with a disabled child lives in a ghetto, no matter how many tulips they plant in it. In the Farewell version, the parents eventually tear the Rembrandt off the wall, walk into a travel agency, take home a bunch of brochures, turn the globe and pick a destination with their eyes closed. It was only much later, long after having read both the parable and its counterpart and after having gone on many trips, that we came to realize: We literally put the critical response into action.

1 THASSOS ISLAND (GREECE) – LANGUAGE

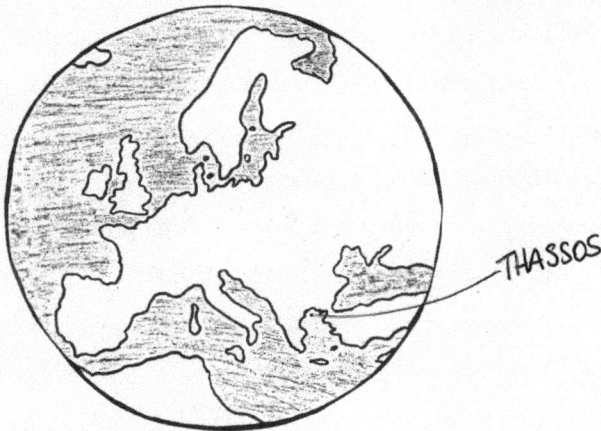

All writing is a sin against speechlessness.

(Samuel Beckett)

The morning after the mother of the autistic adult so effectively conveyed her sense of isolation at the parent meeting, John went off on his bus to preschool and I made myself some tea and started to search the internet for travel destinations. Most offers were for Spain, Italy, and Greece: The three most popular countries for German travelers. I had been to Spain and Italy, but never to Greece. I immediately found an inexpensive offer to fly from

Berlin to Thessaloniki and was then off to the city library to check out guidebooks on different parts of Northern Greece. One was on the islands of Thassos and Samothraki. Thassos could apparently be reached by a three-hour bus ride from Thessaloniki to the city of Kavála, and then a ferry-ride out to the island. It was remote, yet still accessible.

John got up early every morning and he needed to be kept occupied. Thassos seemed large enough for that. We would also need a quiet home base, so I went back online and found a website advertising rooms in a pension run by a German woman and her Greek husband. Quicker than imagined, we were booked for ten days during John's Easter break. I figured we would spend two nights in a hotel in Thessaloniki to get acclimated, then one day of travel to the island, ten days on Thassos, and then one night back in Thessaloniki again before our early morning return flight back to Berlin. Altogether two weeks of travel.

Scott was working and I didn't want to take along family or friends. We had been in a whirlwind of action. The focus had at first been very medical, just to get the seizures under control. When everything had calmed down, John entered preschool and had been diagnosed with autism. I looked forward to spending time alone with him in order to adjust to all the shifts that had taken place. In regards to epilepsy, the course of action had been quite clear. Certain medications were indicated for certain forms of seizures and if one medicine didn't work, one moved on to the next, following a more or less generally agreed-upon process. Autism was a murkier issue. The cause was widely unknown. It was genetic, that much seemed clear. One of the first indications had been a study on twins by psychiatrists Michael Rutter and Susan Folstein in 1977. Out of twenty-one pairs of twins associated with autism, 90% of identical twins were both autistic, while only 10% of the non-identical ones both were. Newer studies had obtained less obvious results, and at any rate only a fraction of the genes involved had been discovered. Due to the uncertainty, there was an array of highly speculative causation theories. Even more disturbingly, there was an array of therapy suggestions as well, many of which seemed to be outright quackery to anyone who appreciated evidence-based treatments. There were as many opinions out there as stars in the sky. I would have to dig into the history and science of autism to make sense of this, but in the midst of the disturbing fuzziness that initially presented itself, I first and foremost needed to focus on John. More than anything else it seemed to me that such a pervasive matter would require familiarization, if only just by time spent together.

John was three-and-a-half years old and not speaking, and we weren't sure just how much he understood. He seemed to get the meaning of some things, but he also often got it wrong. If you said: "Please sit down," he might sit down. If you said: "Please take the spoon," he might also sit down, though, or put something down that he was holding in his hand. He obviously understood that he had been asked to do something, and in his touching effort to comply, he'd try various things.

Even though John didn't speak, he was close to us and others who were around him often. Rather than sitting on his own or next to us, he preferred to sit down on our laps. He enjoyed cuddling. He demanded our attention. Certain stereotypes about autism fitted poorly. John was very attached. Communication was the main challenge with a mostly nonverbal child. I was absorbed by language and John wasn't. Once language has pervaded you, it is always there, inside you. It hovers over everything. You cannot undo it, you cannot lose it deliberately. To a certain extent, we were in different realms, but there was much more to us than verbal language. The difference had to be permeable somehow. Greece appealed to me because I couldn't speak or understand Greek. I didn't even know the

Greek alphabet. For some reason it occurred to me that it might help if we were in a place where I was verbally just as lost as John.

After booking the flight and the room on Thassos, I looked for a hotel in Thessaloniki, printed out the bus schedule to Kavála, and checked out some maps, a dictionary, and a basic Greek language guide at the library. In the evenings, I sat down with John, looked through the guidebooks and explained that this was where we'd fly to. He seemed moderately interested in the pictures, though I wasn't sure just how much of the plan he understood. If any.

On March 31, 2004 we took the subway to Tempelhof airport in Berlin. John was excited. The spacious entrance hall invited him to run up and down. He couldn't get enough of it. As we were allowed to pre-board, John was already sitting in his window seat by the time the crowds piled in. He had flown between the U.S. and Germany, so he knew airplanes. He always enjoyed taking off and landing, it was just the inactivity of the in-between that got him bored and restless. In Thessaloniki, we took a taxi to the hotel, dropped off our luggage and immediately went for a walk. After sitting on the plane, John was anxious to move. We found a playground and he exhausted himself swinging, climbing, and jumping. Afterwards, we ate in the port district of Ladadiká. John went to bed late, which I had expected after all these new impressions, but as usual he got up early the next morning, which gave us an entire day to explore the city.

We passed countless churches, mosques and Turkish baths: Layers of history unfolded as we walked by. Close to our hotel was the church Ágios Dimítrios with its mosaics from the seventh century. We went into the Modiano market hall and saw the Galerius Arch. I pushed the stroller uphill to the old town, and we were rewarded with magnificent views overlooking the city as well as out to sea. On the way, we passed a graveyard with scattered, broken headstones and rubble laying around. I consulted my guidebook. Apparently, the graves were dug up and re-used after only a few years. Many of the old stones and decorations had just been tossed to the side.

After our second night in Thessaloniki, it was time to move on. We boarded the bus to Kavála and this proved to be our first difficulty of the trip. I hadn't anticipated it, because John usually loved to ride on buses, but for reasons unknown, he didn't like this one. Three long hours ensued, during which I had to be creative to keep John entertained and somewhat contained. I tickled him, I sang his favorite songs – never mind the other passengers, this was surely better than John's tantrums. Once we were on the ferry in Kavála, things changed for the better again. John loved water. Looking at the waves swooshing by kept him busy. We entered the island at the port town Skala Prinou an hour and fifteen minutes later and took a bus to the seaside village of Potós, where our pension was located. Unfortunately, the forty-five minute bus ride into Potós was again difficult. My plan to explore the island by using the public bus system would likely have to be adjusted.

Finally at the pension, the owner greeted us warmly and showed us to our room. It had a balcony and a shared kitchenette in the hallway. We were the only guests this early in the year, so we had the kitchen to ourselves. Upon our first exploration of the village, we found that there was construction everywhere. The pension owner explained that they were still preparing for the tourist season. We had come at a time when there were almost no tourists on the island. This was something I hadn't known, but it was just as well. John wouldn't have to deal with crowds of people – something he wasn't too keen on anyway.

On our first morning on the island, I felt full of energy to explore. A traditional mountain village called Theologos was located around six-and-a-half miles inland from Potós. Theologos was the old island capital. It had an old stone bridge and a church worth visiting, St. Demetrios. A German couple ran a small horse farm outside of Theologos offering therapeutic horseback riding. That might be something for John. I took along the stroller for emergencies. John liked to run randomly, rarely keeping a straight path, never following a certain direction. We barely made it out of Potós when John went on strike for the first time. He wanted to get into the stroller, so I pushed him for a while, and then urged him back out again. As the small path trailed uphill, his refusal to walk strengthened. He went back in the stroller. I decided to leave the scenic off-road path, as the pebbly ground was impossible to manoeuvre, and switched to a less scenic but more manageable paved route.

We passed many shrines along the side of the road. This was new to me, but I learned later that they could be found all over Greece. We also passed a goat running around freely. I stopped an old pick-up truck that passed by in the opposite direction, pointed to the goat and asked in English if it might have escaped. When the farmer didn't understand, I fumbled around with my dictionary and language guide, and when he finally understood, he laughed heartily and I understood that he expressed something like: "No, that's okay. That's normal." In the course of our walk, we would then see all kinds of sheep, goats, donkeys, and dogs running around. This was the norm here. No wonder the farmer had laughed at my question. Being in a foreign place for the first time one doesn't have a concept of the norm. So much for the stability and reliability of normalcy, I thought.

I pushed John uphill, we took several breaks in-between, and I let John run around off the side of the road. The gnarled olive trees sparked his interest, possibly because they looked so different from any other tree he had seen. The weather was beautiful, John seemed happy and this was exactly what I had hoped for. A remote setting where he could just be and explore nature, which was something he always enjoyed.

Eventually, we arrived in Theologos, found a small convenience store, and enjoyed a picnic lunch on a deserted playground. We explored the charming, rustic village a little while longer, and then set out for our return. On our way home, we found the horse farm, and indeed, they did offer therapeutic horseback riding. They had a horse that had lived at a facility for persons with disabilities near Heidelberg, Germany for many years and now enjoyed retirement in Greece. Of all places, we met a horse from Heidelberg at this far corner of the world. Scott and I both had relatives there.

I made an appointment for a couple of days later, and we continued our walk back down to Potós, John happily observing everything from his stroller. He surely enjoyed getting away with being pushed around, but I wasn't going to put up a struggle about it. We were here to have fun, not to train behavior. By the time we made it back it was already evening, and before returning to the pension we stopped at the local grocery store where I bought some basic necessities for cooking dinner. While visiting foreign countries it was always interesting to discover new foods and different products. It was fascinating for John, too, since food was one of his favorite subjects. At the check-out register, the woman asked me in English: "Oh! Are you the woman who pushed a stroller all the way up to Theologos today?" She shook her head, half incredulous, half amused. Apparently, our walk had been the talk of the village that day.

We returned to the pension, had dinner and then went to the beach for a while. Ever since John had been a baby he had loved water: Taking baths, splashing in puddles, watching and listening to the rain. Sometimes water made him active, at other times it calmed him. He ran up and down the beach. I, on the other hand, was exhausted. The hike up and down, thirteen miles altogether, had been a little bit of a crazy thing to do. Looking at it later, I was glad that I made it up to Theologos and back. It became somewhat of a guiding expression for me. Whenever I wasn't sure if we could overcome a particular obstacle, or handle a certain situation, I thought back on pushing that stroller up to Theologos.

I made another attempt to walk with John the next morning, this time to the neighbouring town of Limenaria, roughly two miles away. Yet again, John didn't want to walk. I had to find a new solution. I didn't want to struggle with this on a daily basis. I had seen a small car rental office upon our arrival on the island. The pension owner helped me to make a booking, and John and I took the bus back to the port of Skala Prinou and picked up a car. John was elated at the sight of our new means of transportation. Exploring by car was more convenient and less stressful. I turned on the radio and found some music. John sat in the back seat performing his signature *Sitting Rowing Dance*, as we called it – his arms along with his upper torso rocking back and forth as if he was rowing a boat, his smile revealing his utter joy.

The next morning we had our appointment with the Heidelberg horse, but John was terrified and didn't want to go anywhere near it. The owner then had an idea: She had a small donkey that she had found in the mountains. Apparently, a farmer had just left it there to die when it had become too old to work. She had rescued several such abandoned animals. The donkey was very patient, and its much smaller size compared to the horse didn't seem as intimidating to John. He was willing to mount the donkey, a bit afraid in the beginning, but he got more confident quickly. I made an appointment to return a couple of days later.

For our next excursion, we drove out to the peninsula of Alikí and its ruins of a holy site from the seventh century B.C. John was especially impressed with a large Roman sarcophagus. He circled it and looked attentively into the ditch surrounding the huge block of stone. Alikí also had an antique marble quarry site where John ran his hands over the stone. I was impressed at how keen his perception was. If you saw him erratically running around you wouldn't think that he noticed much, but he did. The urgency and purpose of his movements suggested meaning, even if you couldn't interpret it. We were alone on the peninsula and had plenty of time to explore. I allowed John to run around in the ancient ruins, but followed him closely. There was something inherently nice about not having a goal. We didn't have any appointments or commitments. I was able to simply follow along with John's rhythm. I had brought along a picnic for lunch. As long as we had blue sky, it was all we needed.

We fell into a rhythm of getting up early, driving to different parts of the island, bringing along sandwiches, roaming around until the evening (or as I liked to call it: Drifting), then grocery shopping on our way home, cooking at the pension, and taking our evening walks to the beach. John found wells, cisterns and fountains wherever we went, as if he had a sixth sense for them. This wasn't entirely surprising as he had always been drawn to water, but the way he found the sources from far away was still remarkable to me. The pension didn't have TV or internet access, and the local grocery store only carried Greek newspapers, so I had no idea what was going on anywhere in the world.

In the town of Megálo Kazavíti, we happened upon a huge concave sycamore tree. The hole in the middle was so large that it literally separated the tree into two parts. John was fascinated and climbed into the hole to examine the inside. He ran his hands over it, he stuck his nose in to sniff around, and he seemed completely taken with it. He came out and felt the bark and then went back in to again touch the inside, perhaps comparing the two surfaces. I couldn't help but wonder: When he experienced things in such an obviously intense way, how did he process these impressions? Was this an entirely physical experience? A way of being in the world that was exclusively immediate, situational and transitory? It couldn't be. I had noticed many times that John rarely forgot places.

When he was barely two years old, we had visited my grandmother in Northwest Germany. John had taken an interest in the geese in her neighbor's backyard. When we returned several months later, John had jumped out of the car, hadn't even looked around for orientation, but had immediately headed towards her neighbor's yard. Unfortunately, he became distraught in finding that the geese were gone. It was clear that John had a good memory and a good sense of orientation, but how does one memorize without language?

In her book *Thinking in Pictures,* Temple Grandin explained that she thinks more visually than verbally. This often seemed to be the case for autistics. We had started to visualize communication by using laminated photos to show John what we wanted to do or where we wanted to go. John's preschool worked with the *Picture Exchange Communication System,* an approach developed in the mid-eighties by Lori Frost and Andy Bondy. As I watched John interact with that impressive sycamore tree, I couldn't help but wonder: How did John think? His experience seemed so intense. I remembered Austrian author Hugo von Hofmannsthal's travel account *Moments in Greece* in which he emphatically, and so fittingly for John's experience, wrote: "Under this light, the mental is more physical and the physical is more mental than anywhere else in this world."

Philosopher Ludwig Wittgenstein said: "All I know is what I have words for." This rang true for me, bit it didn't seem to be the case for John. We tend to think that an infant or toddler doesn't have language *yet*, implying that the child is in a pre-language developmental stage. John was three-and-a-half years old and his whole system of perception and processing seemed so different. Rather than thinking that he was in a stage prior to language, it seemed as if he was in a stage beyond language. Wittgenstein was right. I couldn't understand how one could possibly think without language, exactly because I was limited by it. Thinking of *Moments in Greece* seemed so fitting. In different works of his, Hofmannsthal raised the question of the relationship between physical experience and language. In his famous *Lord Chandos Letter*, words crumbled in Chandos' mouth "like musty mushrooms." Eventually, Chandos could only further experience the world in bouts of excitation, which in turn overwhelmed him in a way that left him even more speechless. Bouts of excitation: John certainly experienced those interacting with that tree.

There's something dialectical, almost contradictory about autism. We associate introversion with it. We see autism as something that's *inside* a person. Many familiar clichés derive from that notion, for example that autistics are "trapped inside themselves." However, autism is also a syndrome that can clearly be seen on the *outside*. Behavior can be peculiar, autistics can be loud and very physical, their experiences as intense as what I just observed in John. It's understandable that the public view focuses so much on autism's inward aspects. From the admiration of savant skills to the alleged tragedy of someone being "trapped inside," autism's internal aspects evoke a wide range of fascination. The physical and outward aspects aren't equally appealing. We don't understand what autistics are doing when they flap their hands, sniff a tree or make strange and loud noises, but when we pick and choose what we find fascinating or interesting, we don't see the whole picture. It occurred to me that the general attitude of over-engaging with the internal aspects of autism and under-engaging with the external ones didn't do autistics justice.

We returned to the horse farm several times and John eventually upgraded from the donkey. At first, I sat on the horse with him, and in the end he rode all by himself, without a saddle, perfectly balancing himself for a good half hour while the horse trotted along the range. I had noticed before that John had an excellent sense of balance, but this was an astounding feat. It was in large part thanks to the owner's patience that we had even been able to reach that point. Previously, John hadn't liked to be complimented on a task well done. It had somehow been too much for him. I had also noticed that he had done better with certain tasks when left alone. For example, he could pour a glass of water rather well as long as he wasn't being observed. Just the presence of another person distracted him so much that it brought out his dyspraxia and made him spill the water. This was slowly changing. He could now tolerate being seen, and along with it I had started to notice an appreciation of compliments. When I said: "Very good!" he smiled.

Sitting on the horse, John seemed proud of himself. Even just the courage of getting up on it had been remarkable. It was heart-warming and encouraging to experience how he started to interact more and feel comfortable with that.

After ten days, we said our goodbyes to the family who owned the pension, returned the car, took the ferry back to Kavála and the bus back to Thessaloniki and overnighted in the same hotel as upon our arrival before flying back to Berlin. Our vacation had been a success. As long as I had followed John's clues as to what he liked or disliked, we managed well. Of course there was always a level of speculation because John couldn't talk.

We just had to try our best, not only with his basic needs like thirst, hunger, tiredness, or needing a diaper change, but in much broader terms. Sometimes it was easy to see what made him happy and what upset him, sometimes the clues were more obscure.

One could raise a principle question as to how well one person can possibly understand another, but usually there's a certain common ground when using the same language. Our verbal habits are, in the end, based on an implicit assumption of understanding, or at least of the constant possibility thereof. With John, this inherent foundation was missing. We would have to build communication on different grounds. Still, John *was* communicating.

I had noticed things that might have escaped me in our busy daily life. I had been impressed by the intensity of John's experiences. His behavior was his language. He communicated with his body and with constant movement. Affirmation of self, as well as of the world around him, somehow took place beyond the realm of verbal language. The fact that I couldn't understand it had to be acknowledged and accepted as unresolvable. One of the nicest aspects of our trip to Thassos was the discovery of doing nothing. Drifting through the day seemed to be something we could and would do again in other scenic areas of Europe.

SCHEELE KNIGHT

2 HIDDENSEE ISLAND (GERMANY) – PARENTING

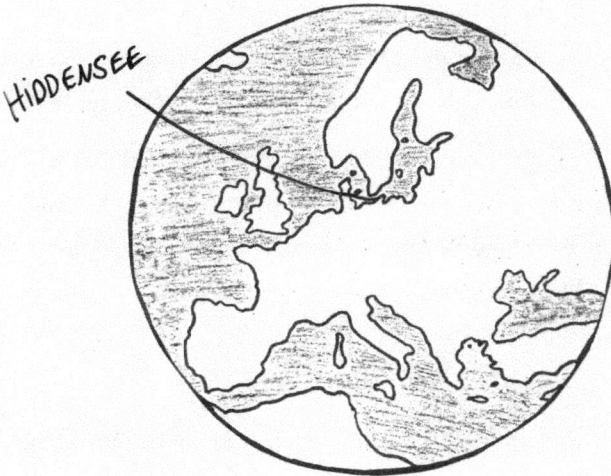

All things in the universe arrange themselves to each person anew,
according to his ruling love.
(Ralph Waldo Emerson)

After the success of our trip to Thassos in the spring, we looked for some place where John could again relax and freely roam about during his fall break. In Germany, children don't go to school for more than six weeks without being on break again. Vacation times, outside of holidays and the summer months, are distributed throughout the entire year. John's preschool was off for two weeks in October of 2004. This time we would travel with all three of us.

Hiddensee is a car-free island in the Baltic Sea and partially a nature reserve, less than four hours away from Berlin. With around 1,000 inhabitants, it is a popular destination for Berliners during the summer months, but not crowded in the fall. The island's name refers back to the Norwegian king Hedin. Hiddensee has a rather colorful history, with several rulership changes throughout the centuries. The original Germanics were driven off the island in the sixth century by a West-Slavic tribe. In the twelfth century, the island fell under Danish rulership, bringing with it Christianity. That lasted until the end of the Thirty Years War. In 1648, the Swedish took control. When Napoleon's defeat in 1815 brought with it the reorganization of Europe, Hiddensee became Prussian, and thus eventually German. In the early twentieth century, an artists' colony developed, with the likes of Käthe Kollwitz and Erich Heckel, and also writer Gerhart Hauptmann.

We parked our car at the long-term parking in the port of Schaprode and boarded the ferry. Arriving on Hiddensee in the harbor village of Vitte, we were immediately taken by the atmosphere of light blue and white fishing boats, and fishermen selling their catch of the day. Due to its location, the island has a mixture of maritime and continental weather patterns, bringing alternating winds and sunshine. When we arrived, the weather was overcast, with a strong gusting wind. It was cooler than on the mainland, but the fresh sea breeze felt refreshing. At the port office, we picked up the keys to our rental apartment.

John was still wearing diapers, and he had recently outgrown the sizes regularly available in stores. We received monthly diaper shipments, paid for by our health insurance, and shipped right to our door. While we had previously been able to buy diapers on-site, we now had to take all we needed from home while traveling. Luckily, the rental association provided trolleys for transporting luggage.

Only a twenty-minute walk from Vitte, our accommodation was on the island's West coast and just a few steps away from the beach. It was a second floor apartment, overlooking a protective dyke and the sea. We had a balcony from where we could hear the waves crashing onto the beach. John was elated, to say the least. We quickly realized that the balcony door couldn't be locked from inside, so we would have to keep an extra close eye on him at all times. What if John quietly got up in the middle of the night? We assessed the apartment and found a simple solution. At night, we could block the balcony door by stacking our luggage and anything heavy we could find on top of a wicker chair, creating a barrier that even Scott struggled disassembling.

Once we settled in, John was eager to go out and we took our first walk on the beach. John ran up and down the edge of the water, getting closer and closer to the incoming waves before eventually being drenched, prompting a return to the apartment.

From the very first day, John felt comfortable on Hiddensee. We had only driven in the car for three hours and had been on the ferry for another forty-five minutes, yet we were in another world. We had left bustling Berlin behind, and on the island everything naturally slowed down without cars. John had freedom to run around without worries of being run over. There was hardly anything to do: There were only four small villages on the island, but the nature was stunningly beautiful with its beaches, wildlife and an exceptional heath landscape. All three of us pretty much immediately changed pace.

On our second day we found a playground close to our apartment. It had a large row boat painted in blue that John enjoyed sitting in. We also found a bike rental shop and rented two Dutch bikes, one with a child's seat on the rear rack. We rode all the way up to the northern tip of the island where the landscape was hilly. The terrain was sandy and we eventually had to lock the bikes and continue on foot. We climbed the path up to a lighthouse and were rewarded with magnificent views over the island and the Baltic Sea.

Scott had brought along his guitar. In the evenings after dinner he played Beatles songs. John had always been taken by music, and he especially loved the Beatles. Like many autistics, John had phases of extremely disturbed sleep-wake patterns, either going to bed late or waking up in the middle of the night for several hours before returning to sleep. Those phases were challenging, as one of us had to be awake watching over John. Scott and I usually took shifts. On Hiddensee, the fresh sea air helped John sleep well. We were more relaxed than we had been in a long time.

Since Greece, John had started to say select words on specific occasions. One morning, breakfast in preschool had been delayed by more than a half hour. John, often hungry, had gotten upset and had positioned himself in the middle of the hallway, where he had then shouted clearly: "Breakfast!"

It remained a singular episode for several months, until one morning John's bus was severely delayed. We stood outside for a long time, and John suddenly burst out saying: "No, no. Bus? No."

The isolated episodes of talking only seemed to occur when John was upset about interruptions in his routines. On the other hand, there were plenty of sudden changes that didn't spark speech. There was no easy explanation as to when the talking might occur. In this particular incidence it had all gotten worse, because a bus similar to John's had driven by without stopping. I tried to explain that it wasn't ours, but he didn't understand. When his bus finally arrived, John had been on the ground kicking, biting himself and crying, while I tried to contain him, afraid that he could roll out into the street.

This kind of situation was something that we had to deal with rather often. Taking a Sunday stroll and just passing a pharmacy could turn into a disaster. John loved the dextrose candy that they normally handed out to children there, but all the stores were closed on Sundays throughout Germany and John had difficulty understanding why the pharmacy doors were locked. He could get very upset about it.

We always had to be alert that something unforeseeable could happen. We knew John well, and we could anticipate many problems. We could also – slowly but surely – help him adjust to situations, like pharmacies being closed on Sundays. It was impossible to entirely avoid meltdowns, though. Life was just too unpredictable for that.

When the world around John became unreliable, and this is what I assumed it boiled down to for him, he dissolved before our eyes. The term meltdown felt appropriate to me, because inside and outside seemed to melt. Disrupted continuity – a closed pharmacy, a delayed bus – affected John so greatly that it shook him to his core. He needed constant affirmation from the outside in order to reach a state of integrity inside. Some researchers think that the notion of self could be a decisive constituent of autism. It seemed that someone who was severely autistic didn't have what could be called our most fundamental certitude: The stability of our self. In that sense, it seemed even more fitting that the term autism originated in the Greek word *autós*, for self.

Meltdowns caused rather intensive stress on everyone involved. It was hard to disassociate yourself from an ongoing situation. For one, it hurt when someone pulled out your hair or bit your arm. Even though it was John's struggle, it also became yours when you were close to him, and if someone hurt himself or others, one didn't necessarily have the distance to consider it an *organization of perception and self* at that very moment. I, at least, tended to be quite affected. I realized that it didn't help and that I had to learn to detach. Scott was much better at handling meltdowns. He didn't get as emotionally involved and could therefore control the situations quicker and with less stress.

Both at home and in school we tried to provide security, rhythm and reliability in order to reduce meltdowns. Part of the problem seemed to be that John struggled with generalization: He had a hard time applying previous experiences to new situations. He could also find it hard to release attention and redirect it. His central problem was to perceive an overview. We worked with a program developed in the mid-sixties by Eric Schopler called TEACCH, structuring time and space. The day was divided into a sequence of picture cards in order to visualize continuity and overview. That helped John's sensory processing as well as his communication skills.

Even though we implemented structure on that superficial level for him, we as parents lived in a state of constant change and insecurity. We revolved around John's needs and routines, ready to react at any given moment. We couldn't foresee what any day would bring. Whatever happened, happened. This to me was another almost contradictory aspect of life with autism: Everybody has routines to a certain extent, but the more severe John's autism was, the more we needed to be flexible.

Intensive parenthood wasn't a transitory phase for us. When I had first become a mother, I had thought that there might be a couple of tiring years, but I had expected life to stabilize as John grew, started to talk, made friends and had sleep-overs, slowly but surely developing his own life. The intensity of the parental experience would lessen over the course of the years, giving us more time again for other interests. Life would somehow fall back into place. John wasn't going through this kind of development. The doctors' letters, from neurologists to psychiatrists, left no doubt about his prognosis. It was unlikely that John could ever lead an independent life. He would need care and help as long as he lived. For us, responsibility wouldn't ease.

Any parenthood is endless, yet it seemed that ours was more extremely so. That was okay, as long as we could care for John, but we often thought about the time when we would no longer be there for him. In all likelihood, he was going to live longer than we did. We felt that it was our responsibility to prepare him for a life without us. We would hopefully have many years to go before separation became reality, but the thought of John's future already lingered in the back of our heads and hearts. All of this connected us deeply with John.

We had a good support system. John liked the social workers and evening caretakers who came to our house, and they in turn showed affection for him. John learned early on to let other people into his life, but in comparing our life with other families who had children John's age, the paths diverged more and more obviously. I realized that I had already started to relate almost any experience to having a severely disabled and chronically ill child. It required a conscious effort to see that parents of so-called normal children had many similar challenges, and that we weren't always different.

We had once attended a concert at the Berlin Philharmonic, and we had arrived rather late. Almost everyone had already been seated, but in the hall's lobby we had passed a woman talking on her cell phone, and I had briefly overheard her explain which lullabies to sing to her child. She had barely made it to her seat before the doors were closed. I had seen how she turned her cell to vibrate. She held it in the palm of her hand for the duration of the performance. During intermission I had again overheard her talking to the babysitter. It seemed that it was her first time on an evening out. It reminded me of the first time I had gone out after John was born. I had been just like her. I had held the cell in my hand on vibrate (although managing not to call the babysitter). Going out had been more stressful than staying in. Still, I had known that it was necessary to learn to let go, and so I had learned, just as many mothers had done before me, and as the woman at the Philharmonic was in the process of doing when I observed her. There was no indication that this woman's child was disabled. Detachment is a challenge for all parents.

It was easy to over-identify with intensive parenthood, because the perception of difference tended to be so overpowering. I sometimes had to remind myself not to create any more difference than there already was. Any parent has to manage difficult nights and sleep deprivation, as well as endure the feelings of constantly being responsible and losing a great deal of independence. At the same time most parents honestly enjoy parenthood. With a disabled child, the unification of these paradoxical feelings is brought to an extreme: We experienced more responsibility, more sleep deprivation, more worries, and more limitations to our freedom. Yet even in that more stressful way, there were deeply touching qualities also to our parenting. I experienced it as a humble strength that was self-content and self-contained in a way that I hadn't known before. It had to do with accepting the fundamental insecurity of life, its deep and inherent unfathomability. We couldn't control life, that had become very clear to us, but it mattered less than we would have thought. While caretaking could become challenging, our attitude towards life in general had become more carefree.

There are certain recurring narratives attached to being a mother of a disabled child. First and foremost there's the "warrior mom" who takes up the challenge and "fights for her child like a tigress." That didn't resonate with me. The military rhetoric pushed me off, and I wasn't a wild animal. I intended to stick with reason, and while it was surely my goal to care for my child to the best of my abilities, I intended to keep other interests as well. Then there's the spiritual narrative that singles out mothers of disabled children as "having been chosen." That didn't resonate with me either. I wasn't a natural born caretaker. It just so happened that my child had multiple conditions: Epilepsy, autism, an intellectual disability, and G6-PD-deficiency. I understood the impulse of the being-chosen narrative. It can be difficult to let randomness remain random. We tend to look for explanations. Calming disturbing difference by directing it towards higher meaning, though, was possibly more useful to an outsider's comfort than to mine. It also seemed rather suspicious to me that fathers of disabled children weren't subjected to such narratives. Maybe the hidden purpose was to keep the mothers on the job?

I didn't like the rhetoric of sacrifice and I didn't like the rhetoric of battle. I didn't want to be looked down upon or pitied, but I also didn't want to be elevated to moral or spiritual higher grounds. I wondered if I could create a place for myself as a mother of a severely disabled child outside of these recurring notions.

On our last full day on Hiddensee, we drove up to the small village of Kloster where German author Gerhart Hauptmann had lived and where he was buried in a tiny graveyard. We visited his house, today a museum, with its impressive wine cellar in the basement. There was only one street in Kloster, unpaved, a dirt road. When we drove by a café, we decided to drop in – it might be the only place we'd find for a while. Only two tables were taken. The waiter was dressed all in black, head to toe, probably in his mid-twenties, with long, dyed black hair in a ponytail. Gothic music was playing, but quietly. The waiter swiftly brought the menu.

We placed our order: "Two regular coffees, a piece of apple strudel without whipped cream, and a glass of apple juice, please."

The waiter disappeared into the kitchen, then returned and stood behind the bar. He leaned against it with a melancholy look on his face. A young woman appeared from the kitchen, dressed all in black, with a piercing in her mouth and her hair also dyed black. She looked as if she had been crying. She walked up to the waiter and the two hugged in a strangely hesitant way. It looked like the final goodbye of two persons who had once been very close. Then she quickly left the café, her eyes fixed on the ground. The waiter followed her with his eyes and just stood there for a while, looking sad.

A kitchen aid brought a piece of apple strudel. The waiter added a generous heap of whipped cream on top of it. Then he started the coffee machine and prepared what seemed to be two café lattes. Finally, he filled a glass three-quarters with apple juice and added one-quarter of carbonated water. He brought everything to our table. "Here's your order," he said quietly. Having observed the nonverbal but moving interaction between him and the woman, we didn't have the heart to tell him that none of this did match our order. We drank café latte instead of regular coffee and shared the strudel with the whipped cream that we had wanted to avoid. John didn't touch his apple spritzer because he was in a phase where he refused to drink anything carbonated, but he didn't get upset, he just pushed the glass away. Even John was in a forgiving mood.

At the end of our week, we took the ferry back to Schaprode, retrieved our car, and thanks to an American's enthusiasm for the partial no-speed-limit of the German autobahn, we raced home. "Downhill Autobahning," as Scott called it. John also liked driving fast. He sat in the back seat, spreading his arms and swerving his upper body, as his laughter built from small chuckles to hysterical joy. On a largely empty highway, the drive to Berlin was cut by about a third of the usual time. Knowing Scott's enthusiasm for speed and seeing John's joy, I had to be the only one relieved when we pulled up in front of our apartment all in one piece.

3 RHODES ISLAND (GREECE) – EPILEPSY

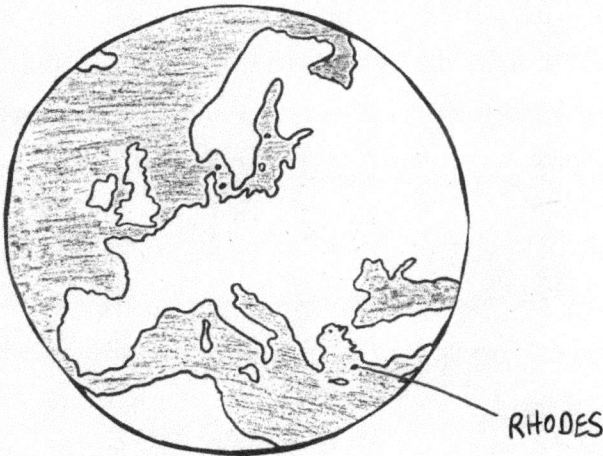

RHODES

Who would deny that when I am sipping tea in my tearoom
I am swallowing the whole universe with it?

(Daisetz Teitaro Suzuki)

We decided to take another trip to Greece in January of 2005 during John's winter break. We found a nice vacation home in the touristy village of Líndos, on the island of Rhodes. When we emailed the owner to book it, he wrote back before confirming: "I wanted to make sure you know that Lindós is much different in the winter season." That was considerate, and it happened to be exactly what we were looking for.

There were no direct flights. We had to fly to Athens and stay overnight before taking a small commuter plane to Rhodes the following morning. We left cold and wet Berlin on New Year's Day. The flight was almost four hours long. John was much more restless than he had been flying three hours to Thessaloniki ten months earlier. He screamed and kicked his feet against the seat in front of him, much to the displeasure of the man sitting in it. For hours, we struggled with John's feet and his loud noises. We wondered if we could ever fly back to the U.S. with him. John was only four years old, but it didn't look too promising. Since Scott's family – John's grandparents, his aunt, two uncles, and a growing number of cousins – lived in the Chicagoland area, this was a sad prospect.

We stayed in an airport hotel. We thought that the most difficult part of our journey was over, but the following morning, we ran into language problems at the domestic terminal. I went through security first while Scott and John waited behind. I planned to receive John on the other side once I was cleared, but a guard urged Scott and John to follow me immediately. Scott explained that John needed to be carefully supervised, but the guard didn't seem to grasp the situation. He just shook his head and pointed to the detector.

Scott tried again: "He's autistic, handicapped. He doesn't speak and will run away."

The guard got more impatient. He didn't understand. He only spoke Greek and heavily signalled with his arms. At the same time, John also got more impatient, maybe because he realized that we were spending another day going from A to B, or just because he felt the tension. I turned back towards them and both Scott and I thought that I was cleared, but then a female guard tapped me on the shoulder for a further search. I turned around towards her in the very second that Scott let John go, so I didn't see him coming. I only heard Scott shout: "Here he comes, Monika!"

In that moment, John had already raced by me heading down towards a corridor to the left. I immediately broke away from the guard and ran after him. The security wasn't pleased, to say the least. I heard shouting, but I continued to run, also shouting, calling John's name and: "Stop!"

If he got lost in the crowd that would be our worst nightmare, but John heard me and stopped. I caught up with him, and two guards caught up with me. We all returned to security, where an English-speaking officer had materialized in the meantime. We properly explained what happened and were finally cleared through to the boarding area. As we left, we could see the relief in the guards' faces that we were someone else's problem now. Scott and I argued briefly at the gate: "Why did you let him go?" and "Why didn't you catch him running by?" It was nobody's fault, though, and we both knew that. Sometimes it was just hard not to cast blame when situations escalated. We then just sat silently, drained.

When we boarded the plane, we realized that only three other passengers were flying with us. It gave us freedom and space to stretch out. Being on his first propeller plane, and flying much lower than in regular jet-engined air crafts, John enthusiastically looked down on the clear, blue sea below us. The flight was a breeze and our stress slowly faded. Flying in at Diagoras International Airport on Rhodes, we appeared to be in paradise. We saw white-washed houses, blue sky, turquoise water and golden beaches.

When we picked up our rental car, it turned out that the company only accepted European driver's licenses. I would then have to do all the driving, because Scott still used his international license. Lindós was roughly thirty-five miles away from the airport. On our way, we saw many half-built houses and were told later that one only had to pay taxes once a building was completed. Builders therefore seemed in no apparent rush to complete their work's finishing touches. We zipped by rugged, hilly terrain and ended up at a mostly empty municipal parking lot above the coastal village of Lindós. With about 1,500 inhabitants, it was a car-free pedestrian zone due to its narrow, winding streets built well before the invention of automobiles. We had rented a house built in traditional Greek seventeenth-century-style in the heart of the village, and since we had agreed with the management on a time for receiving the keys, a handful of locals with donkeys waited for us in the parking lot to transport our luggage from the car park down into the village. We didn't need help, but we felt guilty turning them down as it was off-season and their business obviously slow.

Walking down from the parking lot, our first glimpses of Lindós were stunning. White houses situated below an acropolis that dated back to the tenth century BC. Towering above the backdrop of the Mediterranean sea, the acropolis was built upon a massive rock, dominating the entire village. We could tell how it had been the perfect citadel from which Greeks, Romans, Byzantines, the Knights of Saint John, and the Ottoman Turks had controlled seaborne attacks.

Our rental house didn't look like much from the outside. There was just a large gate, but upon entering we found a mosaic-tiled courtyard and rooms that were distributed around it. When you wanted to go from the bedroom to the living room, you had to cross the courtyard. The outside was the center of the living quarters. The rooms were furnished simply and the kitchen was equipped with old-fashioned appliances, utensils, cooking ware, and dishes. It seemed as if we were transported back in time. People could have lived here in the same way fifty or sixty years ago.

As it had become our routine, we first took a long walk to explore the village. John was interested in the white houses and the labyrinth of narrow streets. We noticed that most shops, cocktail bars, and taverns were closed, and the window shutters of the souvenir shops appeared to have been locked for some time. We seemed to be the only tourists in town. John curiously observed the stray cats. There were dozens of them roaming around, seemingly on every other staircase and rooftop. As on Thassos, John again found several natural springs. Finally, we discovered a grocery store that was open, bought a few supplies and settled into the house by cooking our first dinner.

We hiked up to the acropolis early on our first morning in Lindós. John was eager to move at first, but half-way up he preferred to sit on Scott's shoulders. We arrived at a terrace lined with cyprus trees, and from the walls of the fortress we had a beautiful view down onto the bay. A steep stairwell led to the remains of ancient columns. We explored the Roman temple, the Exedra, and the Athena temple. John climbed around in the ancient ruins, exploring tiny corners and crawling around underneath the signs that explained what we were looking at.

In the evening, we walked to a playground first and then on to the beach. We passed a bar filled with men. A woman walked in and came back out with what appeared to be her husband. We observed a similar scenario with a different couple, and then again the next evening. We asked at the grocery store and were told that the men weren't supposed to drink in the bar before January 6. That was the day of the Epiphany, the last and most important day of the Greek Orthodox Christmas. It was just two days away.

On Thassos, I had been to my first Greek Orthodox church service on Good Friday. I had taken John in the stroller and we had observed it for a little while. The pension owner had told me that it would be okay. She had explained that the mass took hours and that everyone stepped in and out. I had seen many people standing outside, talking to each other: A nice get-together for the whole village. It had been an interesting experience, so we decided to attend the Epiphany festivities. Our main source of information was our local grocery clerk, and he explained that there'd be a procession leading down to the bay for what was called the *Great Blessing of the Waters*. We kept our distance and watched from afar, not to disturb anyone. The priest, dressed all in black, walked onto a pier followed by a congregation of formally dressed men and women. In the midst of the group, we noticed a few teenagers curiously dressed in colorful swim suits. After the priest completed his prayers and blessings, he threw a beautifully decorated cross into the sea. The teenagers then jumped in after it with the winner eventually emerging with the cross and the congregation applauding.

A peculiar custom to an outsider, but then again, as peculiar a custom as this was to us, John's behavior at times was probably equally so to some of the villagers. It reminded me again why stereotyping autistics as living in their own world left a sour taste in my mouth. We all lived in our own world, and anyone who looked at our customs or way of being from the outside could find peculiarity.

When we stepped out of the big entrance door of our house the next morning, the village had completely changed. All the stores were open and the narrow streets rapidly filled up with tourists. The growing and fading sound of the locals' scooters that had become our acoustic backdrop in an otherwise largely silent village had disappeared. Instead, crowds pushed through the alleys and streets. We asked at our grocery store what had happened. An Italian cruise ship had docked and hundreds of tourists were spending the day on Rhodes, mainly in Líndos. We felt like we had been beamed into an entirely different place. We realized we wouldn't want to be here in the summer.

We walked by a news stand that was open for the first time. It carried newspapers in English and we saw that the headlines were still of the tsunami that had hit the Indian ocean shortly before our departure from Germany. We had been cut off from the world, which in a way was always nice, but once we saw the tsunami coverage we felt the need to reconnect and bought some newspapers.

At the house, we had taken up the habit of sitting in the kitchen. Despite blue sky and sunshine it was rather cold and none of the rooms had heating. The owner had given us an electrical heater, but it didn't warm up the living room with its high ceilings. The kitchen was small enough to be heated by it, especially in combination with the warmth that came from the oven or stove-top while cooking.

We sat in the kitchen and read the papers. John sat next to me munching on a sandwich when I suddenly noticed that he seemed to freeze in his movement. His eyes became glassy and his head made a slow nod towards his chest. It was a fleeting moment, altogether maybe two seconds, but it seemed much longer. To me, it happened in slow motion. The knowledge seemed to be in my body much more so than in my mind. I could feel it inside me, growing. It twisted my stomach, it hit my lungs as if knocking the air right out of them. It built a lump in my throat, it flooded my head: The physical awareness that I had just seen the first epileptic event in more than a year. Everything was there in those few seconds, like the flash that some say you see in the last moments of your life. All the EEG's, the medications, the doctors, the hospital beds, and the seizures, day and night. A quick account of events, entirely contradictory to the slow motion in which I perceived the single head nod.

John seemed okay. He proceeded eating as if nothing had happened. I hoped that it would be a singular episode, that I had possibly just imagined it, that it was nothing. It happened again, though, stronger and with a quicker movement of the head. By the evening, the arms got involved, slightly at first, and then more pronounced, coming forward in a gesture that resembled an embrace, his arms meeting in an almost elegant bow in front of his body.

It was building just like it had before, when John had been eighteen months old. We had gotten over it, and now it was back. We always knew that the seizures could return and we had thought about it often, but when it happened it was still devastating. Before long, the seizures were causing dark rings under John's eyes and he seemed worn out. For me, there was an inherent difference between the way I looked at autism and the way I looked at epilepsy. Autism was part of John's personality. Even though many challenges came with it, John still seemed happy. The epilepsy made him disoriented and it exhausted him deeply. We saw how much energy the seizures took out of John. Autism and epilepsy both caused struggles, but autism was more of a way of being, while epilepsy interrupted it.

Twenty weeks into my pregnancy, the ultrasound had shown a so-called choroid plexus cyst on John's brain. The obstetrician had explained: "This is a fairly common thing to happen, and in the vast majority of cases, the cyst dissolves and is gone by thirty weeks. In a very small percentage of fetuses, the cyst is associated with a chromosome disorder called trisomy 18. Don't worry, only one in more than 3,000 babies with these cysts has that disorder." Of course the first thing I had done when I returned home was to go online and search for the worst-case scenario. Even though the internet wasn't as advanced in 2000, I had still been able to find a lot of information. I learned that most fetuses with trisomie 18 were stillborns. If they survived, they had severe organ problems and a short life.

We lived in a Chicago suburb at the time. I had taken my jacket and gone for a walk. I wandered the streets trying to figure out what the cyst meant to me. For all we knew, it was likely that nothing was wrong, but what if my child did have trisomy 18 and would be stillborn, or live just a year, or maybe a few months, or just days? More than anything, my immediate hope had been that I could at least meet my baby alive, even if only for just a few hours. Curiously, I hadn't thought so much about a terminal disorder in itself. What I had worried about was if and how much time we'd have together. I had walked for more than an hour. When I returned home, I knew deeply that the love for my child was unconditional and that I didn't care if he was disabled, sick, healthy, normal, or whatever other categories we tend to think in. It had been an extraordinary moment and feeling. I hadn't been scared or anxious. I had felt liberated.

Looking back at it, my feelings could be perceived as quite irrational and deficient. I had been egotistical, I wanted to meet my child. I could have considered more of the pain and suffering that he could potentially experience. More than anything else my intuitive reaction had probably been a way to deal with a potentially extreme prospect. On my initial way home from the obstetrician, I had thought about the ten long weeks until my next ultrasound. My reaction ensured that I wasn't dwelling on it during those weeks. Before the ultrasound at thirty weeks we had then been mildly curious what the result was going to be, and it turned out that the cyst had indeed dissolved.

Based on what we know today, the choroid plexus cyst didn't have anything to do with any of John's conditions. Retrospectively it was still an emotionally decisive event, though. Once John had developed the seizures, and afterwards when he had been diagnosed with autism, I didn't go through the same kind of loss many parents in similar situations have described. The cyst had triggered lasting affirmative feelings towards a potential illness or disability.

There was no outside explanation as to why the seizures had returned. John had seemed content, he hadn't eaten anything different, he hadn't experienced any more sleep deprivation than usual. We went through ideas of what could have caused the epilepsy to return, but came up empty-handed. Maybe it was just something inside John's body, in his metabolism, in his neurological or genetic functioning. Since we were on an island far from home, we couldn't do an EEG easily, but we doubted how useful it would be anyway. John's EEGs had always been highly abnormal, even when he was seizure-free. There had never been any indication as to cause, location, or cure in it. The epilepsy had always been generalized and refractory. We carried John's emergency medication with us in case he went into a *status epilepticus*. We thought briefly about flying home, but quickly discarded the idea. There was nothing we could do anyway, wherever we were.

After a seizure, John needed to sleep to regain strength. I sat next to him and watched him, his eyes sunken in, a fragile boy whom we couldn't protect. The feeling of helplessness was hard to tolerate. Complete powerlessness is, strangely, one of the most powerful feelings. Hardly ever do we experience our nothingness as strongly as when we are utterly helpless. The two-year experience with John's epilepsy had at least given us confidence in our capability to deal with this, though. We had persevered before, we could do it again. The old sadness returned, but it was a well-worn feeling and control over it luckily re-emerged just as quickly.

Our first excursion after the onset of seizures was to Rhodes city in the very north, the island's principal city. We found the hospital and memorized the way there in case things worsened. Since we were already in town, we decided to make the most of it. The old town of Rhodes city is surrounded by a fortified ring consisting of an outer wall, a ditch and an inner wall. We found a parking spot outside of the fortifications and entered through the Eleftherias Gate. We looked at the remains of the Doric Temple of Aphrodite from the third century B.C. There was hardly anything left, just foundations and a few column drums. Inside the ruins, John had another seizure. We sat in beautiful weather, in a place dedicated to the goddess of love, with a view of the stunning exteriors of the *Palace of the Grand Master of the Knights of Rhodes* ahead of us, while John was sleeping post-seizure in his stroller. Some Knights of Rhodes we were.

Once John had woken up, we continued our walk through the old town with its medieval as well as ancient landmarks: Palaces, churches, mosques, and a synagogue. Considering the circumstances, we had a comparatively pleasant morning and started settling into the reality of epilepsy having re-entered our lives. In the old town's picturesque setting with all its nooks and crannies, we found a tavern and sat down for lunch.

After the seizure, John was calm and patient. His energy level was lower than usual when he was often too impatient and too hyperactive for restaurants. He seemed to be content sitting in his stroller, observing and enjoying the environment. It was amazing to see how strong John was, how quickly he recovered, and how good-humored he was. Our brave four-year-old certainly showed us how to cope, and at least the seizures weren't as frequent as they had been years before when we had barely been able to keep the log for John's neurologist.

For the afternoon we decided to go southwest and then inland via the monastery of Skiádi to one of the original remote villages, Mesanagrós. It lies in the Southern stretch of the Koukouliari mountains, elevation just under 2,000 feet. The road from the monastery to the village was an adventure. It was just a dirt path, a gravel road winding through the mountains. We were relieved when we arrived without any damage to the tires. We walked around the village for a bit, and found it quaint. We then wanted to drive on south in the direction of a village called Kattaviá. According to the map it was only roughly eight miles away, but our map soon left us clueless as we happened upon a junction that didn't show up on it. Which road to take? In this case, not the one less travelled by, we thought. We followed the path that looked bigger but it led higher up. Could this be right? Before we knew it, the path became too narrow to turn around. I didn't feel comfortable putting the car in reverse because of the steep decline to our side. We decided to move on in the hope that the path would widen, but that didn't happen. We passed a flock of sheep and an old hut that looked like a sheep stall, but couldn't get to it with the car to turn around.

We had no idea where we were on the map. The path was winding through the mountains and we were lost. Nevertheless, the scenery was pleasant, so we didn't mind in the beginning, but then we had to stop a few times to remove large rocks which had crashed down from the mountain above. We then reached a point where the entire path had crumbled. Now we weren't only lost in the mountains, we had no other option than to back down all the way in reverse. Scott didn't mind doing it, so we switched seats. The panoramic views were beautiful, but I couldn't appreciate them at that moment. When we passed the sheep and the hut again, I started to feel a little bit better. We had almost made it. We slowly moved on and eventually arrived all the way back at our original junction and took the other path. It was also a dirt road, but not nearly as horrifying as the one that we had just been on. We made it to Kattaviá, and John received an ice-cream as we told our story to the owner of the café. He said that the road was meant only for off-road vehicles. No wonder.

It was late afternoon, but since we were in the South already we drove on to the southern tip of the island. When we arrived, we were taken by surprise. Having passed through four miles of hilly sand dunes, the paltry landscape that looked like a desert suddenly opened up to a peninsula with two picturesque bays on either side. Since the peninsula formed the tip of the island, the wind blew offshore on one side and onshore on the other. On the one side the sea was calm, blue, and as smooth as glass, while high waves crushed in on the other side. In between these two diverse scenarios lay Prasonísi beach, more than a half a mile wide. When we tried to walk, we were almost blown away. The wind was so strong that we almost couldn't breathe. Years earlier, John had been sensitive to wind and hadn't liked it at all. That had only changed after ear tubes had been inserted to reduce his frequent ear infections. Even if John could tolerate the wind now, I was anxious at first that the site might be too loud for him. The waves and the wind on the beach were noisy, but John didn't seem to mind either the wind or the noise. He loved the peninsula just as much as we did. With his hair dishevelled within seconds, he laughed loudly.

Rhodes is quite large, almost fifty miles long. We had traversed its length in one day, starting in the early morning on the northern tip in its principal city, invariably getting lost in the mountains after lunch in the middle of the island, and ending on its southern tip where we watched the sun set behind the wild backdrop of a deserted, breathtakingly beautiful beach. In the car, we had listened to Sting's album *All This Time*. It seemed like the ideal mellow island music (as long as you didn't think about the day it had been recorded). At the end of the day Sting also brought us home to Lindós, driving along the eastern coastline in the dark, with occasional light clusters of distant villages.

When we returned to Berlin, we scheduled an appointment with the neurologist. We made an unsuccessful attempt at an EEG in a regular hospital, which failed somewhat due to John's non-compliance, but mainly due to the technical assistant's impatience. We were then admitted to the Epilepsy Center and managed to get a full 24-hour EEG, but again it didn't yield any new insights. As always, John was put on different medications, which again weren't effective. The specialists were still at a loss for an explanation. Since John didn't want to swallow the medicine regularly, the doctors thought about inserting a PEG stomach tube. We decided against it. About five months later, just as mysteriously as it had started, John was suddenly seizure-free once again.

4 THE FRENCH RIVIERA (FRANCE) – DELIGNY

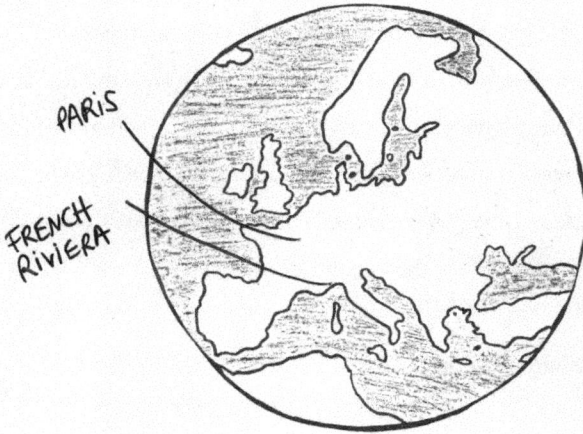

> *One shouldn't search nderneath the phenomena;*
> *they themselves are the teachings.*
> (Johann Wolfgang von Goethe)

Travel's obstacles often don't start with the journey itself. In the case of our trip to southern France in the summer of 2005, Scott exchanged nearly forty emails with the owner of a rental home that he had found online. Logan from Seattle seemed especially worried that we were traveling with a child. We imagined her living in an apartment like Kelsey Grammer in the sitcom *Frasier*, also set in Seattle: A delicate place that a child could ruin within minutes. In the end she agreed to rent us her house in Haut-de-

Cagnes, a small medieval hilltop village roughly twelve miles outside of Nice on the French Riviera.

Logan's house had many advantages. An inexpensive airline flew directly from Berlin to Nice. Unlike the towns at the seafront, the hilltop villages were less crowded, and the house had a large garden that John couldn't run away from because it was surrounded by an old stone wall. While John would be safe, he'd still have plenty of space to roam. He was almost five years old, but running away was still one of our bigger problems, especially because John also still lacked a sense of danger. He was tall for his age and he was physically able to do a lot of things that he cognitively couldn't assess. It escaped him that cars in the street could run him over because his perception was focused on something else – for example an ice-cream stand across the street. At home, all of our windows had security locks.

John was constantly on the move, tireless. His search for new sensations carried him far. He ran, he climbed, he jumped, and then ran some more. Like many severely autistic children, he didn't play with toys in a conventional way. He basically just threw them around. He didn't draw or look at books. He was just on the move, that was his way of being. More than once, I had found myself on the playground with him at the crack of dawn, sometimes as early as five a.m. We jokingly said that we were always on the run, like fugitives. Currently, John was in a brush phase. He focused on finding any kind of brushes or brooms and then rubbed the bristles, incessantly, to the extent of breaking his skin and bleeding. He didn't have an appropriate sense of temperature or pain either. Protecting him from harm was a responsibility round-the-clock. Logan's house seemed just perfect for our balancing act of protection and freedom.

When we arrived in Nice, the temperature was nearing a hundred degrees. At the airport car rental, a line of people trailed through the parking lot and beyond its entrance. Even though we had reserved a car, we were told that the waiting time would be about three hours. In this heat, John wouldn't last the first half hour, we were sure. We quickly decided to split up. Scott got in line, and I got into a taxi with John and the suitcases.

The cabdriver couldn't find Logan's house at first. Haut-de-Cagnes is an old village with narrow one-way streets, zig-zagging and winding. It was confusing. The only advantage was that all of the streets and alleys eventually — and quite miraculously — somehow led back to the village's main square. We drove around for a while, hitting the main square every few minutes. We asked locals several times and finally arrived at our destination. The French housekeeper handed me the keys. She talked about "Logan, Logan," pronouncing the *a* in a French way and emphasizing the last syllable, all the while waving her hands in the air with alarm. Logan seemed to have quite an effect on her.

I spent the remainder of the afternoon worrying if Scott would find us. An American in France for the first time who didn't speak French, didn't have a cell phone with him, no navigational system booked for the rental car, and probably not even a map in it, just the address that we had quickly scribbled down before John and I had gotten into the taxi. Even after Scott had found Haut-de-Cagnes, he still had to locate the house that a local cabdriver hadn't found easily. At some point, I took John for a walk to find a grocery store, we shopped and went back to the house. I started to cook.

Scott arrived just in time for dinner. He had parked the car in the main square after a while and had continued his search on foot. He had met a Moroccan man who was waiting tables in one of the restaurants in the main square. The waiter didn't speak a word of English, but had tried to help Scott in his search. To no avail. Eventually Scott had just found the villa on his own. None of the houses had address numbers on them, just villa names, so he had combed the entire village. Six hours after arriving in Nice, Scott finally showed up at our front door. I was elated to see him, but he was stressed out.

The next step was finding the one-way street that led from the main square up to the house, so that we could park the car in our garage. We knew from Logan's instructions that we would have to drive through a narrow arch. It took us twenty minutes to find the correct combination of one-way turns that led to the bottom of a small, but steep slope, narrowly winding up and to the right before taking a sharp left turn through the medieval arch. With only a few inches of leeway on either side, one had to calculate the correct angle to pass through while giving enough gas to prevent the car from stalling and rolling back down the hill. Scott's first attempt was lethargic. Trying again, the second time with more confidence, he appeared to have found the knack until a young couple suddenly stepped out of the archway just as we approached. Apparently in shock that someone drove up in what appeared to be a pedestrian-only zone, they just froze as Scott hit the brakes, veering slightly to our right. That was when we heard metal crunching. We had hit a granite-stone doorstep just inside the arch, but better the front tire-rim than hitting the young couple. John sat in the back and giggled. He might have thought: "How fun! What are my parents doing?"

Luckily, the damage was minimal and the car was still drivable. The next problem was that the street was too narrow to turn into the garage. After a ten-point turning manoeuvre, we finally made it. Scott, heavily perspiring, asked: "Did you buy any wine when you went shopping, by any chance?"

Dinner was waiting and we ate in the garden. Agapanthuses flourished in pots and flowerbeds throughout. John barely had time to eat, he wanted to explore. We could see how he noticed every detail: The flowers, the bushes, the tiled stone floor near the barbecue pit. He ran up and down, back and forth, touching this and that, and his chuckling *I-am-happy*-sounds told us that he was pleased with our decision to come here. Finally, we could relax. After dinner, we took a closer look at the house. In the garage, we had already seen a carefully covered BMW convertible. The collection of media in the living room was eclectic. *The Doors* paired with Celine Dion. The movie *A Touch of Mink* with Doris Day and Cary Grant, next to the French film *A Chef In Love*. A collection of Walt Whitman poems and Thomas Pynchon's *Gravity's Rainbow* teamed up with Rosamunde Pilcher's *Winter Solstice*.

There were knick-knacks everywhere. In his infinite urge for movement, John tended to knock things over, as unintended as unnoticed by him. So we moved vases, decorations and anything fragile into a room that we locked and wouldn't open again until departure. Upon a closer look at the furniture, we also moved a rather fragile-looking chair from the den into our temporary storage space.

Throughout the next days we visited Cannes and Saint-Tropez. With his restless behavior, John stuck out. Sociologist Rosemarie Garland-Thomson identified four main attitudes in the visual rhetorics of disability: Admiring, sentimental, exotic, and realistic. John being barely five years old, we hadn't reached any of those yet. You couldn't necessarily see straight away that he was disabled. John was still small enough to be interpreted as simply misbehaved. Another child walking all over his parents, another set of parents failing a decent upbringing of their son. The looks that we got were at times critical, but sadly and luckily at the same time it's a rather quick trip from drama to indifference. Intrusive staring was usually swiftly followed by turning away from us.

One day, Scott wore a flashy red-and-white t-shirt sporting the letters ENGLAND, accompanied by the English flag, and suddenly we noticed that people stared more at Scott than they did at John. We had found a new method of diversion. The English shirt was our silver bullet, a perfect lightning rod in France.

Nice then lived up to its reputation familiarly portrayed in the movie *To Catch A Thief*. I had forgotten to take John's passport out of my backpack's front pocket and it was stolen four days into our vacation while we walked through the city. We phoned the German consulate and made an appointment. Its offices were in a house called *Minotaur*. Mythically part man, part bull, minotaur is a man-eating creature. An interesting name for a building housing a consulate. With his casually opened shirt, the Honorary Consul looked like we had pulled him straight off his yacht. He told us that we needed a passport photo of John. The regular German children's passport didn't require one at his age yet, but a picture on the temporary one was needed for flying. Rather than testing a photographer's patience, we decided to drive out to the airport where we had seen an automated photo booth and where we could work on this project at our own pace, or rather at John's pace.

Time was something various professionals often didn't have, but it was the key to any success, and if you anticipated something to take longer, frustration was also considerably lowered. With John, we always had to remain completely in the moment. Our life with him had significantly shifted our attitude towards time. At the airport we fed the machine with coins, getting a variety of hair, nose, and other close-up shots before getting a picture suited for a passport. We then drove back to the Minotaur and the Consul was content with our photo. We could resume our vacation.

We drove to Provence for a day trip. With an ice-cream we bought John's cooperation to tour the impressive amphitheater in Arles. The Roman theater dates back to the year eighty AD. It originally had three stories, sixty arcades, and accommodated 25,000 spectators. Presently, it was used for *corridas*, bullfights typical for southern France and Spain. It turned out that John was interested in the amphitheater's architecture. He walked up the entire arena with us and clearly paid attention to its impressive structure. Whenever we managed to overcome John's initial resistance, we often found that he could enjoy something that he had originally refused.

We took small country roads towards the *Pont Du Gard* aqueduct, one of the most important Roman bridge-building relics in the world. John didn't want to walk there either, yet the surface terrain was too rugged for his stroller. Scott could take him on his shoulders, but we were trying to wean John out of this habit and get him to walk on his own. John eventually cooperated, and standing on top of the *Pont Du Gard*, towering over the beautiful Provence landscape, we all enjoyed the views.

We spent a lot of time in our garden listening to Elliott Smith. His album *From a Basement on the Hill* influenced us to also listen again to his older albums *XO* and *either/or*. John roamed around the garden, and didn't seem to get tired of it. Outside of beach rush hours, we went swimming in *Juan-les-Pins* near Antibes. John was at first scared of going into the sea. We had been to the beach in Greece and on Hiddensee, but those trips had been during times when the water had been too cold for swimming. John was only used to pools. He stood yearning yet perplexed at the shore. We watched him and initially thought that the waves scared him, but then it seemed as if he was concentrating on the shoreline. Leading into the water, pebbles and parts of sea shells were being washed ashore, moving in and out with the waves. Maybe he didn't want to step on them? We found a beach store and bought bright turquoise plastic beach shoes, the only ones available in John's size. We were right, the spell was broken and John could finally enjoy his beloved water. With a nonverbal child, we were always thrown back onto observation and it often felt like we were detectives solving yet another mystery.

One time, a jelly fish swam up to me, only that upon closer view it turned out not to be a jelly fish, but a bulging pantyliner. Not exactly unusual in Europe's biggest public bathtub, also known as the Mediterranean.

Back at the house, French television was filled with reality shows. Scott found them interesting and when I asked him why, he said: "When you watch this without understanding a word that they say, that's when you really realize: Human beings are crazy." Since I speak French, it was harder for me to create that distance, but I realized that he was right. When you manage to fade out the significance of words, you realize the absurdity of certain behaviors. It made us wonder if that experience somehow came close to how John perceived the world at times.

France has a strong psychoanalytical tradition, for example famously represented by psychiatrist Jacques Lacan. It's the only country in the Western world to use its own manual for psychiatric diagnosis. In the French manual, autism was still defined as infantilism when it had long since been acknowledged as a pervasive developmental disorder in the two manuals that are normally used for diagnosis, the *Diagnostic and Statistical Manual of Mental Disorders* and the *International Classification of Diseases*. Autistic children were long considered ineducable in France, and they were often put into psychiatric wards. Even at the time of writing this book, 80% of severely autistic children are officially estimated not to attend school.

Perhaps due to this peculiar tradition, there also existed a distinct anti-psychiatric movement early on as well. A few intellectuals retreated into the Cévennes mountains with a group of autistic children in the mid-sixties. They tried to free the children from the hopeless situation French psychiatry had created for them. Their goal was to weave so-called life nets for the ones who had fallen overboard, to fish them up on a raft. They saw that the autistic children liked to roam around and therefore lived with them in a partly nomadic style, practically following the children's lead. They compared their lifestyle to agricultural transhumance, the seasonal movement of animals between summer and winter pastures. French craftsman Jacques Lin, who lived with his wife and a group of autistic children in the mountains for close to forty years, has written a book about his experiences. So has remedial teacher Fernand Deligny who had come up with the whole idea. I was reading their books while John roamed around in Logan's garden.

Lin described that he didn't speak much when he interacted with the nonverbal children. Because they didn't talk, he didn't want to either. In a world in which verbal language so easily outvotes anyone who doesn't have words, the group wanted to try and understand a nonverbal child's fundamental *Plea for Something Else*, as Deligny phrased it. Even if they – much like the rest of us – didn't exactly understand that plea, they acknowledged that its expression emanated from the autistic children's every gesture. Deligny wrote: "There are and there always will be attempts to search for unexpected opportunities to change gridlocked behavioral patterns. We have made one such attempt, but we even went further: *Life On a Raft*. We wilfully remain in ignorance of what's ahead, and continue an adventure that is different from traveling on a dog-sled to the North Pole. We search for what makes us human."

Jacques Lin described a remarkable incident with twelve-year-old severely autistic Janmari. One night, Janmari woke up and was desperate. He chewed frantically on his pyjamas, he banged his head against the wall, he couldn't be calmed down. Jacques Lin asked him to show what was wrong and Janmari led him outside, and then into the forest, Lin behind him with a flashlight, following Janmari who started to climb a nearby rock in the darkness. Lin realized that Janmari was headed where they had just been earlier in the afternoon. Taking a break on that rock, they had eaten some oranges. Lin had cut them in half, and had inverted the halves to make them easier to peel. Up on the rock in the middle of the night, Janmari searched for something, found the discarded orange halves, inverted them back to their original form, laughed and clapped his hands. Everything was okay then. They returned to the house where Janmari immediately fell into a deep sleep.

It reminded me of an experience with John. I had once woken up in the middle of the night because I had heard John vocalizing. When I entered his room, I found him sitting brightly alert at the foot of his bed. From where he was sitting, you could see a streetlamp's light peeking through between the window frame and the curtain in a slanted angle. You could only see it from that particular spot. How had John discovered that after he had already been asleep? I pulled the curtain and John had readily lain down. He too had fallen asleep quickly then. Another night, I had found him sitting on the windowsill, knees pulled up to his chest, his head tilted towards the full moon, howling like a wolf.

Fernand Deligny started to trace the autistic children's paths in the mountain settlement. He created a map of their constant movement. Other than a conventional map which shows paths that someone has explored and mapped out, the tracings revealed previously unknown patterns. There were *customary lines* reflecting routine activities and *wandering lines* that resulted from seemingly random movements. The lines showed that the children tended to halt reoccurringly in particular places, all of which were in one way or another junctions of life in the settlement. A conclusive interpretation of the lines wasn't possible, but it wasn't intended either. Deligny emphasized that the maps didn't signify anything, that they were devoid of meaning. Interpretation simply wasn't the point, or rather it was exactly his point to abandon it. The maps were shown in Jacques Lin's book. Seeing John roam around in Logan's garden, I imagined that a map of his movements would probably look much similar, and would be equally impossible to interpret.

Like many autistics, John often displayed certain repetitive, self-stimulatory behaviors. He liked to flick his fingers in front of his face, close to his eyes, looking intently at the movement he created. It could be a way to deal with sensory overload, but sometimes he also seemed to just do it for his own entertainment. Deligny described such typical autistic finger movements as a "ballet of hands." It had a slight air of romanticizing an autistic compulsion, but I liked the change of perspective: To just try and look at something in a different way.

Deligny paid close attention to the autistics, for example by noticing the change of intensity and frequency in their repetitive gestures. He realized the moment when a drifting gesture (*geste de dérive*) turned into a steering gesture (*geste dérive*). He called the autistic an original partisan, whether he wanted to be one or not, because his being inevitably escaped anything conjugable, escaped the attitudes of all of our institutions. Deligny never did idealize or romanticize autism. He readily talked about the difficulties of dealing with children who were "insufferable in an impressive way." Being unable to hold speed with the forces of autism was a dramatic experience, he acknowledged. Over the years, the relentless presence of autism caused a certain toughening in the group members. Deligny compared it to soft skin turning into leather by tanning. The autistic's movements formed a drift that took the whole group with it, and the constant experience of friction caused the raft to be callused. Deligny asked: "Are these calluses that we develop just welts and hardenings? Or are they maybe an instrument reverberating harmonies as old as mankind? This is the key question to our quest."

Jacques Lin concluded: "We have spared Janmari and others life in a psychiatric ward. We succeeded in doing so by not relying too heavily on language. Language points to Whys and Becauses, and that doesn't help us when we face autism. We have succeeded in sparing them life in a psychiatric ward by taking a life upon us which wasn't always easy. But we created an environment that allowed these allegedly ineducable, unpredictable, nonadjustable and impractical ones, yet – as we found out – not at all incapable ones, to be quite agreeable companions."

What a nice notion: A portrait of the autistic as an agreeable companion.

After dinner, we usually took an evening walk through Haut-de-Cagnes. In front of the local bar, customers took their stools outside and sat out leisurely drinking pastis, later wine. We met Scott's Moroccan guide and his friends at the boule field. Elderly persons sat in front of their houses. One woman with a flowery apron and a traditional headscarf started to lively talk to John in French. While we were pretty sure that John couldn't understand a word that she said, he still gave her a big smile and appreciated her good nature. Like anywhere John's unusual behavior triggered glances and stares in the village, but people here didn't turn away like we had experienced in the seaside resorts just twenty miles away. Here, they greeted us in a friendly way: "Bonsoir, Monsieur! Bonsoir, Madame!" and some asked us directly:

"What's going on with your son?" Possibly more typical for a village, their language was so direct that it bordered on being rude, but we could easily tell their good intentions. I was happy to explain and preferred this situation to the politically correct, yet more condescending approach in posher surroundings.

We took a day trip to Monaco. Driving back towards Nice, the coastal highway *Corniche Moyenne* trails scenically through the mountains along the coastline. John was thrilled with the magnificent views of the sea. We stopped at the mountain village of Èze where Nietzsche had written part of *Thus Spoke Zarathustra*. Due to the narrow streets, we had to leave our car in a parking lot just outside the village – similar to our experience in Lindós on Rhodes. Èze too was quite touristy, like Lindós, but hadn't lost its charm.

After two weeks we were to fly home via Paris, but first we had to return the keys to Logan's French housekeeper. We cleaned and put everything back into its place. The housekeeper didn't have any complaints. I showed her the chair with the loose armrest and explained that this was how we had found it, and that we had locked it away to prevent further damage. She believed me. After all, she wouldn't even have noticed it, had I not pointed it out. She wanted to be sure, though, and called Logan who in turn didn't want to believe us. She said that the chair was an antiquity and that the price of the repair would have to be deducted from our security deposit. We disputed this for a while and then postponed the issue.

On the flight to Paris I was seated next to a perfectly styled woman who started to care for her hair as soon as the plane took off. She had a lotion with which she literally treated individual tips of hair. She then curled her eyelashes, and diligently rubbed another kind of lotion into her fingernails, one by one. While we landed, she finished by applying an expensive-looking hand cream. An entire flight dedicated to hair, eyelashes and hands – while we had our hands full trying to keep John seated. The spectrum of life in one row of airline seats.

From Orly airport, we took a taxi to our hotel. We had rented a room close to *Shakespeare & Company* in Saint-Germain. Unfortunately, when we got John's stroller out of the taxi and tried to unfold it, a significant part broke. We managed to lift the broken stroller, our luggage, and John up the stairs to the old hotel and entered a room decorated with red silk wallpaper, dominated by a huge red plush sofa. A divider shelf ran through the middle of the room, filled with books, apparently the hotel library. At first sight, we didn't see anyone. Was there even a reception desk? We heard a faint whisper and upon taking a closer look, we saw a tiny reception desk in one of the corners. A bunch of hair stuck up just above its counter. We approached the desk. A hotel clerk was crouched behind it, whispering into a telephone. We seemed to be a nuisance for him, he quickly asked our name and handed us keys, then dove back under the desk.

Having received no hints as to the location of our room, we searched the winding hallways, made up of corners and alcoves. The interior territory of the old building was as obscure as the lobby. We found our room. It was small and didn't have a proper window, just a milky panel that shielded the view of a narrow alley. Once we opened John's folding bed, there was literally no space left on the floor. The bathroom had tiltable mirrors that immediately caught John's attention. We thought that we might have time to unpack while John played with the mirrors and his varying reflections. There wasn't enough space to put our clothes away, however, and so we aborted the idea.

Since John's stroller was broken, we spent a rather large portion of the afternoon trying to convince him to get up from the sidewalk. Accustomed to spending time in Logan's quiet garden, it was difficult for

John to adjust to the big city. Maybe it hadn't been such a good idea to add Paris to the end of the trip. Luckily, we quickly found that John liked the *Jardin du Luxembourg*. The playground in the park charged an entrance fee. We had never heard of a playground charging a fee, but as long as John was happy on the swing, we were happy that he would be more cooperative and open-minded afterwards.

In Haut-de-Cagnes we had been able to cook in the house, but in Paris we had to go out. John didn't like to sit down or wait for food. He also didn't understand yet that he couldn't just grab food off someone else's plate. In Germany, he had once escaped us so quickly underneath the table that he had managed to pick a couple of French fries off a woman's plate next to our table before we caught him. Luckily, she had been a good sport about it.

We chose a small brasserie around the corner of our hotel for dinner. The waitress quickly noticed John's impatience and came over to our table. I was halfway afraid that she would ask us to leave, but to the contrary. She talked to John, made funny faces, and entertained him. She asked us his name.

We told her: "John."

And she exclaimed exuberantly: "Ah! Jean-Luc!"

John enjoyed the waitress giving him a new name. It even seemed as if he adhered to it better. Being called Jean-Luc perplexed him, it pricked his ears. We used this tactic for a while afterwards and came up with lots of new names: Jojo, Don, Johnchen, Johnchenmann, Jack, Jack-in-the-box, Fred, Filou, Schlingel, Schlawiner, Räuber, Struppi, Stöpsel, Piepenpeter, Funky Monkey, Friederike, Bob, Pfifferling, Monsieur le Président. As long as you didn't call him John, chances were pretty good that he'd turn his head. The effect naturally wore off after a while. Nevertheless, to this day, whenever we're in France, eat French food, or watch a French movie, we call him Jean-Luc.

During our first night in Paris, John got up in the middle of the night. In the small room, he crushed Scott's glasses on the night stand before we could intervene. Luckily, Scott had an old extra pair for emergencies. In the morning, we took the métro to the Eiffel Tower. We got in line for the elevator, but an employee quickly walked up to us and ushered us to the front. He must have had a very keen eye. We had come anticipating a difficult time waiting in line, but we had been sure that John would like it up there once we made it. It was then unexpectedly made so easy for us. We got onto the next elevator and John did love the view over Paris. With all the struggles that we sometimes have in public, it's always nice to experience (and remember) such unexpected acts of kindness.

In the end, we even saw the Tour de France. As we waited on the crowded sidewalk, John was entertained by the parade. After two hours and visits to several convenience stores, we were finally rewarded with a group of cyclists flying by. In a split second they were gone, and we couldn't even make out Lance Armstrong as he won his last Tour de France title.

Back in Berlin, the medical supply store had the spare part required for John's stroller in stock, and it was repaired on the spot. The vacation ended a little bit like it had started, with an extensive exchange of emails with Logan in Seattle, this time about the antique chair's loose armrest. At some point, we noticed that we had talked about two different chairs. The one that we were talking about hadn't even been to the upholsterer, so we didn't have to pay anything in the end. When we looked at the house's website a while later, though, we saw that Logan had added: "No children under the age of ten."

5 MALLORCA ISLAND (SPAIN) – PREVALENCE

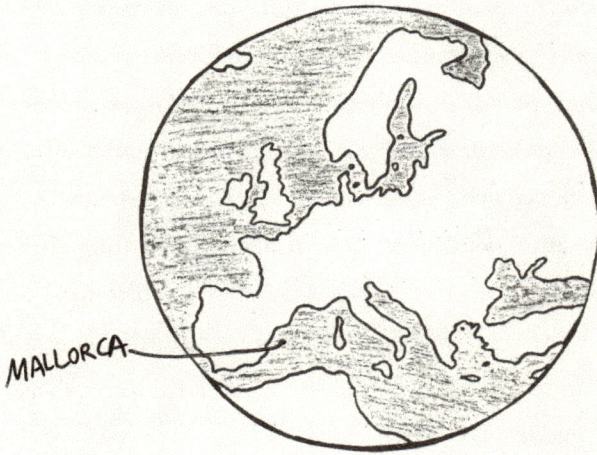

MALLORCA

One should only travel when willing to constantly be surprised.

(Oskar Maria Graf)

It took more than two-and-a-half years until we went on another big trip. We had taken several small road trips within Germany: To Hamburg, Dresden, Leipzig, and Heidelberg. We had visited my parents and friends in northern Germany several times. I had grown up close to the North Sea, and we could take day trips to the tidelands of the Wadden Sea and the East Frisian Islands from my parent's house. Our main focus had been transitioning John into school. We had looked at several schools and I had sat in on a few classes. In 2006, when John would have normally started school, we hadn't found a suitable place for him. A couple of schools in

Berlin specialized in autism, but they only admitted verbal children. John had continued to say a few words here and there, but it hadn't been enough for any of the autism schools. We had extended his stay in kindergarten for an additional year, but that was the most we could do. Schooling is mandatory in Germany and the system only allows for one year of postponement. John had eventually been assigned to a school focused on intellectually disabled children, to begin after the summer break of 2007.

He had been in a sheltered environment in his specialized preschool and kindergarten, just six children in a regular house. In contrast to that, his new public school had more than a 150 pupils and was located in the busy heart of the city center, next to Berlin Alexanderplatz. Since the school's curriculum didn't implement the special structures John needed, we had received approval for a one-to-one aide and we had realized quickly that John was very reliant on him. Three-quarters into his first year in school, for his Easter break in March of 2008, we decided to finally take a trip again. John was seven years old.

We had thought that it would be nice to leave the Berlin winter behind for a few days of Mediterranean sun and had found an offer for a vacation package on the island of Mallorca, including flights, a one-bedroom apartment in a family hotel, and two meals per day. We had never booked a package tour, but it was inexpensive and so we decided to give it a try. Flying in over the island on a bright sunny day and exiting the airport on a street lined with palm trees, it appeared to be just what we were looking for. We picked up a rental car and drove a half hour west from the airport to our hotel in the town of Santa Ponsa. It turned out that it was a holiday resort full of British pubs and restaurants. The town seemed rather deserted at first glance, but when we checked into the hotel we found that it was filled with English-speaking guests. We stayed on the fifth floor, and much to John's pleasure the balcony looked down onto the beach. Since both breakfast and dinner were served as buffets, we didn't have to order or wait for food, which worked out well for John.

Seeing the all-inclusive dinner buffet in the evening, we realized that we weren't going to find tapas here. Instead, it offered a large variety of hearty meat and potato dishes which John happened to love. He looked at the food and started giggling loudly. He must have felt like he was in heaven. Out of nowhere came a remark in a thick British accent: "What's so bloody funny?" We turned around and thought someone was kidding, but behind us stood an elderly gentleman who was apparently serious. Scott shot back: "He's handicapped." The man just turned away, shaking his head. Looking around the restaurant, we noticed a wide range of attention towards John, from annoyed stares to curious looks. We were used to staring, but we realized that it might be taken to a whole new level in a holiday resort. As we saw, tourists like to be entertained. Booking a vacation package meant that you got yourself into a highly social environment in which people sought out any opportunity to start conversations with their fellow travelers.

As usual, John got up early every day and we made good use of our time exploring the island. The East coast of Mallorca is dominated by hotels and housing complexes designed for mass tourism, so we concentrated on the North and the rugged West coast. We took a walk in the artist's hilltop village of Deià that dates back to Moorish times. John especially loved driving the winding mountain roads, with steep rocky inclines and breathtaking views all along the coastline. He sat in the back of the car and was so thrilled that he constantly performed his signature *Sitting Rowing Dance* while we listened to Yo La Tengo.

Driving up to the northern tip of the island, the Cape of Formentor, proved to be quite an adventure when we were suddenly faced with oncoming traffic in form of a large bus. Scott had to drive down in reverse on the narrow and winding road, a steep decline to the sea on one side, and the ascending mountains on the other. When we got to the Cape, we walked up to a railed viewpoint and John was suddenly scared. He clung to my legs. It was the first time that he was noticeably afraid of heights. He hadn't been good at judging heights before. It was one of the many reasons why he needed an aide in school. None of the windows or doors there could be locked. In fact, on John's first day, someone had opened a second floor window and John had tried to climb onto the ledge. Luckily his aide had been right behind him and had pulled him off. The Formentor Cape experience showed us that John now developed some sense of height and depth. We also noticed afterwards that he became a little more vigilant in jumping from playground equipment.

Our guidebook mentioned a remote bay close to the village of Sa Calobra. The bay could apparently only be reached by hiking down a relatively steep path. Shortly after our trip to France, we had been able to get rid of the stroller. It had been a large step for John and for us as well. We were unsure if John would go along with a hike, though. We gave it a try and it turned out that he was so thrilled with the nature that we didn't have any problem. We reached the secluded bay and spent a couple of hours there. John roamed around and examined all of the details: Stones, tufts of grass, sand, reeds, seaweed, earth, and water.

At the Berlin film festival, we had watched a deeply touching documentary called *Her Name is Sabine,* directed by French actress Sandrine Bonnaire. The film portrays her autistic sister Sabine by combining home video footage of Sabine's childhood with current takes in the residential home where Sabine lives as an adult. The childhood footage showed Sabine on several family vacations, where she appeared to be rackety and happy. I had to think of these scenes while observing John's joy on the western coast of Mallorca.

Sabine had eventually become too difficult to travel with. Would the same happen to us? It was hard to imagine when looking at how much John enjoyed himself, but the contrast between childhood and adulthood had also been stark in Sabine's case. I realized again how much we had to appreciate the here and now, because the future was so unclear. In Sabine's case, school hadn't worked out for her, and so she had eventually stayed home. A family move from Paris into the countryside had then further upset her, as well as her siblings moving out one after another as they grew up and started leading their own lives. Sabine had become violent, which had made it even more difficult for her family to take care of her. Eventually, she had been put into a psychiatric ward where she only deteriorated further. The film portrays frighteningly well how a sequence of events that normally happen in life can spiral into an utter loss of control.

Right around the same time, John's transitioning into school had shown us personally how moving from one phase of life to another could be an existential challenge for an autistic person. We tread a fine line. Transitioning was all the more precarious because of the bureaucracy involved. There were a lot of services and benefits, and we appreciated that. Even so, it didn't mean that one received them automatically. As parents, we had to investigate and enforce our rights. When John's school placement had been evaluated, the school board tried to code his special educational need exclusively as intellectually disabled, rather than additionally under the autism code. We wondered why until I found out that autism qualified for higher staff ratio and generally more benefits. We had immediately requested an adjustment of status, but although John had both diagnoses, it had taken us some effort to convince the placement team.

When I raised the issue in the parent group, it turned out that a few children were coded incorrectly or insufficiently. Ours wasn't an extraordinary or singular case. It rather seemed to represent school board politics in Berlin. Yet what administrators might view as a simple matter of saving money could put a child like John severely at risk. Short-sighted decisions like these could cause a deep crisis for a child who was in a delicate balance with the world.

Upon entering school, John had initially struggled with a new phase of aggression. He was at times so easily enraged that damages were unpreventable. Mostly everything in our apartment had been repaired, glued back together, or somehow fixed in a temporary manner until John destroyed it once again. He started banging his head against windows, breaking two panes of glass on our kitchen door. It was obvious that he didn't tantrum out of spite or ill will. In his inability to communicate sufficiently, and/or cope with the world, he was sometimes over-challenged and frustrated. Quite understandably so, but how to deal with it? At seven years of age he had become stronger and much harder to contain. When John sensed that he caused stress or even fear, those signals fueled his meltdown. Insecurity or too much emotion led him further into despair. In critical and dangerous moments he needed a strong counterpart who overruled his loss of control. Dealing with someone who wasn't scared, or better yet: *Not impressed at all* by the scope of his meltdown could often, albeit not always, halt him.

Humor helped, but it was hard to come by. We had developed an affinity to a song called *Monster* by a German band, Wir sind Helden. The lyrics are about a woman whose boyfriend wants to move in with her and she tells him that she doesn't live alone. There's something within her and she repeatedly asks her boyfriend: "Can you hold my monster, can you?" Despite of the strong lyrics, it's a rather cheerful song and John liked it. Sometimes I'd tell him after listening to it: "And yes, we can hold your monster" and he'd give me a big smile.

The main problem was still communication. Using the system of laminated picture cards mostly remained a one-way street. We showed John a picture of what we wanted to do, for example, and he seemed to appreciate that, but he hardly ever used the cards to show us what *he* wanted. Slowly, after years of working on it, he eventually warmed to the idea, but mainly used the cards that involved food and water, his two biggest motivations. For his school lunch, he gave his aide the "more" card when he wanted a second helping. At home, he brought us the "kitchen" card when he wanted to eat, and the "bath" card. He loved taking baths and often brought the card several times per day. He was supposed to always get what he showed as a reward for communicating. One day, after two baths, I told him that it was enough for today and that I would put the "bath" card away. Later in the day, John went to the drawer that contained all of his picture cards. Of course he couldn't find the "bath" card, but after rummaging through his drawer for a while he eventually proudly presented me the card "swimming pool" and walked right up to the bathroom door, with a smile on his face that seemed to say: "I won this one."

By realizing that out of all of his cards the pool came closest to the tub, John had shown symbolic thinking. His triumphant smile suggested that he understood verbal language and social interaction, at least to a certain extent. He understood well that I didn't want him to take another bath, but then he had found a way to trick me into it. It wasn't for no reason that his nickname in daycare had been "Mr. Personality."

It made me think of philosopher Ernst Cassirer, who had written about deaf-blind Helen Keller and Laura Bridgeman. His observations seemed to fit so well for John too: "The specific character of human culture and its intellectual as well as moral values don't trace back to material, but to form. This architectural structure can express itself in various sensual ways. Vocalized language is superior to tactile language, but technical shortcomings of the latter don't negate its general usefulness. Symbolic thinking can also unfold freely by using tactile rather than vocal signs."

On John's clear days, frustration and aggression could be diverted and replaced by a happy boy who was proud of his achievements, but it was a slow process with setbacks and limited generalized effects.

When I had involuntarily been thrown into investigating the politics of education, I had realized that autism prevalence is a highly important issue. It affects the way society looks at autism. We didn't have official prevalence statistics in Germany, and therefore estimates were sometimes based on codes assigned by school boards. Knowing first-hand how those codes were being tampered with and kept artificially low in Berlin, I knew that they weren't representative.

In Germany, autism is still perceived as a comparatively rare condition. The 1999 Fombonne estimate of five children in 10,000 having autism is still widely perceived as a guideline while the *American Center for Disease Control* published autism prevalence numbers at one child in eighty-eight, and most recently at one boy in fifty. We followed how Bob and Suzanne Wright founded the autism science and advocacy organization *Autism Speaks* in 2005, and how they managed to put autism on the media agenda and lobby for it politically. Within just a year, *Autism Speaks* incorporated two established organizations, the *National Alliance for Autism Research* and *Cure Autism Now*. Autism was suddenly everywhere. There were title stories in magazines like *Newsweek, Time Magazine* and *People Magazine*, as well as numerous articles in the *New York Times* and other newspapers. From Larry King to Oprah Winfrey, from *The Hidden Epidemic* to *Autism: The New Frontier?*, it was all over television as well. In her campaign for the Democratic presidential candidacy in 2008, Hilary Clinton spoke about a "national health crisis" in regards to autism: "An epidemic that will demand the next president's attention."

While I felt that acknowledging the prevalence of autism was needed to improve the life of autistics, offensive marketing also seemed to carry the danger of feeding into anxieties. If there was an epidemic, there had to be a reason. The downside of the extensive public talk were ever more wild speculations on causation. Media fed us almost on a daily basis with old and new theories: Candida, lack of certain vitamins or secretin, gluten intolerance, viral infections, aspartame damage, and gut inflammation, just to name a few. Until 2001 vaccines contained Thimerosal, an anti-fungal preservative, which was often suspected to play a role in autism. Since its removal from vaccines, autism prevalence numbers are still rising, though, which makes Thimerosal an unlikely culprit in the end. Nevertheless, the discussions continue and vaccinations remain a favorite suspect, even though there's no evidence of harm. Manipulations were revealed in several studies that had claimed such evidence, and publications were then retracted. Yet even as some of the doctors who conducted and popularized those studies lost their license to practice medicine, the talk about vaccination damage didn't stop.

Was there even an autism epidemic?

Even though Hans Asperger and Leo Kanner had introduced autism as a diagnostic term between 1938 and 1943, the *Diagnostic and Statistical Manual of Mental Disorders* only acknowledged Kanner's Early Childhood Autism as a pervasive developmental disorder in 1980, and

Asperger's Syndrome had only been added to the manual in 1994. Autism is a young diagnostic term. A continuous rise of diagnoses had to be expected as psychiatrists, pediatricians, and the general public familiarized themselves with it. A child with severe autism might have only been diagnosed with an intellectual disability before, and a child with Asperger's Syndrome might have gone undiagnosed and simply been considered a loner or socially awkward. Psychologist Tony Attwood assumed in 2006 that still only 50% of children with Asperger's Syndrome are being diagnosed.

Anthropologist Roy Richard Grinker, father of an autistic daughter, examined in detail how the diagnostic criteria for autism changed throughout the various editions of the *Diagnostic and Statistical Manual of Mental Disorders*, and how these changes contributed significantly to the rise in numbers. For example, between the manual's editions of 1980 and 1987, criteria for diagnosis became more vague and thereby opened the door to more diagnoses. A variety of studies subsequently revealed how much prevalence depended upon the definition of criteria. German researchers Michael Kusch and Franz Petermann came to the conclusion that there were 2,200 autistic children in Germany according to the 1980 edition – and 20,000 according to the 1987 edition. The scale of divergence is staggering.

In the manual's 1994 edition, some criteria were specified as compared to 1987, but they still remained more vague than in 1980. Atypical Autism and Asperger's Syndrome were added and subsequently became heavily used diagnoses. Grinker also notes that during the publication process, *and*'s had been replaced with *or*'s, and the number of symptoms needed for a diagnosis had thereby involuntarily been reduced.

There were plenty of more aspects to consider. For example, distinguishing autism from its differential diagnoses, namely psychosis and schizophrenia, has vastly improved. Also, the rising numbers don't automatically imply that more children are born with autism, as there are many adults among the newly diagnosed, and autism didn't used to be diagnosed when there were other obvious medical conditions. Today up to 10% of persons with Down's syndrome, up to 47% of persons with Fragile X syndrome, and up to 48% of persons with tuberosis sclerosis are diagnosed with autism. Other syndromes with high autism comorbidity include Angelman syndrome, Rett syndrome, Joubert syndrome, and Cohen syndrome. About 37% of diagnosed autistics have another diagnosis.

Grinker visited families in Peru, India, South Korea, and South Africa. Autism was perceived differently wherever he went. In India, autism wasn't as stigmatized as in South Korea, for example. Retreating from society has a more positive connotation in Hinduism, which might be a contributing factor to a more positive view in India. While autism researchers such as Leo Kanner and Bruno Bettelheim in the West theorized that the mother's emotional coldness caused her child's autism – a notion thankfully debunked, discredited and discarded – theories in India assumed autism to be caused by too symbiotic of a relationship between mother and child. (Striking, though, that despite the contrary interpretations of *too distanced* and *too close*, both hypotheses ultimately directed responsibility towards the mother.)

One might also consider autism as part of several more general trends. 6% of German children today have an officially acknowledged special educational need and that number, too, is steadily on the rise. Children are observed and evaluated closer than ever before. In their effort to optimize development, Western societies are driven to detect the slightest differences and we end up discovering a large variety of them. The closer you define normal, the smaller the normal group becomes, creating an ever larger group of abnormality. The *Diagnostic and Statistical Manual of Mental Disorders* knew sixty categories of abnormal behavior in 1952. In its 1994 edition, the number of categories rose to 384. Even though we are physically healthier and live longer, we seem to feel worse. This pertains both to adults and children. A study in one German state found that the number of children under the age of fifteen admitted to the hospital due to psychological problems rose by 43% between 2000 and 2008.

Just to mention a couple of even more global points, researcher Stuart Murray pointed out that the notion of normal or normalcy itself only date back to the mid-nineteenth century when the idea of the 'norm' began to supplant an earlier conception of the 'ideal', and sociologist Majia Holmer Nadeson mentioned that we live in a time that places extraordinarily high demands on social competence, and therefore autism might be perceived more acutely.

I encountered an argument several times that parents might just be more comfortable with an autism diagnosis than with the diagnosis of an intellectual disability. In other words: Autism's prevalence would have increased due to parental choice of words, evading the terminology of intellectual disability. I'm doubtful about this argument's validity. In our case, John is intellectually disabled and we don't feel uncomfortable with that, but autism is a condition that he has on top of that intellectual disability, showing for example in his numerous issues of hypersensibility, his different perception and the different way in which his brain processes these perceptions. If John were "only" intellectually disabled, his problems would probably be considerably less pronounced. I don't see why autism – which in a severe form is more challenging than an intellectual disability without it – would be a preferable diagnosis.

The angle is likely a different one, as social science researchers at Columbia University have shown. They extensively studied the so-called autism epidemic and according to their findings, another change of attitude in the middle-class was especially significant. Up until the middle of the twentieth century, children with intellectual disabilities were almost automatically placed in residential institutions. The percentage of such children not living at home with their families reached its peak in 1967. Ten years later, 83% of intellectually disabled children still lived in institutions. During the eighties and nineties, the U.S. underwent a gradual process of deinstitutionalization. It became not only socially acceptable to keep an intellectually disabled child at home, it was eventually even seen as the better alternative. Integrating their disabled child became a legitimate goal for middle-class parents. When these children lived in residential institutions, society hadn't seen any need for exact or differential diagnoses. The children and adults were somehow taken care of, and that was all society needed (and wanted) to know. As soon as these children lived at home, though, parents needed support and diagnoses helped organize the new family life. When the children started to even attend schools and work as adults, diagnosing became ever more important for organizing all of these developments. Therefore, increased prevalence can be seen as a consequence of empowerment, and further increases in diagnoses can be expected to accompany the ongoing process of inclusion.

A rise in prevalence isn't necessarily a rise in incidence. Most epidemiologists and researchers think that the rising numbers can be explained outside of the notion of an epidemic. However, there are also some who think that this question remains unanswered. What seems most important to me is that the epidemic talk doesn't help the practical situation of autistics. Prevalence, on the other hand, is a worthwhile focus. All factors that contribute to rising prevalence point towards a better understanding of the condition. I agree with Roy Richard Grinker's perspective that rising prevalence means that we increasingly see and acknowledge a difference that has always been there, but that we haven't felt necessary to acknowledge before.

The main city on Mallorca island is Palma with almost 300,000 inhabitants. It has been settled since 5,000 B.C. and it has been both Roman and Arabian. There are many remnants to see and the main sight is an impressive Gothic cathedral, *La Seu*, 330 feet long and a hundred feet wide, dating back to the year 1230.

It was difficult to find a parking spot close to the cathedral, so when we finally found one, we were anxious to get out of the car. Scott walked over to the parking meter while I got John out of the back seat. Since our rental car was only a two-door, I had to flip the passenger seat back and reach behind to unbuckle John's seat belt. I placed my purse next to my left foot and pulled John out of the car. I sensed movement next to me. Someone had appeared out of nowhere and grabbed my purse. A young man ran off. My purse flew through the air as he fled. I couldn't run after him because Scott was over at the parking meter and John couldn't be left alone outside of the car. So I just stood there, hand-in-hand with John next to our car, and yelled at the top of my lungs: "Hey!"

It was just a helpless cry, but loud enough. The young man turned around, looked at John and me for two long seconds, and then dropped the purse and took off. Scott had, in the meantime, started to run back towards us, also alerted by my shout. He ran on to retrieve the purse. I thought that the man had probably somehow managed to take out my wallet, but nothing was missing. The purse was still zipped up and all contents were safe inside. He had really just dropped it after I yelled at him. Why? Had he seen that John was disabled and then decided not to steal from us? I didn't know, but it was the most likely explanation. There was no reason for dropping that purse, as he had already been in a safe distance from us. Scott had been even further away than me, and the young man must have noticed that I couldn't run after him, as I stood immobile hand-in-hand with John.

Our exploration of Palma de Mallorca was cut short by this event. We weren't in the mood for serious sightseeing any more. Being robbed was a bad feeling, but being subsequently and unexpectedly spared from the robbery felt additionally strange. I was happy and thankful to have my purse with all of my belongings back, but at the same time it made me think that by just one look at us even a thief took pity on us. Was that supposed to make me feel good? Or what had happened there? We just walked around the old town for a bit and bought a couple of sandwiches for lunch. We picnicked on a bench in a square, but soon felt ready to head back towards Santa Ponsa.

While driving on the island we noticed many cyclists on the roads, especially in the mountains. We learned that Mallorca was a popular location for preparing their racing season throughout Europe. On one steep slope, in an otherwise deserted mountain stretch, a cyclist's front tire exploded right before our eyes and he went flying over his handle bars. We immediately pulled the car over and ran towards him. He laid on the ground, his hands and knees were badly scratched and bleeding, and he had abrasions on his face. He moved, though, and he tried to sit up.

"Are you okay?," we asked. He didn't respond and had a bewildered look on his face. It appeared that he was in shock. The street was deserted, so he wasn't in any immediate danger. We helped him move to the side of the road and picked up his bike. We wanted to call an ambulance, but realized that we couldn't get a cell phone connection. We would have to drive him ourselves. The trunk wasn't big enough for the bike, so we took the tires off and balanced the frame on Scott's shoulder in the back seat. I reclined the passenger seat as far back as we could, as the injured cyclist struggled to sit down. John squeezed into a corner of the back with Scott and the bike, as I drove.

Once everyone plus bike had somehow twisted into the small car, we carefully drove down and out of the mountains to the cyclist's home base on the northern coast of the island. He was obviously in pain, but nevertheless interested in John and asked us questions about autism. He directed us towards his accommodation, which turned out to be a gated community for professional cyclists that looked like a country club. At the entrance gate, the guard cast one eye on the cyclist and instantly called for help. He took the bike out and several men arrived to take our guy in. He thanked us quickly, but it all went so fast that we could hardly say good-bye.

As always, we had purchased full insurance coverage without deductible for the rental car. That had worked well in Southern France, and was helpful again in Spain. We cleaned the car the best we could, but there were still some blood stains on the seat. Since we were already in the North, we decided to visit the marina in the town of Port de Pollença, which we had only passed by before, and had wanted to come back to anyway.

Before we knew it, our days on the island were over and we headed back to our developing schooling situation in Berlin. John's aide had only been approved for one school year. Upon our return, we had to apply for the extension of his contract after the summer. This wasn't going to be easy. While banks were being bailed out, one-to-one aides for autistic children had fallen prey to Berlin's austerity measures. It had already been hard enough to get the aide approved for the first year, but further cuts in funding had been announced in the meantime. We were afraid that John's aggression would spiral out of control if he lost his aide. We surely wouldn't be able to send John to school then.

About thirty parents of our informal parent group joined to found a nonprofit organization, and I became a member of the board. We talked to all political parties in the Berlin senate to maintain the aides for autistic children. I didn't want to become an activist, but the alternative was to just accept the decline of services and help, and that obviously wasn't really an alternative.

SCHEELE KNIGHT

6 CONNEMARA (IRELAND) – THERAPIES

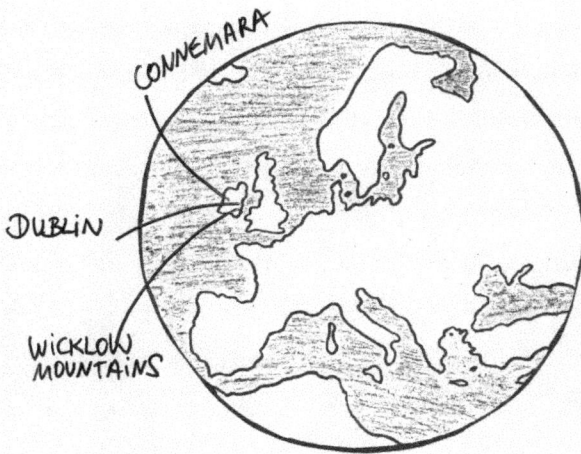

> *Science built the Academy,*
> *superstition the inquisition.*
> (Robert Green Ingersoll)

The summer break started without a definitive answer on the school aide issue. Maybe his contract would be extended, maybe not. It was a terrible situation for all of us, not the least for John's aide who went into the break not knowing if he still had a job afterwards.

John had started to repeat more words and even parts of sentences. There was an autistic girl in his class who was called Owens. Like John, her sensory processing was impacted in a way that made her a sensory seeker.

She liked to climb everything and the teachers frequently had to say: "Owens, get down!" John repeated this over and over at home, for years to come: "Owens, no. Get down. Owens! Owens!" John's speaking was still mostly echolalic. Once, he had been on the swing and had suddenly said: "Ooold!" Since it had been quite chilly, I asked him: "Are you cold?" He replied: "Yes!" It was the only time John ever verbally answered a question.

He had also started to hum melodies that we could recognize, some lullabies, some songs that we listened to often, and parts of classical arias to which he listened with his aide in school. John was very taken with the Queen of the Night aria from Mozart's *Magic Flute*. Especially when he was mad about something, he would hum the melody with a grim look on his face.

He also experimented with his voice, at times making high-pitched sounds and often mimicking adults in a deep and low tone. One day, we were walking on Potsdamer Platz, one of Berlin's main squares. A professionally dressed woman suddenly stopped in her tracks right in front of us. She turned around and looked visibly upset at Scott. It almost seemed like she wanted to slap him. We hadn't understood until John repeated what he had just said seconds earlier in his deep and low voice: "Mhm, delicious!" The woman's angry gaze moved from Scott's face down to John, and then she burst out laughing. We were so used to John's echolalia that we often just tuned it out, but John had at least saved his dad by repeating the growl.

"Mhm, delicious!" was one of his favorite expressions at the time. John had become a huge fan of cheeseburgers and ice-cream. Actually, the majority of words he said were in the food department. When we drove around in the car, listening to music and happened to drive by a gas station, he sometimes got excited and shouted: "Buyin' ice-cream! Goin' buyin' ice-cream!" We had bought John an ice-cream several times while refueling the car, so gas stations had somehow morphed into ice-cream supply stores for him. Whenever we drove by the golden arches, he'd hum the jingle: "Da-da-da-da-daaa!" and we sung back to him: "I'm lovin' it." He knew what a McDonald's looked like, and what it was selling. However, he didn't discriminate between fast food chains. When we drove by a Burger King, he also hummed: "Da-da-da-da-daaa!" and then usually added: "Buyin' cees-burger!" Of course we couldn't buy him fast food at every chain we passed by, or ice-cream at every gas station, so it would often result in an angry hummed version of the Queen of the Night aria from the back seat.

Cheeseburgers were therefore a safe bet to ease transitioning into a new environment when we arrived in Dublin for our summer break in August of 2008. I had been to Ireland before, and I was happy to travel back with Scott and John to see what they thought. The flight to Dublin had been just over two hours. We picked up a rental car at the airport. Neither Scott nor I had ever driven a car with the steering wheel on the right side, having to handle the stick shift with your left hand while driving on the left side of the road. It was easier than we thought. We checked into a bed-and-breakfast that we had booked online and went walking. Within a few blocks we happened upon a McDonald's, and John was in heaven: "Da-da-da-da-daaa, I'm lovin' it." After dinner, we walked through the city and I rediscovered places that I had been to before: Trinity College, Grafton Street, St. Stephen's Green. Back at our B'n'B, we had to be rather quiet in our single room so that John could sleep. We just sat at the open window and enjoyed a glass of wine, the city air flowing in, typical narrow walk-ups across the street, the faded light of the street lamps, the distant sound of an unfamiliar ambulance horn – big city life anywhere, but the sights and sounds at the same time distinctly Dublin.

We got up early the next morning, as we had a long drive ahead of us across Ireland to the western coast. We had rented a house on Renvyle Peninsula in the heart of Connemara's rugged landscape. The American house owner happened to be in Ireland at the time, and was going to deliver the key personally. She had given us precise instructions how to get to the house. After getting off the highway, we enjoyed a wonderful drive through the country towards Renvyle. We still had to ask for directions in two different pubs before finding the house.

The owner explained the necessary details to us. For warm water, one had to push a button and wait for a half hour for it to heat up. The house was charming. The living room had a huge bay window that faced the sea, with mountains in the background just to the right. There was a fireplace and peet to make a fire. Like many autistic children, John liked to take off his clothes. He didn't seem to see the need for wearing them in the first place. In the house, he quickly undressed. We put some shorts and a t-shirt on him and he headed straight for the bay window. Sitting in its corner, he looked outside and obviously appreciated the view.

Ireland took all of our hearts by storm. We explored our peninsula, strolling through old ruins, stone houses without roofs, and a deserted cemetery. We went to Omey Island: During low tide, you could follow a path and reach the island on foot. We weren't sure if we could manage it with John, but he was so thrilled that it was no problem at all. We took a ferry to Inishbofin island and spent all day exploring. We drove the Connemara loop. Wherever we went, the landscape in its many different shades of green offered new breathtaking views. We fell into a rhythm of drifting, much similar to the way we had done years earlier on Thassos. In the evenings in the house, Scott and I took turns working on a jigsaw puzzle of the *Ha'penny Bridge* in Dublin, which we had found in the living room. John wasn't interested, but at least left the pieces on the table. This would have been unthinkable not long ago. He would have swept them off with his hand almost immediately. As slight as his development was, we could always notice it in details.

John seemed to be in his environment. In fact, he was doing so well that we decided to attempt hiking a hill. In Connemara National Park, Diamond Hill is roughly 1,500 feet high. Three walking trails lead up the hill: Yellow being the easiest path, blue the mid-distance, and the red path going all the way to the top. We saw a few families with children at the foot of the hill. John wasn't too thrilled. This wasn't drifting, this had a purpose. Annoyed, he shouted: "Owens, no, get down. Owens! Owens!" He walked reluctantly, taking breaks by the side of the path. Families with much smaller children than John passed us by.

"Doesn't wanna walk, the little fella, heh?" one man asked. "We'll see about these ones!" He pointed to his two children. We shared a laugh and then they were off. Slowly but surely, we did get higher. When we arrived at the cut-off for the yellow road leading back down, we decided to give the blue one a try. At the next lookout point, John was suddenly thrilled. We had reached a point where we overlooked the smaller hills and could finally make out the sea. John did the stand-up version of his *Sitting Rowing Dance*. His "Owens, no, get down. Owens! Owens!" turned from an accusatory tone into an enthusiastic one. His pace quickened and we started to pass the families that had previously passed us. Now their children took more breaks. We shared another quick exchange with the man and his two kids.

"They don't wanna walk, these little fellas, heh?" Scott asked. And pointing to John, I added: "Now this one does!" He waved us on laughing. As we continued on, we didn't think that we would hike all the way up to the top. We would just go on as far as we could and then turn around when we had to. At the junction where the blue and red trail separated from each other, we had the choice of going further up or looping back down. Since John was in his element now, we decided to continue on up. John even led the way. Clouds rolled in and it started to rain. Soon we were drenched and encircled by clouds. We had reached a point where all the families with children had turned around, but we were so close to the top now that we didn't want to give up any more. We took a few more breaks and eventually reached the top in the pouring rain. John was thrilled once we got there.

Going down, it was slippery and steep. We had to hold John's hand. Eventually, we made it back to the blue trail, and John started running ahead of us. When we saw our car, around eight hours after we had started our journey, we felt a sense of real accomplishment. We were soaking wet, but exhilarated. We drove back to our house and dried our rain-soaked clothes and shoes in front of the fireplace. We enjoyed dinner to the smell of burning peet in the dry warmth of our living room. Afterwards, John sat happily in what had become his favorite spot in the corner of the bay window. Watching him, I couldn't help but ask myself if this wasn't better than any therapy. Nature, hiking, a view, and a fireplace.

The pressure to implement therapy early on, and as much as possible, had been on my mind for a while. More and more parents in the parent group tried alternative interventions and suggested inviting so-called experts to our meetings to present treatment options. Schedules of seminars were emailed around. A weekend course with a more than €400 attendance fee would explain biomedical interventions available to "cure autism." It was disturbing to me. Why did otherwise reasonable individuals become increasingly irrational? I suspected that it might have to do with our children getting older, but still being autistic. Conventional therapies brought certain improvements, but didn't make autism disappear. Rather than finally accepting autism as a life-long condition, some parents investigated alternative treatments instead. This seemed to be the next step in the succession of a struggle that I had been observing for years.

It had started with the idea of a time window to act against autism's progress. This is a popular theory derived from the observation that many autistic children first seem to develop normally and then regress. The theory draws on the notion that the first three years of life are decisive for development. Neuroscientists today have doubts how exclusively true this is, though. John Bruer wrote in *The Myth of the First Three Years* that the development of synapses is by far not as over-proportionally important during the first three years as previously thought. Also, anomalies in the brains of autistics have been observed that stem from an early fetal stage. Purkinje cells are smaller and fewer, and the neural cells of the limbic system are also small and additionally more densely packed per unit volume. These differences aren't acquired postnatally and thus speak against a time window. In 37% of autistic children, the brain temporarily grows faster than usual. In 40% of adult male autistics, both hemispheres of the brain are enlarged. Patrick Levitt studied the role of receptor MET that is important for brain functions in the cortex and the cerebellum, but also for the immune system and the gastro-intestinal metabolism. The Autism Genome Project studied 1,400 families and investigated the possibility of neurotransmitters glutamate and GABA playing a decisive role, just to name a few examples. Neurobiological, morphological and molecular research cast doubt on the notion of a time window.

The results of research don't necessarily imply that autistic brains don't function properly, they first and foremost imply that their brains function *differently*. That isn't a negligible nuance. To consider differing brain structures in a purely deterministic way would take nearly all agency away from the autistics. They would be victims of whatever their brain structure inflicted on them, but neuroscience has shown that the functioning of brain and body is way too complex for simple determinism. There's a lot we can do to influence our well-being. The time window, on the other hand, is a deterministic notion. It sets a limit. The parents who bought into it were effectively in a race against time.

Studies have shown that diagnosing too early increases the probability of false diagnosis significantly. Diagnoses at twenty-four months turned out to be wrongly positive for about a third of the children, while diagnoses at thirty months were almost 100% accurate. The idea of "The earlier, the better" doesn't necessarily seem to apply. Seeing autism as a life-long condition instead, one can work steadily and patiently on possible problems like aggression, frustration tolerance, or communication – without time pressure.

In the course of having entered a race for time and having absorbed the mentality that came with the idea of a time window, many parents had become proponents of rigorous therapy regimens, some of them adhering to forty hours a week, even for small autistic children. Most were doing intensive behavioral therapy; one family had bought into the so-called Son-Rise program. I felt weary about that. Did the children have enough freedom when they spent forty hours per week in therapy? Proponents liked to argue that it didn't feel like therapy to the children, because it was presented to them as play. This argument was based on the premise that the child couldn't feel whether someone interacted with them for therapeutic reasons or just to play and spend time with them. We cannot know how children perceive it, though, and for parents it certainly is a therapeutic situation.

To me, it was frustrating when the boundaries between therapy and play were blurred. John loved music, so we engaged with music a lot. Was that music therapy then? I remembered during our winter break, when there had been a lot of snow in Berlin, we went sledding several days in a row in a park close-by. John enjoyed racing downhill so much that we climbed the little hill endlessly. One of us had to ride the sled with him to steer and balance out John's erratic movements. In the evenings we had all been exhausted, but John had slept well through those nights. The way it worked for John, I guess you could've called the sledding therapeutic. Yet we like music and enjoy dancing with John without calling it music therapy, and we enjoy sledding and hiking up Diamond Hill without calling it OT, because it simply isn't. The idea of therapy is linked to expectations and performance evaluation, and those categories don't matter for our family life. We just spend a lot of time with John and try to have a good time together.

Over time, I had watched some parents up the ante. They attended programs that trained them to be co-therapists. I wondered how that might affect the relationship between parent and child. Wasn't the emotional attachment in a parent-child relationship much different from a therapist's? The question reappeared whether the child could discriminate between therapy and non-therapy. If the child could do so, the previous argument that therapy was just play would be obsolete. On the other hand, if the child couldn't discriminate between the two, he or she would be faced with an irritating mixture of messages from the parent, some therapeutic, some parental. Mixing the emotional stability of a mother-child or father-child relationship with therapeutic goals seemed rather risky to me, especially when considering how important reliable attachment figures are for autistic children. How did the co-therapy concept affect family life, especially if there were other siblings involved: When was the home a place of education, and when was it a shelter from demands? Was that obvious to everyone in the family at all times? When could autistic children just be themselves? Was a home still a home when it doubled as a therapy location?

Then, alternative treatments had become popular. Quite a few parents in the parent group fed their children supplemental nutrients, put them on diets without gluten and casein, performed intestinal cleansings, and heavy metal detoxifications. They were interested in all kinds of biomedical interventions and paid high fees for consultations and expensive lab tests. Our parent group only mirrored a general trend as, for example, in the year 2000 only a handful of children had been subjected to chelation, a form of detoxification, and five years later the number had risen to 10,000. Evidence-based science was still in a stage of basic research and therefore couldn't provide any answers. Alternative interventions, on the other hand, were in the market of providing answers, and some parents longed for a cure desperately.

Michael Fitzpatrick, British doctor and father of an autistic child, pointed out that many biomedical interventions draw on previous medical dead ends like biological psychiatry from the sixties and seventies. Lab tests award a scientific aura while also alluding to core occidental themes, like the nineteenth century belief that we are poisoned by our own excrements, which in turn carries remnants of the Christian Fall of Mankind. In the beginning of the twenty-first century, these feelings are exacerbated by the notion that next to our own bodies poisoning us, the environment has also turned against us, invoked by industrialization and the increase of natural disasters. "While science haggles over alternative medicine, it has long since become a rapidly growing branch of economy," journalist Dirk Böttcher wrote in an article titled *Hope in small dosages*. The sales market for vitamins, minerals, and enzymes has become a multi-million dollar business.

Over the years I had seen how some parents had completely exhausted themselves, but there was almost no common ground to speak to each other. The mindsets were so different. One father in the group had been especially adamant about cure and questioned me about what interventions I had tried. When I said: "None," he laughed at me and said: "Oh my God, what ordeals you still have ahead of you. There are so many things to try. It took me years to get to this point."

I told him that I didn't intend trying them. He was shocked. "But how can you let your child down like that? Don't you see that you have to, because one of the interventions *could* work?" he asked. I tried to explain that it was scientifically unlikely and that I didn't want to waste our time chasing after a ghost. Especially because I didn't feel it to be ethically right to subject my son to all of these ordeals, as even he himself had called them. The man looked at me as if I came from a different planet. He had basically dedicated his whole life to healing his autistic son. I would see him occasionally at the group meetings and he would say how much better his son was doing after this or that intervention. On one occasion, just ten minutes after claiming improvement again, he told us that the occupational therapist had resigned due to his son's increased aggressiveness, and that he was looking for a new occupational therapist. Hadn't he just claimed improvements? I truly didn't understand it, just like he didn't understand me.

Researchers David Gal and Derek Rucker from Northwestern University published a study according to which counter-evidence, paradoxically, tends to turn people into even stronger advocates for what has been disproved. Such advocacy is based on belief rather than reason. Even if nothing works over the course of years, and even if they've spent all of their money and time, I saw how some parents remained convinced that their interventions had been the right thing to do and that they should carry on in the same manner. If it made them happy I would understand, but even that I wasn't sure of. The father who had argued with me several times was at some point admitted to the hospital with multiple organ failure. His wife said that he had completely exhausted himself searching for cure.

Two mothers were doing Holding Therapy with their autistic child. In a multi-disciplinary book, psychologist Ute Benz compiled research from various medical and judicial fields with regard to such approaches. The results are distressing. Forced holding for a prolonged period of time causes incredible stress on the child. It promotes fear, helplessness, desperation, and it violates the child's autonomy as well as dignity. The procedure that is supposed to "loosen blockages so that love can flow again" – one therapist's rhetoric – destabilizes the child's personality and leads to disturbed social interaction and deep loss of trust. It isn't clear how a forced identification with an aggressor should help a person who already has a fragile sense of self.

In disguise of therapy, at times a level of violence is acted out which wouldn't be tolerated by society under other circumstances. Therapy isn't a protected term. While the job title therapist might sound trustworthy, it doesn't vouch for any humane or professional quality. Proponents of various alternative interventions at times seem to loose a sense of danger and abuse. As a result of her research, Ute Benz called for a public debate about what constitutes violence in therapy. It's sadly ironic that autistic children were treated with a level of insensitivity or emotional numbness that was otherwise, wrongfully, ascribed to autism.

Next to violence, society also often supports exploitation of suffering and hope. A popular case in point in Germany is Dolphin Therapy. It's being promoted in TV documentaries and newspaper stories. Reporters follow families with disabled children to Florida, Turkey, Israel, Curaçao, and other places that offer the therapy. The children swim with the dolphins and supposedly make developmental leaps, or so the story goes. The destinations are far away and on-site therapies costly, so parents often collect donations beforehand. For example, our bakery one day suddenly had a donation jar on its counter.

Entire communities are getting involved. Once the funding is successful, that creates an underlying obligation of success. Who would return and tell a local reporter that the intervention didn't change anything? Which newspaper wants to publish *that* story? Which reader wants to read it? Didn't they donate money to relieve suffering? On many levels, a feel-good dynamic evolves that clouds any objective look at the intervention. A myth of effectiveness – purely anecdotal, of course – is being created.

One family in John's preschool took their daughter for Dolphin Therapy in Miami, returning convinced that it had helped. More than anything I could see that they wanted to believe so. I couldn't see the differences that they raved about. However, the newspaper coverage was enthusiastic. During a parent meeting following the newspaper coverage, one mother was very emotional: "Dolphin Therapy is such a wonderful thing, but it's so expensive. I can't believe that there's help for my son, and he doesn't get it, just because we can't afford it. It breaks my heart."

At that moment, I realized how harmful even the feel-good dynamics and rhetoric can be. Convincingly represented in the media, pressure is created for other parents to follow the path and stage their own fundraising effort. I've met autism therapists who argued in favor of such interventions, stating that any creation of hope is positive. Unfortunately, this seems a somewhat short-sighted point of view. Even though these interventions superficially create hope, parents sooner or later realize that a specific intervention didn't help the way they had hoped it would, and so they move on to the next. The hope created is highly transitory. It leads to a succession of disappointments, thereby eventually creating suffering, not the least for the autistic child who doesn't have any say in being dragged from one thing to the next.

Looking at science, Dolphin Therapy is doubtful. Most dolphins in the centers aren't kept species-appropriately. This is, of course, an animal rights issue. The levels of chlorine are unhealthy for dolphins, but necessary when humans are in the water, due to risks of water pollution and disease transmission. A general ethical debate about using undomesticated animals for therapy has been raised since the early nineties. In this case, it even concerns an endangered species that is even brought in from nature because breeding in captivity is unsuccessful.

Biologist Karsten Brensing and his colleagues studied swimming-with-dolphin programs and therapies between 2003 and 2005. Uncoordinated behavior of the marine mammals, speed of movement, frequency of breathing, and depth of diving all pointed to elevated stress levels in the dolphins. The researchers did find that the ultrasound resonating under water could have an effect on biological tissue under specific circumstances, but the dolphins in most centers didn't emit the effective frequency under the poor conditions that the mammals were kept in. Even in centers where they registered transmission of effective frequency, it wasn't long and consistent enough to be helpful. Results in centers varied according to how appropriately the dolphins were kept. In large free-water compounds they were less stressed, but even there only one in five showed any preference for a disabled child.

The University of Würzburg conducted a comparative study between 1998 and 2006, and came to the conclusion that Dolphin Therapy isn't more effective than any other animal-based therapy option that they compared it to. It was only in the category of *Parental Perception* that Dolphin Therapy scored higher than, for example, horseback riding. Independent instruments of evaluation, for instance interviews with caretakers and video footage, showed no significant changes with Dolphin Therapy.

Relatives and therapists continuously have to decide what needs therapy and what can be left alone. I always tried to keep in mind that scientists and society have often been wrong about which behavior should be treated: Left-handedness and homosexuality being two prominent examples. For guidance, I thought it was useful to look at what autistics themselves have said about therapy. Autistic Michelle Dawson, for example, suggested an ethical evaluation to precede any treatment or therapy on non-consensual patients. Autistic Jim Sinclair wrote: "If an autistic person is engaging in behavior that is dangerous or destructive, or that interferes with the rights of others, then certainly this is a problem that needs to be resolved. If an autistic person lacks a skill that would enhance that person's ability to pursue his or her goals, then every effort should be made to teach the skill. The problem I see is when autistic people are subjected to intensive, stressful, and often expensive treatments simply for the purpose of making them appear more normal: Eliminating harmless behaviors just because non-autistic people think they're weird, or teaching skills and activities that are of no interest to the autistic person just because non-autistic people enjoy those activities." German autistic Angelika Empt wrote: "Looking back on all the counseling and therapies that tried to break through my autism, they have hurt me more than they were useful. What I needed was a careful and slow building of inner structures to take down my autistic wall. My current therapy, which I've been doing for two years now, is a gentle, quiet, and delicate process of restructuring."

John was almost eight years old. He had been in early intervention programs as soon as the epilepsy had started at age eighteen months. Conventional therapies had helped us, sometimes more obviously than others. Occupational therapy had been helpful early on, but only at age two and three. Speech therapy had long been a dead end, until a new speech therapist had worked with a method developed by a Brazilian speech therapist named Beatriz Padovan. It noticeably improved John's speaking and he enjoyed the new sounds that he could make. Sometimes structured approaches had worked, and at other times dynamic ones. There were no set routes.

Each autistic child is different and sometimes development also just happened by itself, without any credit to therapy or anyone but John himself. He discreetly developed and discovered on his own, just like any other child, even if slower. I thought that we sometimes didn't appreciate this enough in children with intellectual disabilities. The focus on therapy tended to be so overpowering. Naturally, we wanted to help John learn to express himself and overcome his frustration. On the other hand, we also wanted to give him time and space for his own discoveries; to just let him be. It was a balancing act. Returning from school in the afternoon, I could see that John was just happy to be home and we realized that we would like to leave therapy to the school hours. Of course, this would only be possible if the services for John's needs were kept in place – something still up in the air for the start of the upcoming school year.

In Ireland, we were happy and relaxed, drifting through nature, day after day. We had originally planned to see Galway, which was only an hour and twenty minutes away. We never made it there: There was just too much nature around us to explore. Letterfrack and Clifden were as far as we got city-wise, and only for groceries and supplies. Before leaving the West coast, we did want to see the Cliffs of Moher, though, and so we set aside one day for a trip, driving through the Burren to Doolin and Liscannor. Much like we had experienced at the cape of Formentor in Spain, John was scared of the height as we walked along the famous cliff-tops. He still enjoyed the views when Scott carried him, but he wasn't in the supreme mood he had been in earlier in the week. The touristy activities never seemed to turn out as great for us as the remote and unknown ones did.

On our way back towards Dublin, we drove via Limerick to the Wicklow Mountains. We had booked a couple of nights in a bed-and-breakfast there. Many years earlier, in my student years, I had been to the Wicklow Mountains with my friend Susanne. We had taken the bus from Dublin to Enniskerry and had hitch-hiked on to Glendalough. It had taken a long time for a car to come by in Enniskerry, and while we waited for a lift, I found a four-leafed clover on the side of the road, which I dried and to this day keep in one of my books. Driving through the Wicklow Mountains with John, the days of carefree hitch-hiking were clearly over, but Glendalough and the Wicklow Mountains were just as beautiful as I remembered them. The former life and the current one connected in the shared beauty of the landscape. Sometimes one has to come back to places previously visited, just to make that connection. A system update.

The bed-and-breakfast consisted of a family house and a garage next to it that had been turned into a guest room. The cheery owner quickly handed us the keys: "I'm off, lads. I have a date tonight, but my son is here if you need anything." We did need something, as we missed a third mattress in our room, but we first took a ride to buy some food and then rang the doorbell to the house. Nobody answered. There was loud music, though, so the son had to be home. We walked around the house to knock on the living room window. Listening to Pink Floyd, he was drinking and smoking with a couple of friends. Startled, they jumped up with guilty looks on their faces, but were readily helpful in finding us another mattress.

The owner was back for breakfast the next morning, looking tired, but in a good mood. She was affectionate with John and told us that she, too, had a disabled daughter. We had a nice conversation with her before setting out to explore the area. When we checked out the following day, she gave us a discount on the rate that was quoted online. "Out of solidarity," she said and smiled. This was another thing about Ireland: Wherever we had gone in the past ten days, from the grocery store to the gas station, and wherever we had talked to anyone, from people we met on our excursions to the owners of the places where we stayed, everybody had been extremely nice to us and also to John. We were sorry that our vacation was coming to an end.

On our last night, we went into Dublin's Temple Bar District for our farewell dinner. In the street, a band played Johnny Cash's *Ring of Fire*. John stopped abruptly, stood immobile and watched them with a keen eye. When the song – which to our knowledge he had never heard before – was finished, he turned around wide-eyed, obviously impressed, and flawlessly hummed the melody of the chorus without the words: "And it burns, burns, burns, the ring of fire, the ring of fire."

Little did we know that it was going to replace the Queen of the Night aria. Eventually, John even perfected the horn section of the song. He would use it in times of frustration, for example when being denied the third ice-cream of the day, blurting loudly from the back seat of our car: "Daaa-daa-daa-dadadadada-daa-da-daaa, the ring of fire, the ring of fire!"

7 SOUTH TYROL (ITALY) – NEURODIVERSITY

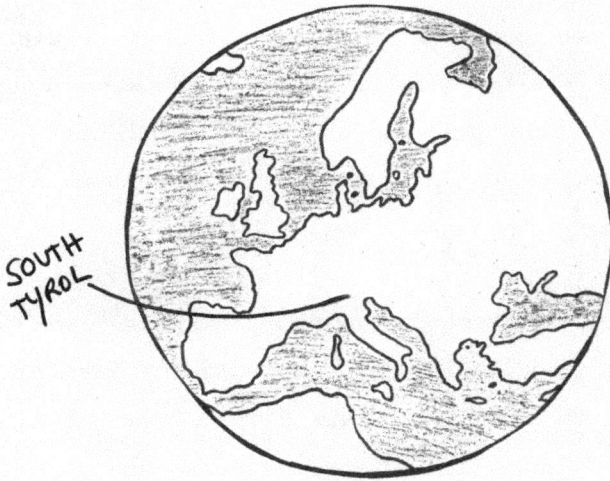

The question is not how to get cured, but how to live.

(Joseph Conrad)

John's aide was approved for his new school year after lots of struggles with the Berlin Senate's educational department. For the fall break, we decided to travel to Northern Italy, just over five hundred miles from Berlin. Since John loved to ride in the car, that seemed easier than flying somewhere. In the summer, on our way home from Ireland, we had run into problems on our return flight. We had flown Aer Lingus for the first time, and the flight had been severely delayed. The boarding gate had been changed twice, making the transitions difficult for John, who still had problems waiting in the first place. Then the staff hadn't allowed us to pre-board and had insisted on us boarding last. It was according to their safety policy. The whole situation had been a disaster.

On our way to South Tyrol, we overnighted half-way in the city of Ingolstadt in a small motel just off the highway. We proceeded the following day via Munich towards Austria where the Brenner pass took us over the Alps towards Italy. Having arrived there, the infamous Alpine *Jaufenpass* was open, and so we drove the winding, scenic route rather than the quicker highway. The views of the mountains along the way were gorgeous, and since this was Scott's and John's first time in the Alps, we stopped several times along the way to take in the scenery. John was appreciative as always of a new grand landscape.

South Tyrol was part of the Austro-Hungarian Empire of the Hapsburg monarchy until it became Italian in 1919, following the treaty of Saint-Germain after World War I. Today, it's an autonomous Italian province in which more than 70% of citizens still speak German. We had booked a small rental apartment in the province's south on the premises of an old wine-processing facility, within the village of Tramin that has a population of just over 3,000 inhabitants and is known for the vine *Gewürztraminer*.

After checking in, we went to scout the area. Wine terraces ascended gently on the mountain slopes. A church with a square and a fountain made up the traditional center of town. We saw people dressed in traditional mountain apparel while palm trees indicated the southern location. Just above town, only a ten-minute walk from our apartment, we found the chapel of St. Jacob. A guide just happened to open the church as we arrived. We joined the group and inside the chapel found well-preserved, colorful Romanesque frescoes, dating back to around 1220, in relatively good condition. They showed hybrid creatures: A centaur, a cynocephalus, a skiapode, and other creatures from medieval myths. It made me think back to our minotaur in France. From the church grounds, we enjoyed magnificent views over the valley, and then walked on further up the mountain. Soon we were in a remote setting where the forest seemed to swallow all sounds. We sat in a clearing and the silence was so thick that it seemed as if you could physically feel it. It felt almost unreal.

When we returned to the rental apartment, we discovered that we had wireless internet access, opened up our laptop, and were bombarded with the news of the day. I thought back to the silence we had just experienced in the mountain. What a clash of nature and contemporary amenities. We could spend the days roaming in the middle of nowhere, and then reconnect with the world upon our return.

Since our apartment owner's family still worked as vintners, we were able to taste different wines that the family harvested. In order to get to our apartment, we had to walk through a hall furnished like a wine cellar. Shelves had been built into large wine barrels, cut in half. They were stacked with dozens of unlabelled bottles, mostly white wines. On a wooden table lay a piece of paper and a pen. Whenever we wanted, we could just take a bottle and put a mark next to our apartment number. Anyone was invited to use this honorary system. At the end of your stay, the owner just counted the marks and tallied the amount.

South Tyrol was full of diversity between the Italian and the German, the Alpine and the Mediterranean culture, the bustling city of Bozen – the capital of South Tyrol province – and the serenely quiet mountains, and with its hybrid creatures, half human and half animal, as portrayed in the chapel of St. Jacob. Even the German heritage in itself reflected diversity, because everything seemed so old-fashioned compared to Berlin. It reminded me of elderly expat Germans I had met in Chicago while working at the German Cultural Center. We had organized lectures, talks and exhibits, and a number of elderly Germans regularly attended these events. They had been living in the U.S. since the fifties, yet when they spoke English, their German accents were still evident and they used old-fashioned terms. They had been living outside of Germany for decades and had lost touch with the language development. In South Tyrol, I read the *Dolomitenzeitung*, a local newspaper, and the obituaries were also written in a style that had long since vanished from German newspaper obits.

On our way out of the vineyard, we met the owner and chatted with her. She asked at some point: "And will you also visit Italy during your stay?" Her question caught us off guard, we didn't immediately understand it. We *were* in Italy, after all. Then we realized that she didn't look at it that way. She was asking if we wanted to drive beyond South Tyrol. I told her: "Yes, we think we'll drive to Verona. It's supposed to be nice, right?" She shrugged and said: "It's okay, I guess." Her enthusiasm for a city of which its old town was a UNESCO World Heritage Site was quite moderate.

When I had called her from Berlin, I had first asked on the phone: "Do you speak German?" I had heard the indignation in her voice when she had replied: "Of course, we *always* speak German." Yet in the grocery store in Bozen, when I had spoken to the cashier in German, she had been offended and had replied angrily in Italian that she didn't speak German. It was difficult not to be insulting in one way or another. It showed us how deep the identity questions ran in the region.

The identity politics and the diversity we encountered reminded me of autistics striving for autism to be accepted as part of their personality in what has been coined the *neurodiversity* movement. It first received momentum in the early to mid-nineties, notably by autistic Jim Sinclair's essay *Don't mourn for us*. Sinclair wrote: "It is not possible to separate the person from the autism. Therefore, when parents say, 'I wish my child did not have autism,' what they're really saying is, 'I wish the autistic child I have did not exist, and I had a different (non-autistic) child instead.' Read that again. This is what we hear when you mourn over our existence. This is what we hear when you pray for a cure. This is what we know, when you tell us of your fondest hopes and dreams for us: That your greatest wish is that one day we will cease to be, and strangers you can love will move in behind our faces."

The term neurodiversity was coined by sociologist Judy Singer from Australia, herself on the spectrum. She looked at what feminism had accomplished for women and what the movement for the rights of homosexuals had achieved, and envisioned a similar emancipatory movement for autism. Although Judy Singer and Jim Sinclair received some public attention, theirs remained somewhat singular voices until the rise of the internet eased the distribution of ideas. Harvey Blume published the term neurodiversity in 1998 and in the new millennium autistics started to organize themselves under this term with increased public attention. To cherish autism as part of one's personality doesn't mean that autistics claim a right to withdraw from society. Quite to the contrary. Beyond demands of social assimilation, they desire to be seen as a worthy part of the community. On the show *Anderson Cooper 360 Degrees,* Sanjay Gupta asked autistic D.J.: "Should autism be treated?" D.J. replied: "Yes, with respect."

As part of the disability rights movement, autistics scrutinized treatment interventions and rhetoric. The rampant, if unproven theory that vaccinations cause autism is criticized for reducing the autistic personality to being a vaccination damage. When the NYU Child Study Center started an ad campaign for autism research in December of 2007 by using ransom notes and portraying autism as an abduction, advocates reacted immediately. One ad read: "We have your son. We will make sure he will no longer be able to care for himself or interact socially as long as he lives. This is only the beginning... Autism." Ari Ne'eman, president of the *Autistic Self Advocacy Network,* called out the harm of the "stolen child" stereotype: It violates the dignity of autistic being when you equate it to a loss. The ads resort to old prejudices against autism and disabilities. They imply an insufficiency, and by associating autism with a kidnapper, they relate it to a criminal action. The protest found huge support and soon the *New York Times,* the *Washington Post* and the *Wall Street Journal* reported. Less than three weeks after its start, the campaign was pulled.

In 2010, an Australian autism campaign called "Communication Shutdown" asked people to shut down their social media for one day to help understand the isolation autistics might feel. The charity was supported by various countries but never involved autistics themselves. Many of them felt that the internet helped them communicate and that staying off social media for one day couldn't appropriately convey autism. In protest to the campaign, autistics renamed November 1 "Autistics Speaking Day" rather than "Communication Shutdown."

In general, the internet has emerged as an ideal platform for autism advocacy, especially self-advocacy for autistics who might have social difficulties in direct contact. Before digital networks, who would have thought that autistics would form effective social groups? In these groups, one can observe typical social mechanisms, for example the development of their own colloquialisms. Autistics refer to themselves as aspies, and call non-autistics NT's, for neurotypicals. German autistic author Nicole Schuster expressed on her website how being diagnosed has given her a positive new attitude toward life: "Since early childhood, I have felt different from others. I have never felt at home, I have never felt like I belonged. By coincidence, I happened upon Asperger's Syndrome. I knew immediately: These are my soulmates. People who feel and think like I do.

Today, I know that I have Asperger's. The day of my diagnosis was a new beginning. My life as an aspie started on November 2, 2005."

Neurodiversity is an emancipatory movement. Psychologist Tony Attwood also emphasized this aspect. In his *Complete Guide to Asperger's Syndrome*, he recounts how he took up the routine of accompanying a diagnosis with a positive remark: "Congratulations, you have Asperger's Syndrome!"

Is autism really part of the personality, though? Even autistics themselves don't agree on that assessment. Autistic author Susanne Schäfer, who has experienced significant improvements in her perceptive problems, mentioned during a conference in Germany: "I always thought that autism was part of my personality. I can only say now: What constitutes autism, disturbed perception and concentration and so forth, if you remove all that, I am still here. It's not an autistic personality, my life is now much easier and more beautiful. Today, I no longer find anything worthy in autism. I'm thankful for that." On the other hand, some high-functioning autistics even want Asperger's to be entirely removed from the *Diagnostic and Statistical Manual of Mental Disorders*, following the example of homosexuality which was removed in 1973. (The separate diagnosis of Asperger's Syndrome has incidentally just been removed from the new edition of the *Diagnostic and Statistical Manual of Mental Disorders* DSM-5, published in May of 2013. The occurrences are still pathologized, though, they have just been moved under the autism spectrum. Whether under Asperger's name or under the umbrella of an autism spectrum, the crucial question was and will remain: Where is the borderline to pathology?)

Author and critic Gary Westfahl, himself identifying with Asperger's Syndrome, published a text in 2006 called *Homo Aspergerus: Evolution Stumbles Forward.* According to his observation, the internet creates a time-consuming and highly complex continuity of endless communication: Interactive, fragmented, non-linear, and dynamic, the internet and especially social networks hinder focus and thereby eliminate creativity and productivity. Autistics, though, because of not being so pre-disposed to social interaction, could resist this unproductive environment and excel. Westfahl's arguments are somewhat reminiscent of earlier theories. Media theorist Marshall McLuhan hypothesized an invisible contamination by media as early as 1964. The melting of the organic and the technological would be inevitable, creating technically structured individuals. In Westfahl's argument, it's the technically structured autistics who then remain creative and original. Plus the autistics can use the new technology to distribute their ideas and creativity without having to get into direct social contact. That argument also reminds of McLuhan who described media as a prosthetics as well. Westfahl concluded his text: "I am now prepared to argue that Asperger's Syndrome should not be regarded as a handicap or as a debilitating condition; rather, it is a tremendous asset, a set of beneficial traits that may someday be recognized as the characteristics of a new, and superior, form of humanity." Looking at the experiences that autistics have shared in recent years, Westfahl's conclusion seems rather over-enthusiastic. We heard and read about feelings of isolation and depression, even in high-functioning autistics. They've told of their struggles with sensory overflow and how stressful it can be to navigate the world. Not all individuals with Asperger's would likely characterize their condition as a tremendous asset, and performing at a higher level in a specific area doesn't establish a superior form of humanity anyway. Humans turning into ever more productive, well-functioning autistics: Westfahl's *Homo Aspergerus* as the next step in evolution would rather be a dystopian perspective. Apart from his unduly evolutionary meandering, Westfahl's argument of autistics as "capable workers" did somewhat fit into the realm of the neurodiversity context, though. Some autistics had shown certain assets and strengths that they were increasingly able to use in order to lead a self-determined and independent life.

Mathematical philosopher Mike Lesser, Dr. Dinah Murray and Wendy Lawson – all three autistic – considered an "attention tunnel" central to both the cognitive strengths and weaknesses of autistics. According to their idea, autistics can exceptionally focus their attention and this allows them to excel in specific and repetitive tasks where attention to detail is necessary. Their monotropism idea resonates with expressions of other autistics. Australian writer Donna Williams for example talked about "mono-processing" in a similar way. A tweet I happened upon summed up these strengths of high-functioning autistics in a nutshell: "It's inevitable that the wikipedia site for Asperger's is one of the most detailed and best organized of all." Persons with Asperger's often seem to soar in mathematics, and they often seem to have an extraordinary understanding of complex structures and an affinity to technology, especially information technology.

A growing number of employment agencies are drawing on these strengths. Since 2004, the Danish company *Specialisterne* exclusively looks for employment for autistics. The company has spread to Switzerland, Austria, Great Britain, Iceland, and most recently to the U.S. Similar projects have been founded in Germany. Hajo Seng, an IT programmer and administrator diagnosed with Asperger's, runs an employment agency called *autWorker* in Hamburg. In Berlin, *auticon* is Germany's first company to exclusively employ autistics, currently working with eight IT consultants. *SAP* announced that they are looking to hire hundreds of autistics. A German autism research cooperation called "AFK," in which autistics work together with researchers of the *Max-Planck-Institute* at the Free University of Berlin, found that the lack of social competence remains a key problem in job placement, though. Despite their capabilities, even high-functioning autistics often still don't make it past the highly social situation of a job interview. Such weaknesses are least important in an environment that highly concentrates on mathematical-technical talents, and therefore autistics often end up in self-selecting communities. Temple Grandin alluded to that dynamic when she described NASA as "the world's largest sheltered workshop for persons with autism."

Silicon Valley is another such self-selecting community. Asperger diagnoses are apparently increasing significantly there, leading to the suspicion that children of engineers might be especially prone to autism. Journalist Steve Silberman wrote: "The chilling possibility is that what's happening now is the first proof that the genes responsible for bestowing certain special gifts on slightly autistic adults – the very abilities that have made them dreamers and architects of our technological future – are capable of bringing a plague down on the best minds of the next generation." Yet quite simply, highly specialized thinkers who lack social skills might not have had as many children in former times, because they didn't live in an environment where they met like-minded thinkers to build a family. In that sense, Silicon Valley wouldn't be a reason for increased autism prevalence, but rather just its host. Cambridge psychologist Simon Baron-Cohen elaborated on both possibilities with the so-called "assortative mating" hypothesis on the one hand, and on the other hand the hypothesis of an evolutionary process in which the increased demands for specialized tasks over time reshaped the male brain to focus on systemizing rather than empathizing. Evolutionary biologist Bernard Crespi and sociologist Christopher Badcock argued with a slightly different focus in their "imprinted brain theory." They described an evolutionary tug of war between motherly and fatherly genes. When genes of one partner dominated significantly, a brain imbalance would evolve. Schizophrenia would be an indication of dominant female genes, autism an indication of dominant male genes.

These ideas aren't entirely new. Hans Asperger suspected as early as 1944 that the autistic personality might be an extreme expression of male intelligence. Sociologist Theodor W. Adorno described the individual as a biological substrate of his new work environment. Sociologist Max Weber famously elaborated on "trained specialists." Today's autism theories to a degree seem to be reiterations of previous lines of thought, now projected on autism. They largely remain in the realm of experimental thinking, and many of them seem suspicious in terms of gender stereotyping.

Discussions of autism are almost always highly ambivalent and the neurodiversity movement is still comparatively young. Many questions still have to be negotiated. Utilitarian arguments that try to establish autistics as "capable workers" exclude low-functioning autistics on the severe end of the spectrum, like John. The original argument for neurodiversity was one that tried to acknowledge all autistics for who they were, beyond their ability to contribute to the GDP. The biggest challenge for the idea of neurodiversity seems to be a careful phrasing of a differentiated attitude: To claim rights, respect and dignity for a way of being without underestimating the potential need for support in care, schooling, therapy, respite, work, and residential placement. We do live in a system that honors such extensive multi-level support only for pathologized states of consciousness, after all. The neurodiversity movement also has to be careful not to draw too much on ontological differences. Sociologist Majia Holmer Nadeson pointed out that distinguishing between biological groups establishes two separate entities and suggests that they might be irreconcilably different from each other. This neglects the dimension of permeability and the possibility to learn social behavior. Autistics have shown that they can learn, even the so-called low-functioning ones.

John being severely autistic, chronically ill, intellectually disabled, and prone to dangerous, aggressive behavior, sometimes people were surprised that I didn't swiftly discard the idea of neurodiversity. Once someone told me that he thought it was pure cognitive dissonance, that I just didn't see how miserable our life with autism was. However, I felt that he was missing the point. I did see how difficult our life with autism was (I wouldn't call it miserable). I lived it every day and night. There was no sugar-coating going on in my mind, but assuming what you could call a Nietzschean affirmative attitude towards life and its circles, dying and living, loving and hurting, suffering and enjoying, did create freedom – even if our life didn't always allow for this perspective, which could seem rather cynical in moments of despair. Sociologist Donna Haraway described how HIV-positives shifted the focus on *living with the virus* and how this helped them overcome the role of victims and reunite with a world that had turned away from them. I hoped that something similar could happen with the neurodiversity movement. If we managed to emphasize the necessity of services and help within the neurodiversity discourse, we might also be able to address the dignity and worth of life on the spectrum.

I had been around eight years old, like John was now, when my brother and I had also vacationed in Tramin and had hiked the Tramin Hiking Path with our parents. Upon successful completion of the track, we had received a hiking pin called "The Golden Backpack." Would John be able to do that? The hike was long, and it would take us higher than Diamond Hill in Ireland. At the tourist info we found out that the path still existed, even though there were no longer any "Golden Backpacks." They still carried booklets to collect stamps in the mountain huts along the way, and they gave out simple hiking pins when you had completed the task. We decided to give it a try.

The enthusiasm and ambition John had developed on Diamond Hill didn't kick in the same way. He walked, but not fast. Along the way, we took many rests, especially when collecting stamps at mountain huts. Altogether, the distance was more than eleven miles, and we had to overcome a height difference of about 2,000 feet. We had started around nine o'clock in the morning and for the last section, a rather steep descent through a gorge, it was getting dark already. I was a bit afraid that we wouldn't make it out by daylight, and stupidly enough, we hadn't brought along a flashlight. I guess we never thought it would take us that long to return. With John, you never knew when you'd come back from an excursion. In the future, we would always take a flashlight on long hikes, lesson learned. Nevertheless, we came out of the gorge just as it was finally dark. While we cooked dinner back at the apartment, John ran and jumped around as if we hadn't done a thing all day. The amount of energy he had was amazing. I couldn't tell if John felt a sense of accomplishment, but he certainly seemed happy. This hike wouldn't have been an easy task for any eight-year-old, let alone a severely autistic boy.

We did take that day trip to Verona and enjoyed the city. John even posed in front of the amphitheater with two men dressed as gladiators – a rare touristy activity for us. It wasn't easy to take good photos of John, because he never looked at the camera, but the gladiators' costumes cracked him up, and so we managed to get in a good one. On our way back to Berlin, it had already snowed in the higher altitudes of the Alps, reminding us that another winter was just around the corner.

8 SOUTHERN SWEDEN – INCLUSION

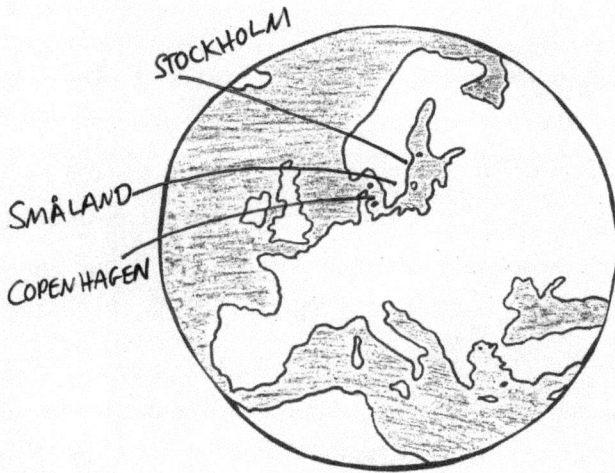

"Don't stare!"

(Everybody's mother)

By spring of 2009, we had to apply for another extension of John's school aide. Next to further spending cuts, the Berlin Senate increasingly focused on mainstreaming children. What little funding remained was needed there, so the Senate had become even more determined to phase out the aides in special ed schools. The way politics were going in the city we weren't going to find stability for John, so we started to look for schools outside of Berlin. After two years, the constant fight over John's school needs being met had seriously started to wear us down. My volunteer work had become excessive and my paid work suffered from it.

We revisited a private school that we had looked at three years earlier. At the time, we had thought that it was too far away, about forty-five miles, and had decided against it. It took us almost an hour and a half to get there in thick traffic and I was disheartened again. This wouldn't work, but when we saw the classes, we realized instantaneously just how much better it would fit John. The school worked with continuous structure in all rooms, modelled after the TEACCH program. The curriculum was tailored to nonverbal children. All teachers worked off of the same approach. In the Berlin public school system, teachers valued their pedagogical freedom, which meant that every teacher did things differently, which in turn meant that it was almost impossible for John to find routine and overview, the kind of safety he needed. The private school wasn't bound to pedagogical freedom. I knew we just had to get John in there, even if it meant that we had to move. The principal was generally open to the idea. However, she didn't have space for the fall. We would have to wait one more year and then she could take John in, starting after the summer of 2010. Once again, we would have to get the aide contract approved in Berlin.

A friend of mine had been on vacation in Grisslehamn, on the East coast of Sweden, not too far from Stockholm. The place where they had stayed, a typical red Swedish house, had been spacious and situated in a relaxing rural setting. We had never been to Sweden, so we decided to fly to Stockholm and stay in the same house for John's Easter break, just for five days. We had booked the smallest size car at Stockholm airport, but when we arrived the car rental only had upscale Volvo sedans available, and so we received a free upgrade. We were off to a good start. We drove in the large car through the countryside towards Grisslehamn. Since we were so much further North, the land was still covered with ice and snow, which we had already left behind in Berlin. We were transported back into winter.

The family on whose premises we lived had two Golden Retrievers. John had a curious relationship with dogs. He loved observing them, but he didn't like them getting close. Here too, he was afraid of the retrievers, but interested nevertheless. Since John was so sceptical, we called the dogs Double-trouble. It cracked him up. We'd say: "Uh-oh, here comes Double-trouble!" and John would snicker and sway back and forth – often a sign of appreciation. This could only be topped when we took a walk and someone with three dogs approached: "Triple-trouble!"

There was an open chicken coop in the backyard. Contrary to the dogs, John had no problems with the chickens. He enjoyed running among them. It seemed illogical, because their movements were more unforeseeable than those of the dogs, but in the case of the chickens, John didn't mind.

We took a day trip to Stockholm and after walking through the old town *Gamla Stan*, we decided on a rare adventure with John, a museum. It consisted of a large ship called the *Vasa* and a building that had been built around it. The *Vasa* is a Swedish galleon that sunk on its maiden voyage in 1628. It had been discovered under sea in 1956 and recovered in 1961. The wooden ship is 230 feet long, thirty-nine feet wide and 170 feet high. It once held sixty-four canons and was decorated with 700 sculptures of Roman warriors, Greek gods, lions, mermaids, and fantasy figures. You could walk all around the ship on seven different levels. Walking was something we could do, and while John normally wasn't interested in smaller museum piece objects, he had been interested in the amphitheater in Arles. The ship being a large structure as well, we thought that it might be comparable in a way.

It was dark inside the museum. John just wanted to run around. Scott and I didn't get a chance to read the area descriptions, but we did manage to see all levels. It wasn't the greatest excursion for John, but we never knew what would spark his interest. We always guessed as we went along. Sometimes we hit the jackpot, sometimes we made wrong decisions that triggered a meltdown, and sometimes John was mildly interested or reluctant. The latter was the case with the *Vasa*. At least he didn't mind. I hadn't thought that I would find a ship that interesting, but it turned out that I was impressed with it. As was Scott, and so it worked out just the opposite of what we had expected.

Grisslehamn is the ferry town for transport to Åland, an island off the Swedish coast that belongs to Finland. We contemplated a day trip and went to the port, but John was in a shaky mood. To take the risk of a full-day excursion where we had to rely on the ferry's departure time back to Grisslehamn, effectively being stuck on Åland, didn't seem to be a good idea. We always had to decide according to the moment, and the island wasn't for us, we were afraid. John enjoyed being driven around in the Volvo, listening to music. Lately, he was especially taken with Sufjan Stevens' album *Come and feel the Illinoise*. We could practically listen to it day and night, as far as John was concerned. We put the CD in, and instead of visiting Åland, we drove up North alongside the mainland's coastline.

We had lunch in a Swedish fast food restaurant in Östhammar, just off the highway, a curious place, as it was full of people but almost silent. We found a quaint old town, Karlholmsbruk, to take a walk and then continued inland towards Uppsala. Thinking back to our five Easter days in Sweden, it seems as if we spent the entire time listening to Sufjan Stevens while the Swedish landscape, monotonous yet still appealing, rolled by. In the seemingly endless sameness outside of the towns one had to look for details, like a small café off the side of the road or a farm nestled in the distance in order to find the way. Maybe the landscape's appeal arose exactly out of its monotony, in combination with the colorful *Illinoise* album. Something about it was soothing. I could understand John's happiness with it.

On our last day, we explored the unique small islands of the archipelago off the Swedish coast. The ferries that took you from one island to the next were public service, you could just drive on and off as you wished. John enjoyed going between skerries and ferries, perpetually moving between water and land.

We enjoyed Sweden's serenity, so we jumped at an opportunity that happened to present itself within just a couple of months. An acquaintance owned a small garden house in Småland, Southern Sweden, and sent around an email asking if anyone wanted to rent it for the low price of €200 per week in the summer. She wouldn't be able to go, and so she looked for someone to mow the lawn and keep up the place. At that inexpensive price, we could stay for three weeks.

The house was close to the city of Växjö in an area known for its furniture trade and glass-making, comparatively easy to reach by car from Berlin. A two-hour drive to the Baltic Sea, a ferry ride to Denmark, then approximately six more hours of driving. When we arrived at the harbor to set over to Denmark, the port was filled with cars. Summer vacation had just started, so the highways and ferrylines were in high season. We were lucky to have pre-purchased ferry tickets, because any cars that didn't were turned away and sent to another port town more than two hours away. It took a long time to sort out the chaos in front of the ferry. It was hot and because our car didn't have proper air-conditioning we put towels over the windows to shield us from the sun.

John was almost nine years old but still incontinent. To take diapers for three weeks, we had stuffed our small Renault Modus with the packages. There had barely been any space left for clothing, because we also needed to take bedding. John, bored when the car didn't move, ripped open the diaper packages and sat in the back throwing around diapers. Reaching Sweden by car wasn't as easy as we had thought, but as soon as we were on the ferry, things started to brighten up. John enjoyed being out at sea and out of the car. To split up the long trip, we overnighted in a bed-and-breakfast in Denmark.

We reached our destination the following afternoon. The house was located about twelve miles outside of Växjö, driving through a village called Rottne and then turning right at a faded sign that read Målajord. The garden house belonged to a bigger estate called *Solhagen*, of which otherwise just the main house remained. It couldn't be seen from the garden house, though, because of the vast grounds of the estate. Nature had been left to its own devices for many years. The original owner had been a Swedish pioneer in South Africa, the rather famous whale fisherman Carl Ossian Johnson, who had co-owned the *Southern Whaling and Sealing Company*, founded in 1909. Johnson's first wife had refused him a divorce for thirty years. *Solhagen* was a country home where he had intermittently lived with his new partner Esther and their mutual daughter. The ghost of the woman who never became his wife was said to still rumble in the main house's attic. We were assured, though, that no sightings had been made near the garden house.

Later, the premises had been used as a boarding school for delinquent teenagers. An overgrown soccer field and old graffiti at the base of the garden house were reminders of that period. The wooden garden house, painted in yellow, turned out to be bigger than we thought. On the ground floor it had a kitchen, a bedroom and a living room, and on the upper floor, there were two more bedrooms with a bath. There were no amenities, though. The only heating was a fireplace in the living room, and there was no TV, dishwasher or washing machine. The latter was the most difficult aspect with an incontinent child. We would have to spend a lot of time washing by hand.

A strip of land around the house had been mowed and thereby carved out of the wild nature. It made up the yard. An assortment of garden furniture was stored in a shed, there was an open fire pit with a grill to hang directly above the flames, and in a large tree hung a long swing that swung very far with its long ropes. John would eventually spend hours every day in it. Inside the house, there was a turntable and a selection of old LP's. We enjoyed rediscovering music of our past throughout the evenings whenever it got too cold to be outside. The only CD we found in the house was the album *Dreams* by the band The Whitest Boy Alive. We listened to it frequently and it became attached to the memory of the yellow garden house. At night, we heard the rumble of trucks in the far distance. The owner of the main house told us that there was a Volvo plant close-by and that they sometimes did test drives at night close to *Solhagen*.

A half-hour walk away, there was a lake where we could go swimming. However, once John had taken the walk he knew the path, and the second time around he was so anxious to get to the water that he couldn't control himself. He had gotten himself so worked up that when we made it to the lake, he couldn't calm himself and we had to turn back. He had a meltdown even though it was something that he wanted to do.

John still had significant problems with delayed gratification. We could usually adjust to such situations and find solutions. For example, when we cooked dinner, he had previously not been able to wait for it to be ready. As soon as one of us started cooking, he wanted the food immediately. We had bought a service bell and started to ring it at the dinner table when the food was ready. John had eventually been able to redirect his attention to the service bell signifying the food, and not the act of cooking. It wasn't worth it to get creative about a temporary situation, though. Apart from the lake, there were plenty of other things to do.

During the second week of our stay, a rain front with colder temperatures took about seven days to move through, and we had to spend more time in the house. Birds had nested in the chimney, so the only fireplace in the living room couldn't be used. The Berlin couple that had stayed in the house before us had left a note on the kitchen table. They had gotten smoked in when they had experienced a cold weather streak, and their note warned us not to operate the fireplace. They had bought some extra blankets that they had thankfully left under the note. The house was cold and damp. The laundry washed by hand took three days to dry. We hit a rough patch. We drove around and found a campsite in Växjö that had a public laundromat.

Since we couldn't understand the Swedish radio and there were only Swedish newspapers in Rottne, we occasionally checked up on the world by driving the twelve miles into Växjö where the public library offered wireless internet access. I had found a Swedish cookbook in the kitchen, so I checked out a Swedish-English dictionary during one of our trips to the library, translated word by word and made a traditional Swedish herring salad that I was quite proud of. During another visit to the library, we chatted with an employee of the tourist information that was located next to the library. She recommended a visit to *Huseby Bruk*, an old ironworks and mill settlement from the 17th century. You could apparently visit the water mill, lumber mill and the blacksmith's shop. As soon as the weather cleared up, we drove out there. Naturally, John wasn't interested in the historical aspects of the village, but we had a nice walk around the settlement, bought him some ice-cream and then happened to see a bike rental that had an adaptive bicycle with a wheelchair in the front. John had outgrown the children's seat and couldn't ride on his own, but this could work. The clerk at the bike rental told us that we could ride around the adjoining Åsnen lake, the second largest lake in Småland province, and we spent all day doing so. We took frequent stops to let John run, and ate along the way. It was a great and unexpected experience. John rather enjoyed his prime seat and was in a good mood all day. We had thought that we would just walk through the settlement and then drive back to *Solhagen*. Who would have thought that a bike rental had such a specialized and obviously expensive rental bike on offer?

It fitted to what we had noticed before, though: Sweden was an extremely handicapped-friendly country. In Växjö, we had looked for a playground and had coincidentally discovered one that had a swing accessible for wheelchairs. It was the first time we encountered a public playground equipped for children with disabilities, but it made so much sense. Part of the reason why children with disabilities weren't frequently seen in certain public areas like playgrounds, was that these places didn't accommodate their needs.

The difference we noticed was more pervasive than just having the right equipment, though. People were generally more comfortable with disabilities. They hardly stared at all. When John was loud and made his funny movements, they would look at us and smile. Of course people in Germany and other countries were sometimes friendly as well, but here it was the widespread norm. Only once in our entire trip did we encounter difficulties: When we visited a glass factory in Kosta, a group of tourist teenagers from Germany ridiculed John. In contrast to that, John once had a meltdown close to the Växjö library, and a group of Swedish teenagers had smiled compassionately, and two girls had even talked to John. We generally saw many individuals with differing disabilities throughout our stay. I was pretty sure that Småland province didn't have a higher percentage of persons with disabilities – they were just out and about a lot, which I thought might have to do with comfort.

Germany, like most Western countries, signed the United Nations *Convention of the Rights of Persons with Disabilities*. It took effect in 2008. Politics since then focus on mainstreaming children into public schools, call it inclusion, and then claim that they're fulfilling the spirit of the UN convention. In reality, more often than not, it's a convenient way to save costs for special ed needs: A rather clever way to disguise austerity measures as progressive politics. Inclusion is much more than – and different from – throwing a severely autistic child into a regular classroom with twenty-five children who can talk, calculate, read, and write. John, for example, needs an environment that fits his perceptive challenges and that allows him to learn by offering the structures that he needs.

I'm aware of the segregating effect of special ed schools. A vast number of children with disabilities – including autistic children – could attend regular schools but aren't yet doing so. In general, mainstreaming is a necessary effort. (Incidentally, a similar problem of segregation presents itself in adulthood when adults with disabilities work mainly in special facilities.) How should people learn to be comfortable with disabilities when they're never exposed to them in the first place? Comfort largely seems to evolve from exposure. There aren't going to be any easy solutions for the ones who are most severely disabled, though, and especially so when they have multiple conditions. Maybe one day inclusion will get so far as to accommodate a child like John, but it's unlikely to happen while John himself is still in school.

Thinking about this in Sweden, I realized that my main concern was for John not to deteriorate because the demands on him were too high, the surroundings too overwhelming or the feedback too negative. This, too, was a balancing act. Rather than focusing on school, which for us seemed far-fetched, I predominantly hoped for our inclusion to be one of public acceptance. I hoped that it would be natural one day to have playgrounds that accommodate all children, like the one we saw in Växjö with a swing for wheelchairs; or that regular bike rental shops accommodate cyclists with special needs like we experienced at *Huseby Bruk*. I hoped that one day people wouldn't critically stare at us quite so much, and that more judgemental looks could be replaced by compassionate smiles, as we experienced in Sweden. I was annoyed with myself, as this all sounded so boring and I felt like I was becoming too much of a complainer, but it was one of our central problems: Not John, but the world around us.

When John had been two-and-a-half years old, I had met a Russian mother whose child had been admitted to the same hospital ward as John. She had told me that where she came from in Russia, they always threw a black coat over someone who had a seizure. She asked me if I had tried that with John and had seriously suggested doing so, because she was convinced that it might help. I almost couldn't believe it, and it had made me sad that she lacked any comprehension of how the black coat was hiding a seizure rather than curing it. I was certainly grateful that we didn't throw black coats over anyone in the West, but we weren't quite at the end of the road yet either.

It was in Sweden, while experiencing the significant difference of attitude towards persons with disabilities, that I understood the pervasive effects of constantly having to negotiate feedback from the outside. In the middle of it, I had lost sight. Marginalization had become natural to me. People were usually annoyed by us. We disturbed their peace. We were a nuisance that they didn't need to sit next to in a restaurant, for example. They were busy enough as it was, and they didn't need a child like John on top of it. Those were the messages we often received. I had gotten tough towards the constant staring and had thought that I was able to largely ignore it, but when it disappeared I realized how much it had still influenced me. Without what appeared to be constant negativity towards us, I was less tense and felt more at ease in my entire being. A burden that I hadn't even known to be so big, fell off me.

Three weeks gave us a long time to explore southern Sweden, especially because John still got up early every day. We were mostly on the road by eight, spent the morning and early afternoon driving somewhere, and then the later afternoon back in the garden. We walked around Teleborg castle in Växjö, Kronoberg castle in lake Helgasjön, Kalmar castle, and the Borgholm castle ruins on the island of Öland. In the southern part of Öland, we discovered the strange beauty of the *Stora Alvaret*. The Alvar is a barren, flat landscape with little vegetation, unsuited for agriculture, a rocky chalk plain formed by the ice age. *Stora Alvaret* is one of the last remaining karst landscapes in Europe and the largest European Alvar extent. It was a perfect area to explore by walking with John.

We tried canoeing one day, but it didn't work. John's movements were too uncoordinated. It was a miracle that we didn't tip over before we made it back to shore after just about five minutes. During one of our driving excursions, we stumbled upon a historical sign for what was called the *Hörnebo Slate Quarry*, and our day became adventurous. We climbed down a steep hill and came upon a long and dark tunnel. Since we didn't have a flashlight, Scott scouted it out by using his lighter and then came back to get us. "Wait till you see what's on the other side!" he exclaimed. Next thing, we found ourselves walking through the cold dampness with just one lighter, more or less oblivious to what was lurking around in the complete darkness. We emerged into the light on the other side and found an abandoned quarry overgrown with fluorescent green vegetation. It was like an abandoned paradise. We stepped over large stones and through ponds to survey the old work-site. John, of course, liked the continuous sound of running water.

We also visited a moose farm. It was okay, but seemed more like a tourist trap and was to us far less interesting than discovering the unadvertised quarry. We took a long trip North, towards the towns featured in the children's stories of Astrid Lindgren, most well-known for *Pippi Longstocking*. We saw where the *Six Bullerby Children* lived, fictitiously of course, and we visited the farm where the movie versions of *Emil of Lönneberga* had been shot. John took a seat in the shed full of wooden figurines which Emil carved when he was locked in the shed for punishment after having pulled one of his tricks. John didn't know the story or the film, but it made me smile how he sat down on Emil's stool. After all, he could be a little Emil sometimes himself.

Southern Sweden was generally flat, but there was a hill called Hanaslöv, a ski resort during the winter months. We took a gorgeous hike up. We didn't have to coax John at all, he was all up for it from the start. Up on top, we were rewarded with a beautiful view over the green pastures and the blooming landscape.

On our way back home, we overnighted in Denmark's capital, Copenhagen. Upon checking into our room, we noticed that we missed the bedding for the children's mattress. We called reception. Scott was just getting the luggage from the car when someone knocked on the door. I had put John into the bathtub, which we often did after long drives. Since John loved bathing, it helped him transition to new surroundings. I opened the door and let the maid in. It might have taken a minute, probably less, to attend to her. While she closed the door, I was already on my way back into the bathroom and encountered a flaming red child. John had switched the handle to its hottest, and the water in the hotel was almost boiling hot. Lacking an appropriate sense of pain and temperature, John sat underneath the super hot stream, pouring it over himself. I lunged over to turn the water to cold, which I then realized was too abrupt, because John started to have chills. I turned the water to warm instead, and tried to slowly decrease his body temperature. I wasn't sure if his skin was so badly burned that it needed treatment. I was relieved when Scott arrived. We wrapped John in a towel and laid down on the bed with him. We decided to give it a few moments to see if we had to call an ambulance. John still had the shivers, but we noticed that the flaming red color slowly got paler. We didn't have to go to the hospital in the end, but it took a long time for all of us to recover.

Later in the evening, we walked out to Copenhagen's signature sculpture – the Little Mermaid – in a mellow mood, picked up some food on the way back to the hotel, and that was the extent of Copenhagen for us. An end to a wonderful trip that reminded me once again that we couldn't leave John alone for a minute. I shouldn't have answered the knock on the door, and just stayed with John in the bathroom. The maid would have come back later. I just hadn't anticipated that anything like this could happen.

We returned to Berlin on a Sunday, and since Germany has strict regulations on opening hours, shops were closed. We had to drive to the main train station where grocery stores are allowed to stay open on Sundays for travelers. The store was always crowded and we usually avoided going there. We stood in a long line, John was anxious and everyone stared at us. The contrast to Sweden was extreme. We should have split up, one of us going into the store, the other one staying with John in the car. Another mistake, while the one I had made the previous day in Copenhagen still lingered in my mind. When we finally exited the store and got back to our car, I couldn't help but cry.

The real end of the Sweden trip was only discovered two weeks later, though, when Scott developed a strange round rash on his thigh and was diagnosed with Lyme disease, caused by a tick bite. Ticks were common in rural Sweden. I had pulled one out of John's leg during the trip as well, but Scott hadn't even noticed that he had been bitten until it swelled up. He had to be treated with antibiotics for eight weeks. A not so nice souvenir of an otherwise enchanting place.

9 NORMANDY & ALSACE (FRANCE) – HISTORY

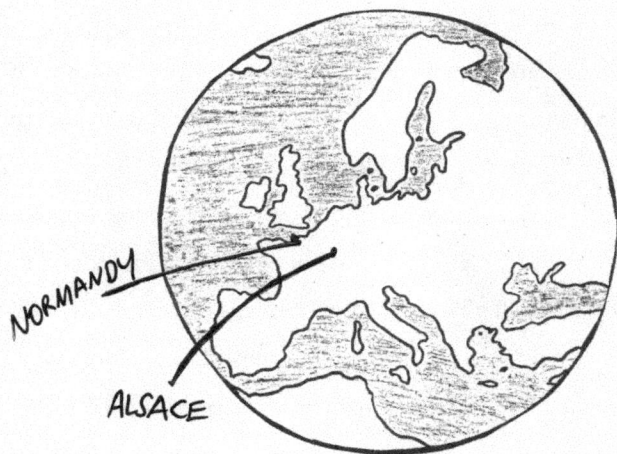

Each life reveals itself eventually, and also each landscape,
fully so, but only to the shaken heart.
(Hugo von Hofmannsthal)

For the beginning of John's third year in school, his aide was only approved after filing an appeal in court. It took weeks of work and it was good to know that this was the last time. Soon enough, John would attend the private school outside of the city. For his fall break in October, we were all ready for a vacation in France. We loved France and hadn't been there for more than four years. Scott found a cottage on Normandy's Cotentin peninsula in a village called Siouville-le-Hague.

We drove towards Western Germany first, and overnighted in the city of Aachen, close to the Belgian border. Aachen's emblem is its cathedral, dating back to the year 800. We walked there, and were strolling back through the quaint old town towards our hotel when we happened upon a fountain called *The Circulation of Money,* created in 1976 by artist Karl-Henning Seemann. Life-sized bronze sculptures that looked like cartoon characters surrounded the fountain. John was fascinated by them. He climbed up, gave them a hug, smiled, and we took some great photos. What was it that he saw in them? As so often, we didn't understand, but we were happy that John enjoyed himself.

The next morning, we proceeded through Belgium into France. Just over the border, the highway was closed due to construction and the detour took us through small villages for about twenty-five miles. Almost every village had a cemetery centered around a memorial to World War I. We weren't too far from Verdun. Eventually, we reached the *Pont de Normandie,* a cable-stayed bridge over the Seine river, more than 7,000 feet long, and spanning almost 3,000 feet in between the pillars. The bridge arches high, with the widest bridge span in all of Europe, and John was thrilled driving over it. It got us from Le Havre to Honfleur in Normandy.

Entering the Cotentin peninsula, the highway ended and once again we took small country roads through villages. High hedgerows lined the streets and created a unique atmosphere. With the rustic charm of old stone cottages, each village had its own appeal. The first thing that impressed us when we reached our village, Siouville, was the light. We drove around a curve, and a gap in the hedgerow suddenly opened with a view of the sea. The way in which the sunlight reflected, it tinted the air in a purplish blue, and the old buildings shone in a flat, yet warm beige color. Combined with the hedge's saturated green, the backdrop seemed almost magical. This was nothing like the hidden charm of the monotonous Swedish landscape, this was breathtaking upon first sight.

Arriving at the cottage, the caretaker asked us for an unusually large cash security deposit. We looked at the contract and it wasn't listed. However, the caretaker showed us that it was in the broker's terms and conditions, which inadvertently hadn't been sent to us. Since it was just a deposit, we drove into the village center, looking for an ATM. After this unexpected formality was resolved, we could finally settle into the house. It was an old cottage, with a garage to the side and a shed in the back, all buildings made of stone. The garage and the shed were original inside and out, but the main cottage had been renovated. A large yard with several apple trees surrounded the house, and old concrete telephone poles added to the ambiance of the scenery. We were glad to see that the yard was walled off by stacked stones. The entrance was secured with a wooden gate.

We walked down to the beach. The high tide had left clumps of dark seaweed behind, decoratively strewn across miles of sandy yellow beach. The wind was strong, and we learned that the peninsula was popular with surfers, who camped out on the beach that was otherwise abandoned at this time of year. We let John run around barefoot and after a while went shopping at the local *Super-U* grocery store where the selection of cheeses, yoghurts and other dairy products turned out to be exceptional. The house's caretaker had shown us a supply of firewood in the shed, and so we started the fireplace upon settling in. The cottage's ground floor was an open plan, the kitchen connected to both the living room and the dining area. A setup in which we could all be together, even while cooking dinner.

In the morning, Scott took John for a walk to the local bar that simultaneously served as the bakery, two rooms connected by an open door, run by the same person. Placing the baguette on the kitchen counter upon returning, Scott looked amused and told me that there were locals sitting in the bar at 8:00 a.m. drinking wine and shouting: "Bonjour" to everyone who entered, as if they had just stepped out of a French movie cliché. "Also," he informed me, "we have three sheep in our yard."

We hadn't closed the gate at night and the lush grass had apparently drawn them onto our premises. John was curious and watched them from a distance, and so we spent some time in the yard observing sheep.

The newspaper that Scott had brought with from the bakery featured an article called "What remains of our orthography?" Its author complained about the wayward status of spelling competence, especially amongst young people, and quickly found the internet to blame. I had already encountered "deterioration of orthography" being discussed in 1992 when I had stayed in France for a few months as an Au Pair. At the time, there had been just the complaint. Now that the internet had emerged, it was a great source to be held responsible for anything that supposedly went wrong, or so it apparently seemed in France just as much as in the U.S. or Germany.

We took a day trip to the peninsula's East coast to see the D-Day sites. We thought that it would be interesting, but we had no idea how strongly these sites were going to affect us. As much as one might know about or understand history, it still felt overwhelming to stand on Omaha Beach. On this site, one of the most significant battles had been fought, eventually liberating most of Western Europe. Of course, the Russians had been fighting under Stalin's dictatorship against Germany for three years already by the time the Allies landed in Normandy. June 6, 1944 as opposed to June 22, 1941. Yet the significance of Normandy to us was that democracy had reentered Western Europe here. We thought about the men who had sacrificed themselves. John ran up and down the beach while we stood with a knot in our stomachs. The contrast between the somber history and the current beauty of the bright and perfect beach was incomprehensible. We looked out to sea and tried to imagine, but couldn't fathom how it had been possible to enter land here. The magnitude of the endeavor revealed itself in a completely new way while standing there.

At the American cemetery in Colleville-sur-mer, John was loud, ironically just as we happened to see a sign: "Silence and Respect." We would have liked to pay our respects in silence, but we couldn't keep John quiet. Were we still allowed to enter? As happened quite often, we were in a limbo as to whether or not we were okay or crossing an invisible border of what could possibly be acceptable to others. An American family walked by us, and the mother smiled at me. I felt much better after her encouraging gesture. It seemed that we weren't unduly disturbing.

We visited Utah beach and the German cemetery. We went to Sainte-Mère-Église where John Steele's parachute had snagged on the church spire, and explored the Pointe-du-Hoc cliff, an eerie site full of remnants of fortifications. Exploring the curious landscape between the bomb craters and the forts was made more bearable by John just being himself. It took some of the weight off. Memorials, museums and explanatory signs lined every village and town in the area. The entire coastline was one huge, powerful warning against war. In the evening, we sat silently at the fireplace. John relaxed by watching the crackling flames, as we thought back on what we had experienced.

I was brought back to thinking about autism's history, too. One of the reasons for Hans Asperger to come up with autism as a diagnostic term had been to protect the children in his care from Nazi eugenics.

The *Viennese Society for Racial Hygiene* had been founded in 1924. Doctor Alois Scholz, who was later to become the society's chairman, explained the organization's goals: "Just as the term implies, this society deals with our people's gene pool. Only if we promote the strong and that which is able to live, and wipe out that which is unable to live, as demanded by nature, do we promote hygiene, which is useful to the whole." The society didn't have a lot of power until Nazi Germany annexed Austria in 1938. The society sided with the Germans and started to teach their ideology at the University of Vienna. In Germany, a *Law for the Prevention of Genetically Diseased Offspring* had already taken effect in 1933 and it was likely that it would be implemented in Austria soon enough as well.

Asperger had written a letter to colleagues in 1934, contemplating autism as a diagnostic term, yet it was after the spread of eugenic ideas in Vienna in 1938 that he decided to go public. On October 3, 1938 Asperger held a lecture on "autistic psychopaths" at the University Hospital of Vienna. (Incidentally, the term psychopath wasn't used derogatively. At the time it rather just implied that autism was part of the individual's personality.) In his lecture, Asperger said: "We should ask ourselves: What can we do for these individuals? When we fully dedicate ourselves to helping them, we also serve our people best. These children are underdeveloped intellectually, but their practical ability – in short: Everything that has to do with their instincts, and therefore their practical usefulness – is developed relatively well. And so is the value of their mind. These children's cases are important to note, or will especially be, once the *Law for the Prevention of Genetically Diseased Offspring* will take effect here in Austria." Asperger emphasized that abnormal children weren't necessarily inferior. By identifying the group of "autistic psychopaths," Hans Asperger tried to save the children who were in his care by creating an argument for their practical usefulness. He even addressed how doctors could handle evaluations once the *Law for the Prevention of Genetically Diseased Offspring* would take effect. Asperger suggested: "When a doctor is asked to evaluate

146

a child, he shouldn't judge solely on the basis of a questionnaire or the results of an IQ test. In his report, he should first and foremost convey his knowledge of the child's personality and this knowledge has to consider all capabilities, not only abstract intelligence."

Today, we still encounter arguments that Asperger already expressed in 1938. For example, special employment agencies for autistics are reminiscent of what Asperger said in his lecture, and so is Gary Westfahl's argument of "capable workers" that also emphasized usefulness, but from a different angle, coming full circle and leading back to evolutionary arguments. It's interesting that many of our current arguments and debates can be traced back to autism's origins, just as the wide spectrum of occurrences traces back to the diagnostic term's almost simultaneous double-origin in Europe and in the U.S.

One night on French television, a series called *What Is Love?* reported on autism. Several families were portrayed; the focus was on the caretaking and mainly on the parents and how they dealt with the challenges. Shouldn't the autistics be the center of the story, I asked myself? I didn't find an answer to that question until I started to write about our story. I realized that nonverbal children like John seemed elusive when you tried to convey their being. I didn't know what John was thinking, and he couldn't say it. In terms of what he liked or disliked, we guessed from his actions and reactions. It was only natural to revert back to the parents, because they could speak.

The program was followed by a political talk show in which a group of participants discussed French patriotism. Some participants assumed that French people had some kind of inferiority complex. They argued that citizens of other countries were proud of their nations, while more and more French people no longer even participated in singing their national anthem, the *Marseillaise*. Many allegedly only discovered their French identity while living abroad. You could have substituted the "French" with "German" and the discussion would have fit right into a German television program. There had also been a similar discussion in France during my stay in 1992, and then again during an internship at a cultural institute in France in 1994. As with the reoccurring debates about orthography, it seemed as if France was just as stuck as Germany in ever the same identity discussions.

The following morning, looking out of our window, we found that a pony had wandered into our yard. We had again forgotten to close the gate the previous night and the horse seemed to have been attracted by the apple trees. We immediately got dressed and took John out to say hello. He was apprehensive at first, but eventually warmed up to the pony, even posing for a few photos while clearly keeping an eye on what our guest was up to. When we eventually drove off to go shopping, we left the gate open so that the pony could leave again. I had imagined it being a little bit like Thassos where the animals had roamed around freely. I assumed that here, too, animals would wander, but upon returning from the store, we saw several people trying to catch our pony in a field outside of Siouville. If we had only known, we could have just closed our gate and called the police. Normal in Greece obviously wasn't likewise in France.

Siouville-le-Hague is located between the coastal villages of Flamanville and La Hague. What was apparently normal in Normandy, on a different note, were nuclear power plants. Flamanville was in the process of building a nuclear power plant, and La Hague had a nuclear reprocessing plant, infamous in Europe for its castor transports of reprocessed material. Increased levels of radioactivity register while the containers are transferred from trucks onto trains, and there was a wasteline leading from the reprocessing plant miles out to sea. One chatty fellow whom we met on a walk in Cherbourg told us that the water sometimes also registered increased levels of radioactivity.

We found it difficult to understand why anyone would want to put these contaminating structures right onto the most marvellous coastline, but we apparently missed the point. Normandy was an economically underdeveloped region. Almost everyone we talked to mentioned that they didn't mind the nuclear plants because they brought dearly needed employment. Even knowing that the locals seemed so comfortable with them, it was still an eerie feeling to see these large facilities in the middle of this stunning landscape.

Over the course of the week, we explored the hilly dunes along the West coast of the Cotentin peninsula in our drifting style. John settled in nicely and as in Ireland, he slept superbly through the night. We took a day trip to the Mont Saint-Michel monastery just on the border between Normandy and Brittany. The monastery was built on a rocky island in the Mont Saint-Michel bay, and had originally only been accessible during low tide. The Bishop of Avranches had ordered a small chapel to be built on the island in the year 709. It had been extended into a Pre-Romanesque church by Benedictine monks, who were sent there by the Duke of Normandy in 966. The grounds had evolved further throughout the centuries, with a Romanesque abbey being built in the eleventh century, and another Romanesque extension in the twelfth century. A Gothic section, a cloister and a refectory were added in the thirteenth century. The impressive complex had become an important center of Medieval pilgrimage, and during the French revolution it had been transformed into a prison. Marking its millennial anniversary, Benedictine monks moved back into the monastery in 1966, and since 2001 brothers and sisters of the *Monastic Fraternities of Jerusalem* have lived and prayed on the premises. Being a

UNESCO World Heritage site since 1979, the monastery attracted about three million tourists each year.

We arrived early to avoid crowds, which was easy for us because John still got up early every day. Upon entering the island, there was a narrow street with stores, and John immediately looked for candy or ice-cream. We bought him a donut and managed to walk by the other stores. We were able to explore most of the monastic premises. The panoramic views over the miles of low tide were stunning. The sand glittered golden-brown in the partial sunlight. As we walked back down to the narrow street which was the only access to the parking lot, busloads of tourists were just arriving, of all nationalities as it seemed. We had to fight the oncoming crowds to even manage walking in the opposite direction. John started to get anxious and eventually began to bite his hand. We got out as quickly as we could, and were thankful that we had arrived early. With the later crowds, there would have been no way for us to visit the monastery with John.

Normandy impressed us deeply in regards to both nature and history, and we were sorry to leave after a week. We had planned to trace our way back towards home by stopping for another week in the Alsace, a French region bordering Germany. We had booked a log cabin in the wine region that nestled in the foothills of the Vosges mountain range. Alsace is one of France's economic strongholds, a bustling metropolitan area. It's a bit similar to South Tyrol, not only because of it being a wine region, but also historically because borders changed several times and the land had switched between being German and French. The difference in Alsace was that German was no longer the predominant language spoken, even though many people still had German surnames.

We took a ride along the wine road. In the rather populated region, it was more difficult for us to find secluded places where John could roam. We found an off-the-beaten-track walking path in the mountains near Obernai, circling a vineyard. We made it about half-way when John suddenly didn't feel like walking any more. John laid on the path, with his ear on the warm asphalt. He just laid there for some time as if listening to something on the asphalt or underneath, and we sat down next to him and waited, appreciating the views of the vineyard until John was finished with whatever he was doing. He eventually agreed to walk on, slowly progressing into a good mood, and out of nowhere began flailing his arms, flapping his hands, and smiling as if nothing ever happened.

We drove up to the cloister of Mont St. Odile and enjoyed the sunset, looking out over the valley and its already changing fall colors. Another day, we spent in the city of Strasbourg, seat of the European parliament, featuring an impressive cathedral and an old town with sixteenth-century half-timbered houses. When John had been younger, he had liked to go into empty churches, where he vocalized and loved listening to the echoing acoustics of his own voice. As he had grown older, though, that fascination had diminished. In Strasbourg, John was rather impatient inside the cathedral, and it was crowded and didn't give him a chance to experiment with sounds anyway.

We had originally wanted to see the Isenheim Altarpiece in the Alsacian city of Colmar, but considering our experience with the cathedral, we let it suffice with a walk through Colmar's old town. In Normandy, we had skipped seeing the Bayeux tapestry. We had to concentrate on outdoor activities, and roaming through nature still seemed to work best.

On our drive back to Berlin, John grew increasingly restless. About thirty miles outside of the city, he erupted into desperate crying, screaming and attacks from the back seat. I was driving, and John suddenly grabbed my hair from behind and pulled hard on it. It was far too dangerous in the heavy traffic. I took the next exit and pulled into the first street. We waited it out for a while, trying to calm him, but it didn't work. What was wrong? Maybe he didn't want the vacation to end? The situation had intensified the closer we had gotten to Berlin. Scott took the driver's seat and I sat in the back with John, still trying to calm him. After finally making it home, we immediately put John into the bathtub, but he continued to flail his arms around in a mad rage, screaming, and setting the entire bathroom under water. Our neighbors certainly knew that we had returned home. Then suddenly, John's mouth started to bleed, but curiously he calmed down at the same time. I found a large molar underneath his tongue, one of his last baby teeth. That's what he had struggled with. We had been so clueless. He hadn't even touched his mouth, so there had been no indication. The attempts at interpreting his behavior could be poured down the drain with the blood-strained water. It had been nothing but a coincidence that the situation had intensified while approaching Berlin. John now seemed happy to be home.

I thought back to Fernand Deligny, and the idea of defying our urge for interpretation. It was a good idea, and one that I reminded myself of frequently, always appreciating the change of pace it brought along, but it was also just impossible in a moment of desperation. You had to come up with ideas in order to resolve a crisis. It hadn't occurred to us that John's meltdown was a reaction to physical discomfort. I had noticed before that I had a tendency to search for psychological reasons.

It was the most upsetting to us when John was in pain and couldn't communicate the source. "Show us where it hurts," we'd say, but he couldn't do it. Since John sometimes used our bodies rather than his own, we also asked him to show it on us, but he couldn't do that either. I read in accounts of autistics that they can have problems identifying where pain stems from because they just feel it so pervasively. That seemed to be the case for John as well. To me, this was one of the most difficult aspects of his autism. It led to situations of utter helplessness where we wanted so much to help and couldn't figure out how. When we finally did, sooner or later, we felt happy yet the distress was exhausting and lingered long.

After returning to Berlin, we had to tackle some profound changes. We lived in the heart of the city, and the private school that John was going to attend the following year was too far to drive on a daily basis from our apartment. The school had boarding facilities, so some children lived there from Monday through Friday, but we weren't ready to take that kind of step. John was only nine years old. We had managed to get him into the private school, now everything else needed to fall into place. As soon as we returned from France, we started to look for a new apartment in areas of Berlin that were easily accessible to the highway that led towards his future school. We also needed to live on the ground floor, because John was jumping up and down so much that we couldn't have anyone live underneath us. After three months, we found an adequate place.

In order to get approval for the out-of-state bus transport, we had to get a certificate from the school board stating that John was unable to attend a school in Berlin. To help convince the administration, we just took John with us to the appointment. John didn't like to go into any buildings that looked like doctor or therapy offices. As soon as we sat down, he wanted to get up and leave. It didn't take long until he ran up and down the hall, making loud noises. When the head inspector asked us into his office, we unexpectedly met a kind and compassionate person. Like I had observed with other parents of disabled children, the years of negotiating public reactions and bureaucratic necessities had made us a bit too defensive. The inspector took a close look at John and asked us what we needed. He said: "I see that your son has very special needs, and I see that you take good care of him. If there's anything at all I can do to help you, I will be happy to do so." Within ten minutes of stepping into his office, we walked out with the paperwork we needed. In my mind, I had already been prepared to take the matter to court if need be. My thinking had become too negative by default.

In February of 2010, we moved into our new apartment in the Southeast of Berlin, cutting John's travel time by thirty minutes one-way, while still living in an area accessible by public transportation, for my work with travel groups throughout Berlin. The apartment fit all of our new needs, but we were sad to move out of our old neighborhood where several of our friends lived and would now be half-way across the city. We moved a half a year before the school transitioning in order to split the move and the change of school into two separate events. It meant that the whole year of 2010 turned into one big transition, but we needed to establish a stable situation delicately, which would be reliable long-term. It would be worth the effort for years to come. Since we now lived considerably further from John's current school, the bus company wanted to pick him up at six a.m. for school starting at eight. We decided to drive John ourselves for the remainder of the school year instead – each resolved logistical effort usually being swiftly followed by a new one.

10 VALENCIA (SPAIN) – CULTURE

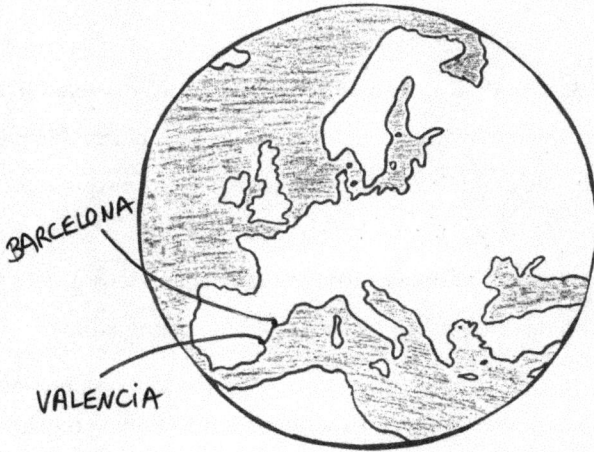

Culture is not so much what you plan
but what you get away with.
(Marcus Westbury)

Before John's new school start, Scott found a rental house near Valencia for our summer break. Since John had grown considerably, we were even more apprehensive about flying and decided to undertake a massive drive; almost 1,500 miles one-way. For almost three weeks of travel, we once again needed to take a car load of diapers, so instead of driving our own small car, in plus ninety degree heat, we rented a spacious station wagon with air-conditioning to avoid the chaos we had experienced on our summer trip to Sweden.

On our first day, we drove from Berlin to Besançon in France, usually a nine-hour ride that took us more than twelve hours with the stops that we had to make. The second leg of the trip was from Besançon to Montpellier on the Mediterranean, a considerably shorter distance of six hours. Since we started early in the morning, we arrived in the early afternoon and were able to see a lot of Montpellier. I had spent almost a year there, five months in 1992 and six months in 1994. We walked by my old apartment, the university where I had studied and the cultural institute where I had worked. We ate dinner on the picturesque main square *Place de la Comédie* and afterwards watched the beginning of the soccer world cup final between Spain and the Netherlands at a large public viewing area that was filled with hundreds of people – our autistic boy feeling happy in the colorful crowd.

Driving through the Pyrenées mountains the following morning, we soon reached Catalonia. The further South we got from there, the more considerable the landscape changed. The soil turned from dark brown to a brownish red and there was considerably less vegetation. It was hot, very hot. The ride from Montpellier to Valencia was normally about six-and-a-half hours, but it took us a good nine hours. John started to get restless, this being the third day in the car. We realized that he was reaching his limit, even though he otherwise loved driving. When we stepped out of the air-conditioned car during breaks, John was unhappy with the heat. If we couldn't fly any more, and if we couldn't spend several days in the car, our reach was going to be quite limited in the future.

The house was located near the town of Llíria, outside of Valencia. It belonged to an English-Spanish male couple living in London. They had explained in detail the directions, because even the navigational systems wouldn't find the location. You had to drive out of town and through open fields that almost seemed like a desert. We passed over a dried-up creek, continued on an unpaved gravel road, and then eventually reached a settlement of around a dozen houses, one of which was going to be our home for two weeks.

An English woman who lived in Valencia took care of the house and awaited us. One of the first things she explained was that the shade around the house attracted the wildlife that surrounded the settlement. We should keep all doors closed, and not even leave the entrance door open while fetching groceries from the car. As a precaution, we should always shake out our shoes before stepping into them, even inside the house. She explained: "We have tarantulas and scorpions here, and they like to hide in shoes." This wasn't exactly encouraging to me. We saw a gecko running up a wall in the hallway while the caretaker was showing us around. She happily pointed to it: "It's always a good sign to have these fellas around the house, because they feast on tarantulas!" When she left, I told Scott that I wasn't sure if I could stay here for two weeks. He didn't seem to be too worried, he said: "I'm sure it's gonna be fine. Otherwise they wouldn't rent this house out. We have neighbors on both sides who live here permanently, so it couldn't be so bad." His pragmatism didn't leave me any line of defense.

John was most thrilled with the pool in the backyard. Since his school class went swimming once a week, the health insurance had provided us with neoprene swim trunks for incontinent children, specially tailored to John's measurements. We had never rented a house with a pool before. It felt luxurious, even though it seemed standard here. It was simply too hot not to have one. We heard the neighbor kids plunging around in theirs, and their mother shouting at the top of her lungs from inside the house. The neighbors on the other side were loud as well. As we quickly discovered, this was to be the every-day decibel level. Since one of the neighbors was called Jesús, and his wife constantly called him, we got used to the acoustic backdrop of continuous "Jesús, Jesús!" shouting.

The pool was especially nice in the evenings. On the backside, it was fenced off towards nature, and in the front, the yard cascaded downhill, offering views over the valley, into the sunset. Swimming in that atmosphere became the highlight of every day's end. However, the pool also carried a lot of potential for conflict. John didn't yet understand that he couldn't spend day and night swimming. In the first days, getting used to the Spanish food, John had diarrhea and so we couldn't let him swim for a couple of days. Even with the special swim trunks, it seemed too dangerous. Surely they weren't made for diarrhea. John didn't understand why he couldn't swim, and it got hard for all of us. It was best not to be home so that the pool outside the window wouldn't tempt him. At the same time, an almost ten-year-old child wearing diapers and having diarrhea wasn't exactly the situation in which you wanted to be out and about all day. Our first few days in Llíria were the roughest we've had on vacation – even more so than the rainy days in the damp and cold Sweden house.

Once John got over his diarrhea, we picked up exploring the area. We visited a town close-by in the mountains, Chulilla. The walking was steep, and the church where we could have enjoyed some shade was locked. In the heat, we decided to postpone sightseeing and rather drive to one of the beaches around Valencia. The sea was pretty rough and the current was strong. We had to watch John closely. I found it to be difficult and physically demanding to handle him in the sea. John loved it, though, and luckily Scott managed it well.

We usually went out early in the morning and late in the afternoon, since we realized that it was best to follow the Spanish routine and stay home during mid-day heat. We could take advantage of the air-conditioning, even if we couldn't hold a siesta. John had quit taking naps before he was even two years old. The house's owners had an extensive DVD collection. John discovered *The Sound of Music* and was hooked. Whenever we were home he wanted to watch it, over and over again. Scott and I soon knew by heart not only the lyrics but also the dialogue. We tried to put in *Ratatouille*, we tried to sneak in *Finding Nemo*, but John knew exactly what he wanted, and when he concentrated on something, nothing in the world could distract him. We were stuck with Maria, Herr von Trapp and his seven children.

After a week, we had gotten used to the hot climate and felt ready to explore Valencia. With the help of John's pediatric psychiatrist, we had recently received a disability parking placard that was valid all over Europe. In Valencia, we got to appreciate it greatly, as the parking situation in the old town seemed worse than in Berlin. We ended up seeing much more than we could have without it. We were thankful that our life had been made significantly easier. (Even though there were limits to public understanding. In Berlin, someone had already shouted angrily at us: "Hey, but your child can walk!")

Our highlight in Valencia was *The City of Arts and Sciences,* a futuristic complex of entertainment and science buildings by architects Santiago Calatrava and Félix Candela. It housed an open-air oceanographic park, an opera house and a museum of science, with a suspension bridge and large fluorescent sky-blue pools connecting the buildings within the complex. The pools were inviting for John, especially in the heat. As soon as he put his foot in to test the water, a security guard ran from across the complex, blowing a whistle. John didn't understand why he wasn't allowed to use such a beautiful large pool. Luckily, we discovered a few ice-cream stands throughout the complex, and managed to distract John just enough.

Our sightseeing was often hindered or helped by unexpected factors, and as always, we just had to see what was waiting and then go with the flow. John was amazed by the futuristic buildings, he looked up and down their structures. After the amphiteater in Arles, this was the second time that he seemed genuinely interested in architecture. We took a lot of photos and later at home researched the location, thereby realizing retrospectively where we had been and what we had seen. We had come to do this quite a lot: While we were somewhere, like the *City of Arts and Sciences*, we concentrated on what John wanted to do, and by roaming around we just developed a feeling for a place. With the help of the photos, we could then later find out more about where we had been and what we had seen.

An interest in architecture seemed not too unusual for autistics. Even though John was far from being capable of putting such an interest into any kind of project, it reminded me of many popular autistics' interests. British architectural artist Stephen Wiltshire, diagnosed with autism, is known for drawing cityscapes with geometrical precision. Gilles Tréhin, a French savant artist with extraordinary mathematical talents, envisioned a highly complex, yet imaginary city called *Urville*. He has been drawing it for twenty years. With a population of around twelve million, nearly 300 drawings of different districts reflect architectural styles and provide historical, geographical, economic, and cultural information. The Vichy regime in France, World War II, and globalization are all accounted for in Tréhin's imagined city. Savant James Henry Pullen, born in 1832, had spent seven years working on his masterpiece, the ship *The Great Eastern*. Autistic artist George Widener is known for his complex paintings of landscapes and numerical palindromes. His works were first shown in the realm of outsider art in Germany and later as exhibits in their own right. Larry Bissonnette is an autistic artist whose work has been exhibited regularly in local and national exhibitions. Autistic savant Daniel Tammet has extraordinary mathematical skills and has learned the Icelandic language within one week. He's often compared to Kim Peek, the real-life model for Dustin Hoffman's *Rain Man*.

There was a lot of coverage on Daniel Tammet in German media. Public engagement with savants seemed to spike in a time in which neuroscience advanced to a leading science, possibly because autism is one of its frontiers: We feel as if we know so much about the brain, but still cannot explain these extraordinary talents – no matter how many fMRI studies are being conducted. Yet only about 10% of autistics have extraordinary capabilities and special talents. It sometimes seemed to me that we paid a large amount of attention to a comparatively small group of autistics, but it was a group that was admittedly easily fascinating.

Autism's founding father Hans Asperger said: "It seems that for success in science or art, a dash of autism is essential. For success, the necessary ingredient may be an ability to turn away from the everyday world, from the simply practical, an ability to re-think a subject with originality so as to create in new untrodden ways, with all abilities canalized into one specialty." Somewhat reminiscent of this observation, a vast number of posthumous diagnoses have emerged in recent years. Hans Christian Andersen, Jane Austen, Belá Bartók, Ludwig van Beethoven, Alexander Graham Bell, Anton Bruckner, Marie Curie, Charles Darwin, Emily Dickinson, Albert Einstein, Glenn Gould, Vincent van Gogh, Thomas Jefferson, Wassily Kandinsky, Immanuel Kant, Stanley Kubrick, Vladimir Lenin, Michelangelo, Wolfgang Amadeus Mozart, Isaac Newton, George Orwell, Spinoza, Alan Turing, Andy Warhol, and Ludwig Wittgenstein might all have been autistic. Looking at the diversity of characters represented, one could argue that it reflects the wide autism spectrum that we perceive today. If one believes that autism's prevalence hasn't increased, but rather just the awareness, then there have to be a lot of undiagnosed autistics throughout history. On the other hand, how reliable can posthumous diagnosis be? Not very. Yet it's clearly part of the current identity politics of autism to reflect on its cultural history.

In the seventeenth century, philosopher Thomas Hobbes in *Leviathan* described man in his natural state as violent, unproductive, lonely, and animal-like. Poet John Dryden, on the other hand, fashioned a somewhat contrary idea around the same time in his heroic play *The Conquest of Granada*: That of the Noble Savage, a true existence in nature and autonomy, beyond the manipulations of civilization and culture. Autism could be placed at both ends of the human condition, could be perceived both as a raw force and as true nature. It can serve as a paradigm for the suspense between cultivation and destruction that humans are perpetually caught in.

The term *Idiot Savant* was already coined in 1887 by John Langdon Down. Researcher Uta Frith referred to the history of Russian *Blessed Fools* in terms of autism. Then there are the so-called *Wild Children* who were found living on their own in forests, some of whom had supposedly been adopted by animals. A seven-year-old boy had been found in the German state of Hessia in the fourteenth century, an Irish boy in 1652, referred to in medical literature as a sheep boy, and a girl in Holland in the eighteenth century. One could also include *Wild Peter of Hameln* and *Kaspar Hauser*. The latest case of a wild child was the *Wild Boy of Burundi*, found in 1976, supposedly raised by apes. Psychologist Harlan Lane diagnosed him with autism. Many of the previously mentioned wild children are today assumed to have been autistic as well.

Autism and its image are often culturally intertwined. When we look back in history – whether it be towards *Wild Children*, *Blessed Fools*, or posthumous diagnoses – our attempts address autism, but inevitably become symbolic at the same time. François Truffaut's movie *The Wild Child* recounts the true story of a twelve-year-old boy found unclothed in the forest of Aveyron in the eighteenth century. Victor couldn't speak or understand language, he lived like an animal and was probably intellectually disabled. Truffaut sent his lead actor Jean-Pierre Cargol to study autistic Janmari, whose story of the inverted orange halves I told earlier, to model Victor's character after Janmari's behaviour. The blurring of syndrome and image receives yet another twist when we add fictitious characters that were modelled after an original affinity to autism, but have then been removed from the syndrome and used to create characters that hardly have anything in common with autism any more, like for example Edgar Rice Burrough's *Tarzan* and Mowgli in Rudyard Kipling's *Jungle Book*. The question has also been raised: Is Sherlock Holmes autistic?

A traveler on one of the trips that I led as a travel director recommended to me the 1934 short story *Silent Snow, Secret Snow* by Conrad Aiken. Autism didn't even exist as a diagnosis in 1934 yet, but told from the boy's perspective, the story describes a child's slow retreat into his inner world. However authentic of an autism account it could be – being purely imaginative and avant la lettre – it did deliver a powerful sense of young Paul slipping away from the world.

Herman Melville's great refusinek character of *Bartleby the Scrivener* has been related to autism for more than thirty years. A full-scale study of Bartleby's clinical condition has recently been undertaken by a researcher from Stanford Medical School who found that the markers for Asperger's were apparent. Amit Pinchevski, professor at the Hebrew University of Jerusalem, wrote in his text *Bartleby's Autism. Wandering along Incommunicability*: "Melville's depiction of the forlorn scrivener, originally published in 1853, serves as a historical validation to the fact that individuals with these symptoms have been with us throughout history and probably before." Melville himself was suspected to have had autistic traits – another one to add to the ever lengthening list of posthumous diagnoses. Even when we interpret Bartleby's behavior as autistic, it still also serves as a place holder for every man's and woman's existential mode of being alone. In that sense, Bartleby's autism is inevitably symbolic. It carries a meaning that points beyond the syndrome. This is not unusual. Stuart Murray analyzed autism in a variety of books, for example in Charles Dickens' *Barnaby Rudge*, Joseph Conrad's *The Idiots* and *The Secret Agent*, Anita Desai's *Clear Light of Day*, J.M. Coetzee's *Life & Times of Michael K.* and William Faulkner's *The Sound and the Fury* (even though Faulkner based Benji's character on a real-life man with Down's syndrome, the character also has many autistic traits). In literature, the autistic difference is mainly used as a tool for telling stories, as a proxy to spruce up the story. Quite similar to the argument of the internet being a prosthetic for autistics, autism is a prosthetic to the story. Murray concludes: "Autism is endlessly fascinating, these novels seem to say, but never more so than when we might quickly characterize it and use it to look at something else." This changed somewhat with the film *Rain Man,* in which autism is central to the story. However, there too, autism is arguably used as an image. Raymond, played by Dustin Hoffman, actually has the condition, but his brother Charlie, played by Tom Cruise, exhibits markers of autism as well: Problematic social interaction, repetitive language, and aloofness. Though in this case, they don't refer to autism as a real syndrome, but are used to characterize the reckless era of the eighties. In the end, Charlie's dysfunctional character is catalyzed by his brother's autistic presence – *Autism as a catalyst* being another frequently found cultural narrative.

Then, there's a particularly special connection between autism and science fiction. Steve Silberman described the elaborate, technically accurate science fiction universe as "an autistic playground." This technological autism aesthetic has entered more mainstream publications. Characters with technological affinities in Douglas Coupland's novel *microserfs* are referred to as being autistic. In his novel *jPod,* protagonist Kaitlin calls her colleagues and her boss autistic. In Stieg Larsson's successful millennium-trilogy *The Girl with the Dragon Tattoo,* the character of Lisbeth Salander has Asperger's, a photographic memory and is a computer genius. These character elements play no small part in the trilogy's allure.

Autism as a symbol reflects back on the psychiatric category both positively and negatively. On the one hand, the term's heavy usage puts the syndrome in danger of being perceived as merely a fashion. As early as 2004, journalist Niall Ferguson stated in a newspaper article: "America has Asperger's," alluding to the condition's contemporary ubiquity. He claimed that people were just using it as an excuse to be egotistical and socially rude. On the other hand, there are also publications that contribute to a better understanding of the spectrum: Books like Mark Haddon's *The Curious Incident of the Dog in the Night-Time* incorporate the syndrome's complexity better than has usually been done before. As part of a conference on intellectual disabilities and moral philosophy, Ian Hacking held a lecture at Stony Brook University in September of 2008. In *How we have been learning to talk about autism* he said: "The new multimedia genre of autistic narrative–autobiography, parental biography, fictions, stories for children, and above all blogs, is an essential part of transforming the conception that severely autistic people lead 'thin' emotional lives into a vision of a far richer mode of existence."

We had brought along the DVD collection *Spain – on the Road Again* featuring Mario Batali, Gwyneth Paltrow, Mark Bittman, and Claudia Bassols. Whenever we could get John away from *The Sound of Music,* we watched an episode. One day, we happened upon Mario Batali and

Gwyneth Paltrow cooking paella with the Zen Master in the Albufera, just south of Valencia, close to where we were. The cook started by preparing a fire, and when Batali asked him how many minutes it would take until the fire was ready, he replied: "I do not direct the fire, the fire directs me." I liked that. It reminded me of the way we lived: John was our fire. Don't ask how long something will take, that's not the way this works.

Our rental house had a traditional Spanish Paellero next to the terrace, a small room with a wood-fired cooking grate. We had to try this ourselves, so we were off the following morning to the rice fields of the Albufera. On our way home, we stopped at the Valencia central market hall to buy the required assortment of seafood. In the evening, as Scott started the fire, it quickly got ridiculously hot and steamy inside the tiny Paellero. I peeled the shrimps and brought them outside, and a swarm of black flies immediately attacked the plate. The flies had already made us give up eating dinner outside, now the cooking in the Paellero proved to be equally difficult. While Scott cooked, John and I watched *The Sound of Music* inside the air-conditioned house. Who had the better job? Me listening to Maria singing *Do-Re-Mi* for the thousandth time, or Scott in the sauna being attacked by hundreds of black flies? In the end, the paella turned out delicious. We ate it right out of the pan, as they said it should be done. On the DVD, the Albufera Zen Master had taken some paella on his spoon and had held it upside down. The rice had to stick. Our paella even passed his final acid test.

We drove out to the quaint city of Chelva the following morning, walking from one shady spot to the next, and then on to a waterfall outside town. The cool mountain water coming down from above was something for our water-loving boy. John did an exquisite stand-up version of his *Rowing Dance*. However, the ground was slippery and even though Scott held on to John, the two slipped and landed right underneath the water.

Scott's shorts were ripped, but nobody was hurt. John didn't mind the fall at all, in fact he was giggling. I happened to take a photo just as they were going down.

When we returned home in the evening, the caretaker of the house came by. She asked us if we could open the gate for the bi-weekly water delivery in the evening. The remote settlement wasn't hooked up to the water and sewage system, so the houses had waste tanks underneath the buildings and water tanks that were regularly refilled. The delivery would take place around ten. "That's ten tonight, right?" we asked.

"Yes," she assured us, laughing. It wasn't too surprising. Our neighbors didn't even start their dinner until then. We waited, and ten o'clock came and went, and so did eleven. When it got dark, it was pitch-black outside. There were no street lamps, and in clear nights, the view of the stars in the sky was magnificent. We went to bed, thinking that they would probably come another day, but we woke up to loud noise at one a.m. A rattling truck with a big water tank had arrived, and everyone was shouting: The neighbors, the workers, and the truck driver. Bright lights generated by the truck lit up the neighbor's yard, and they were refilling his tanks. Next thing we knew, a half-naked Jesús jumped over our fence and ran towards our gate to let the water truck in. The floodlights now illuminated our yard, then there was more shouting, and suddenly the roar of running water. The entire terrace overflowed, but eventually they were done and moved on to the next-door neighbor's house. Jesús waved good-night as he jumped back over the fence into his own yard. Curiously enough, our light sleeper John hadn't even woken up. The next morning, it seemed to me as if the whole scene had just been a dream.

There was something to be said for picking your cocktail lime right off the tree, but I was still somewhat relieved when we checked out without having encountered a tarantula or a scorpion. On the way home, we would do four instead of three days of traveling, thus reducing the daily amount of time spent in the car. The first day, we only drove up to Barcelona, a ride of about three-and-a-half hours and stayed in a small hotel just off *Las Ramblas*. According to the hotel's website, we would still be able to drive through to unload our luggage. As we made it into Barcelona, just after noon, traffic was heavy and the streets were filled with people. We drove in circles trying to find the street leading to the hotel, and we had to double back to a gas station, and then once again drove back through the maze of crowded streets into the pedestrian zone. John was patient, but close to reaching his limit when we finally checked in.

I had spent a couple of months in Barcelona during my studies and had lived with a Spanish family while attending a language course. I looked forward to seeing the city again: The seafront where we had gone rollerblading and the cafés in which we had spent our school breaks. However, it was hot and crowded and John wasn't especially pleased. We took the subway out to the cathedral *La Sagrada Familia*, where it was a little bit less crowded. The *Sagrada Familia* dates back to 1882, but the building process is still ongoing, according to the plans that architect Antoni Gaudí left behind, fully aware that he wouldn't be able to finish the work in his lifetime.

Since we stayed in the heart of the city, our hotel's parking garage was located a few blocks away. As Scott went to pick up the car the following morning to load our luggage, he brought along his backpack. While driving back through the pedestrian zone at walking pace, a man stuck his hand through the window and opened the driver's side door. He seemed anxious and rambled about fluid leaking from the front of our car. Scott managed to shake the man off and close the door, but he reached in again and grabbed Scott's shirt. Again Scott pushed him away and was finally able to continue on to the hotel where John and I were waiting with the luggage.

We had just passed the Spanish-French border when we pulled over for a break, and Scott wanted to get his camera out. "Where's my backpack? It was on the back seat, did you put it in the trunk?" he asked. I hadn't seen it. We searched the car and realized only then that someone must have opened the back door and stolen the backpack while Scott was confronted with the man back in the pedestrian zone. They must have worked in a team of two. The backpack contained books, DVD's, Scott's cell, my filofax, a carton of cigarettes, and most hurtful of all our camera with probably around six hundred photos, including some precious pictures from Berlin. Scott's oldest brother and family from Chicago had visited us just before our trip to Spain, and we had taken rare photos of John with his cousins in Berlin. In Spain, I had only taken few photos with my old camera. Those were the only ones left now – a small fraction. We thought about driving back and going to the police, but what could they possibly do? It wasn't worth driving all the way back to Barcelona with John. We simply drove on to our next stopover city Nîmes.

One of the reasons for overnighting there had been the amphitheater, but with our luck on this trip, it was closed due to a concert in the evening. We walked around the old town and ate dinner at a Chinese restaurant. John enjoyed a carousel close to our hotel. He could have ridden it over and over again for hours. At some point, the employee even gave us a free ride. Back in our room, I checked my email and found a message from a man called Jesús. I first thought of our neighbor in Llíria, but it was a different Jesús, a man from Barcelona. He had found a backpack, and in it my email address in the filofax. He wrote that there were also books and DVD's. It looked like Scott's cell phone, his cigarettes and the camera were gone. The thieves had apparently taken what they wanted and just left the rest. Jesús offered to send us our backpack.

We drove through France and into Germany the next day. John wasn't doing too well, he became aggressive and Scott had to sit in the back with him most of the way. We stopped over in Heidelberg where we both had relatives. We could sleep at my aunt and uncle's, and Scott's aunt and uncle's hosted a barbecue. John eventually fell asleep on the couch. After a huge rainstorm had calmed down, we returned to my aunt and uncle's house – only to discover that their basement was flooded. Scott carried John into the guest bedroom and we all worked together for a couple of hours, wiping the basement. Back in Berlin, we received another email from Jesús with UPS contact information. He had already dropped off the backpack at an office close to his apartment. I called them and wired the postage. Four days later, our backpack arrived in Berlin. We offered Jesús a reward, but he adamantly declined. He wrote: "I feel so terrible about all the thefts in Barcelona, and I'm aware of how badly it reflects on my city. I love Barcelona and I'm glad if I can correct the image at least a little bit." He certainly did. We were impressed that he hadn't only taken the time to find us, but also to return our things.

Spain was an exhausting and somewhat contradictory experience. We had wanted to see how far we could go by car and had possibly stretched our limit. We had expected hot weather, but couldn't know that it was going to be an extra hot summer. John had enjoyed the sea, but the strong waves had made it difficult. Having a pool in the yard had been nice, and at the same time arduous, because of John's lack of understanding. The house had been too much into-the-wild for my taste, but Scott and John hadn't minded that. The theft in Barcelona had been a bad experience, but at the same time we had made the humble experience of Jesús getting our backpack mailed to Berlin. The trip was our biggest undertaking of any vacation with John and we probably wouldn't ever drive that far again, at least not in the near future.

The biggest surprise occurred ten months after our trip. We received an email by the owner of the house that we had rented. He had been contacted by the Valencia police, who in turn had been contacted by the Barcelona police, who in turn had found valuables in an apartment during a raid. Among these valuables was a camera, and while they had searched it for evidence, they had discovered photos of a father and son in a pool. The name of the house was spelled out in the mosaic tiles of the pool. They had googled the house's name and had then contacted the owner about a family that had stayed in his house during the dates saved on the camera chip. We sat speechless in front of the email. Our photos were back.

We emailed the police that our camera had been stolen, and that we hadn't filed charges at the time, because we had already been in France when we had noticed the theft, but that we would like to get at least the chip back if at all possible. The Barcelona police had apparently uncovered a ring of organized crime. They had contacted the house owner to find out if there was any connection. Once they knew that the camera had just been stolen and that the people on the photos were unconnected tourists, they apparently dropped their interest. We offered to wire the postage and sent the police our address, but since we hadn't filed a theft we never heard back from them and the chip never arrived. We had come ridiculously close to getting our photos back.

11 PRAGUE & TEREZÍN (CZECH REPUBLIC) – ETHICS

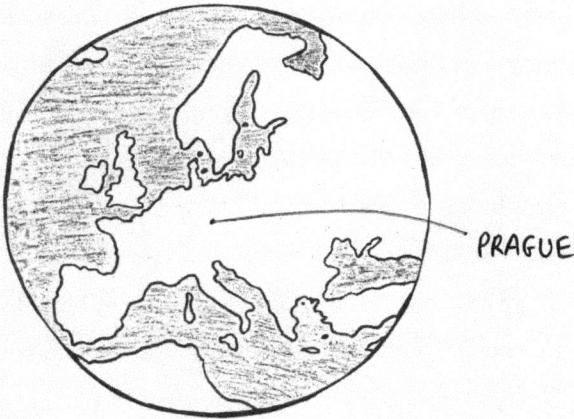

PRAGUE

We are here to notice each thing,
so that each thing gets noticed
(Annie Dillard)

John started his new school after the summer break of 2010. We transitioned him in slowly, but he did exceptionally well, much more quickly than we had anticipated or dared to hope for. He thrived in the extremely structured surroundings. A three-year long burden was lifted from our shoulders. After observing John for a couple of weeks, his teachers surprisingly said that he could manage full days of school without an aide.

One mother I talked to urged me to apply for one anyway: "John will always learn more when he gets one-to-one attention. He qualifies for an aide, so you should apply." We weren't so sure. John also needed to learn to fit into a group without getting exclusive attention. It depended upon what you were looking for. An aide could train specific skills more closely with John, but being in the class without someone at his side at all times could improve more general social skills. In the old school, the environment had been too dangerous and too unstructured to even think this far, but if the new school could manage it, there was a new perspective. Social skills were important for John's future, considering that he would always depend on people around him. Also, having someone at his disposal at any given moment afforded John with a somewhat wrong idea about life. We decided not to apply for an aide.

John had previously been home at three p.m., so we had needed caretakers in our house four times a week in the afternoon. Now John returned at five p.m. and we only needed help on Friday's when school ended after lunch. I hadn't noticed beforehand how much different life is when you always have someone come and go. Even though we liked our social workers and caretakers very much, we found a new freedom and privacy.

Within a couple of months, we had reached such a stable situation that I was able to work more. It made me realize yet again how our entire lives depended upon John's stability, and that while we could do everything for him at home, it wouldn't be enough if the outside didn't fit as well. Hopefully, he could stay in this school until he was eighteen. We would have to make plans early on for the next transition then, but in the meantime we would hopefully have a few stable years ahead of us, which I intended to take full advantage of. I plunged into work with enthusiasm.

When the company that I had been employed with in Chicago asked me if I could do a trip outside of Berlin, five days in Prague, Scott and I thought about it and decided to give it a try. I hadn't been separated from John in many years. The caretaking situation had led to a close, almost too symbiotic relationship. John was ten years old. He seemed, now more than ever, interested in his classmates and he didn't like to hold hands any more when walking. He still didn't have an appropriate sense of danger and would run into the street, but no matter how problematic his refusal to hold hands was, it also seemed to be a rather clear sign that he wanted to be more independent.

I took my first trip as a travel director abroad since John was born. I had imagined how nice it would be to have more freedom, to be your own person again, but when it happened it felt strange. No John plopping down on top of me, or pulling my arm to get something that he wanted. We pretty much lived with constant noise and body contact. Not having that around left a void at first. It reminded me of when John had first started preschool, after we had been in and out of hospitals for two years. The seizures had left no space for anything else. When John was first picked up by the bus for preschool, I had sat with the newspaper in my hands at the kitchen table and couldn't read it. My concentration barely lasted a few sentences and my thoughts constantly drifted. I couldn't process what I was reading. I had adjusted quickly, though. It was similarly strange to get used to the extended amount of time on a business trip. No diaper changes, no feeding, no bringing John to bed and laying down with him, and above all: No night duty. Five full days and nights felt eternal. It surprised me how quickly I got used to it. I slept like a log. The work in Prague was extensive, but it wasn't stressful at all. It made me realize how high the stress levels were that I was used to at home.

While it had been comparatively quick and easy to adjust to new freedom, it was hard to get back into caretaking when I returned. The lack of sleep drained me much more than it had done before my trip. John's domination of my time and energy felt exhausting. It took me more than a week to get re-adjusted. Caretaking was something you got used to. Taking a rest from it inadvertently meant that returning to it would be hard. I also realized that I had started to idealize the demands within the short time period of my absence. I had returned to Berlin with a weird, somewhat vague idea in my head that it wasn't all that difficult. It's strange how the mind works. After years of experience, a few days had clouded my assessment.

John had handled my absence well enough, even though his teachers said that they had occasionally sensed a certain disorientation in him. He had cried a little bit in school, but overall he seemed to have been okay. The bus driver said that it had been more difficult the longer I was gone. Scott had managed without any problems. He repeatedly explained to John, as he was showing him a photo of me, that I was only going to be gone for five days. We weren't sure how much of it John understood. When I returned, John barely acknowledged me at first, but later in the evening he was cuddly with a large smile on his face.

Prague wasn't only a significant experience because of the break I got from my caretaking duties, it was also a beautiful city. I had visited the Prague Castle, Charles Bridge, the Astronomical Clock, Wenceslas Square, the Jewish Quarter, and in my few hours of free time, I had taken the subway to the Franz Kafka Museum. I couldn't wait to come back with Scott and John, so we did during John's break for the long Pentecost weekend. Even though Prague wasn't as inexpensive any more as it had been right after the Velvet Revolution of 1989, hotel and restaurant prices were still comparatively modest if you knew where to go. We had found an inexpensive hotel online, in one of the large Soviet-style prefab complexes just outside the city center. At fifty dollars per night including breakfast, they offered a family unit of two adjacent rooms with a connecting door. The parking lot was secure, as we were told that car theft was still a worrisome issue in Prague. A public bus stopped a short distance from the hotel.

As always, we put John into the bathtub upon arrival to ease his transition, and then headed outside. The city was full of tourists for the holiday weekend. We just walked around a bit, mainly in the side streets. If we wanted to see the main sights, we would have to get an early start the next day to avoid the crowds. The hotel's breakfast room opened at six a.m. John was making loud noises while inspecting the buffet. The staff and the few other guests in the room reacted with friendly smiles. By now, John had grown enough for people to immediately notice that he was disabled rather than just misbehaved. Understanding and compassion increasingly replaced the critical reactions that we had often encountered in public when John was smaller. In some respects, things got easier as John grew. Obvious physical clues apparently helped people understand disability.

We had noticed that before during a visit to Ikea in Berlin. Using John's disability ID, we had checked out one of Ikea's wheelchairs. John always enjoyed being driven around, whether it be in the car, on the bus, or as we happened to find out, in a wheelchair. He happily looked around the store, laughing and doing his *Sitting Rowing Dance*. We were comfortably able to look for furniture while wheeling him around. We were surprised to find that everyone around us was accommodating. When we went into the cafeteria to get Swedish meatballs, a woman offered us to go in front of her at the cash register. I said: "Oh no, thanks, we're fine," because John was still in a good mood and we weren't in a hurry. She replied: "I insist. You should go ahead!" When John had problems in the check-out line at our local grocery store, it was rare that someone would let us go in front. The wheelchair completely changed our experiences. Wherever we had been in the store, people had stepped to the side and had smiled compassionately. It hadn't been just one incident, it had been a pervasively different experience. At breakfast in the hotel in Prague we noticed that there was a shift now even without as clear of a signifier as a wheelchair.

We took the bus down into the center and walked over the Charles Bridge without having to nudge into people. The morning air was still damp and the city just awakening. We walked up to the castle and around the vast grounds. We saw the room where an assembly of Protestants had thrown two Catholic councillors and a secretary out of a palace window in 1618, the defenestration which contributed to the start of the Thirty Years War. We enjoyed a wonderful view over the city. John stood on the terrace looking down at the cityscape with its many spires and giggled. It was interesting that he didn't seem to be afraid of heights here, which had scared him at Cape Formentor on Mallorca and at the Cliffs of Moher in Ireland.

When groups of tourists started to pour in, we left the castle grounds and walked back over the Vltava river into the Jewish Quarter. On the second floor of the Pinkas synagogue, a whole room was filled with children's drawings from Terezín concentration camp. I had been there with the travel group and it had impressed me deeply. I had looked forward to showing it to Scott, but when we arrived a lot of people were pushing each other through impatiently. John felt the stress and started to bite his hand. We had to leave quickly to avoid a meltdown. We took a streetcar back over the river into the not so frequented Lesser Town and New World where we found a playground and spent almost an hour. We eventually ended up near the Loreta and dropped into a typical Czech beer hall for dinner, the *Pivnice U černého vola*, To The Black Ox.

We had spent a full day walking all over the city, from six-thirty a.m. to six-thirty p.m. We had easily found places to change John's diapers regularly. Every restaurant and hotel we had asked had let us use their washrooms without any problems. Drifting even worked in a rather big city now. It had been difficult in Paris, but in the meantime John's interests had somewhat shifted – mainly, as we suspected, because of food. Walking around in a city, there were plenty of kiosks, stands, and stores with sweets and ice-cream, and of course John would occasionally get something.

On our way back to Berlin, we left the highway to drive to Terezín concentration camp. Almost three years earlier, we had overnighted in Nuremberg on our way back from South Tyrol, and after walking through the quaint old town, we had visited the grim Nazi rally grounds on the outskirts of the city. Walking rather too quickly with John through an exhibit that partly touched on the Nazi euthanasia program, we had gotten interested in researching this more upon our return to Berlin. The knowledge that a child like John in Germany would not have survived the 1930's and 1940's had always lingered somewhere in the back of our minds, but it hadn't seemed to be an urgent thought until we visited those Nuremberg rally grounds. The reality had hit us there in an immediate way, maybe similar to the impact we had felt while standing on Omaha beach. It was one thing to know and read about history, it was another to be in a place that conveyed a different sense to that knowledge.

In the 1860's, both liberal and socialist circles had started to use scientific knowledge, namely Charles Darwin's theories about natural selection and the survival of the fittest, as arguments against aristocracy. One's position in society shouldn't be determined by birth, but by achievements. Alongside industrialization, a pervasive ideological shift towards performance and productivity had taken place. By the early twentieth century, arguments of racial biology had grown widely popular and were found internationally and in all political spectrums. For example, Karl Kautsky propagated "socialist eugenics" in 1910. In the U.S., the director of the Eugenics Record Office, Harry Laughlin, published *A Model Eugenical Sterilization Law* in 1914. Twelve states had already passed sterilization laws by that time. In 1933, Germany passed its own, modelled after Laughlin. The University of Heidelberg in fact awarded Laughlin with an honorary degree for his work in eugenics in 1936.

The Nazi Euthanasia program was called *T4-Action*, named after the address of the building where it was coordinated, in Tiergartenstrasse 4 in Berlin. Persons with disabilities and mental illnesses who were deemed unfit were murdered in gas chambers, altogether about 70,000 until 1941. The so-called *Hartheim statistic*, named after one of the execution clinics, proclaimed that 141 million Reichsmark had been saved in caretaking expenses. There had been protests against the program, especially by the Catholic church. The *T4-Action* was therefore officially discontinued in August of 1941, but continued unofficially. Some of the gas chambers in the psychiatric clinics were still being used, but to a lesser degree. The obvious killing was mainly replaced by more subtle methods such as starvation, withheld medication, and overdoses. Altogether, there were about 200,000 Euthanasia victims and among them were 5,000 medically euthanized children.

Upon returning from Nuremberg, we had visited the *Museum of Medical History* at the Charité hospital in Berlin. A section of it reflected on the Nazi racial hygiene theory and euthanasia practice. We had then discovered an entire exhibit dedicated to the topic at a psychiatric hospital in the North of the city, at the the former *Wittenauer Heilstätten*, later renamed *Karl-Bonhoeffer-Hospital*. There, we had happened upon a photo of a young boy who had been euthanized and who looked similar to John. In the documents that remained about him, he was described as "severely mentally retarded," but the descriptions of his behavior sounded like he might have been autistic. Children like John and parents like us had lived here not too long ago facing challenges that we couldn't imagine. It had become impossible to evade the thought. Visiting these sites for us became a way of dealing with the feelings that these thoughts evoked.

When we arrived at Terezín concentration camp, a woman at the entrance told us that there would be a guided tour later. We explained that we couldn't do that with John. She nodded understandingly and handed us booklets containing a map with explanations. She also gave us recommendations on where to go. We then walked for about two hours, and only encountered three other people. The emptiness felt eery.

Today's situation couldn't be compared at all to such atrocities, of course. Yet even presently, our life with John confronted me with ethical questions. When the Dutch government decided to pass legislature on medically assisted suicides in 1990, they appointed Prof. Jan Remmelink, attorney general of the Dutch Supreme Court, to chair a committee investigating the issue. The first results of the so-called *Remmelink Report* were reported in 1991 and led to legislature taking effect in 1994. Since then, several investigations into the development of medically assisted suicides in the Netherlands have been undertaken, the latest one published by Lancet in 2011. Overall numbers of medically assisted suicides were pretty stable throughout the years, even though there was some concern that doctors didn't report all cases. The preferred method changed from lethal injections to a much higher rate of *deep-continuous sedation*, a method of withholding fluids and food and thereby eventually leading to death by dehydration. The rate of *deep-continuous sedation* more than doubled in the Netherlands since 2001 and rose by 50% since 2005, while the overall numbers remained at around 4,000 medically assisted suicides per year. The issue of euthanasia came into the picture when looking at the cases in which the medically assisted suicide was carried out without the patient's consent: About 1,000 per year; one fourth of the total. These cases were mostly connected to dementia, psychiatric disorders, and disabilities. 41% of them were murdered at the request of relatives. 14% were fully conscious and even able to communicate. 11% would have been able decide, but hadn't been asked. In 32% of the cases, the relatives justified their decision by saying that they couldn't cope with the caretaking any more.

A doctor in the Dutch city of Groningen euthanized twenty-two children aged zero to twelve with parental consent between 1997 and 2004, according to his own published records. Eduard Verhagen's report gave reasons for killing the children: Their quality of life was low; they would never be able to live self-sufficiently; most of them were unable to communicate sufficiently; and some were frequently hospitalized while not having a reduced life expectancy. Verhagen's evaluations led to the so-called *Groningen Protocol* of 2004, in which euthanasia of children with disabilities aged zero to twelve was regulated: Since then legal in the Netherlands. The reasons listed for euthanasia were arguably all applicable to John as well. How could that not make me question our acceptance in society?

In Germany, pregnancies can be terminated without time limit in order to protect the mother's psychological well-being when the fetus shows severe disabilities. If the child is developed enough to potentially survive the abortion, the doctors first administer a lethal injection into the fetus' heart while still inside the mother's womb, in order to terminate the baby before retrieving it. Autism is shielded from that issue only by the fact that it cannot yet be detected prenatally.

I asked myself how far my own acceptance went. If there were a pill that John could take every morning and it would make his autism disappear, would I give it to him? Yes, I would. The answer was easy and clear. I knew well the frustration that autism caused John at times, the struggles and the challenges. Science didn't yet understand it, but it was clear that there was a multitude of malfunctions in his mind and body. Of course it was a highly theoretical question anyway, because science was nowhere near the introduction of such a pill and in all likelihood wouldn't be in my lifetime or in John's, but thinking about it made me realize again that there were no easy answers. En route to developing medication, research would probably first understand autism's genetics. As soon as autism could be detected prenatally, though, the problem would likely take care of itself. Around 90% of pregnancies detecting Down's syndrome are terminated today, even though children with Down's syndrome are generally perceived as good-hearted and non-aggressive. If so many parents decided against those babies, in spite of their comparatively good public image, one could only imagine that the percentage of abortions would be higher in case of autism with its more negative reputation.

Nonprofit research investments of tax money and donations can biopolitically turn into veritable for-profit ventures: For the profit of a society with less differing offspring and thereby reduced caretaking and medical costs incurred. Science and technology always carry an inherent dualism. While they can help they're also, inevitably, a matrix of complex power dynamics. As Michel Foucault, who studied biopolitics so extensively, wrote: "Power is not something you gain, take away, share, something that you keep or lose, power is something that is put into effect from countless points, in the play between unequal and ever-moving relationships." Progress in science increases ethical questions, and decisions will likely get harder to make. The more science and technology *can* do, the more we have to ask if we *want* them to do it: A dialectical development spiraling ever faster. Philosopher Giorgio Agamben addressed this concern in 2002 in his book *Homo Sacer*. We worry so much about life that these worries turn absolute and melt with eugenics.

Parents, autistics, therapists, caretakers, doctors, researchers, and politicians are all players in the power dynamics of autism. As research progresses, we will continue to raise and defend arguments within our unequal and ever-moving relationships. Autistic self-advocacy and the emancipatory neurodiversity movement seem ever more important in this light. By now, it has become clear that autistics will have a voice in any debate – "Nothing about us without us" – and while we might not always agree, it is imminently important to listen and learn. In December of 2009, President Barack Obama appointed the president of the *Autistic Self-Advocacy Network* Ari Ne'eman to the National Council on Disability. Obama is the first president to pay increased attention to autism. On his agenda for disability after entering his first term, autism was the only syndrome explicitly listed. Obama's agenda also recognized disability as its own entity, separating it from health care: A significant acknowledgment that disability isn't necessarily an illness, and that men and women with disabilities are a political minority – a point that disability rights and studies have tried to make for a long time.

One also has to remain realistic, though. As philosopher Thomas Metzinger wrote: "We shouldn't kid ourselves: Prohibition has never worked. Experience teaches us that for every forbidden desire humans have, for every demand, there is a black market. For each market, there will be an industry supplying it." A recent case in point is "stem cell tourism." Experimental stem cell therapy is for example reported from Russia, Costa Rica, China, and Mexico: Countries with comparatively high technical capabilities that conveniently lack the scientific quality control and ethical standards of Europe and the U.S. With regard to autism, it became known and discussed in the case of an autistic boy named Matthew. His parents took him to Costa Rica for stem cell therapy in an attempt to cure his autism and wrote a weblog about their experiences. The assumption that merely by injection these cells would miraculously know what exactly they were meant to do in the body reflects a strong therapeutic optimism commonly found in proponents of alternative interventions. Bruce Dobkin of the University of California said: "It is extreme nonsense to think that cells can be incorporated into the complex nervous system and do so much, when we cannot even get cells in mice and rats to do very much."

Just how dangerous alternative interventions can be became apparent in 2005 when a five-year-old boy in Pennsylvania died after an attempted detoxification called chelation. In 2003, an eight-year-old boy had suffocated in Milwaukee during a church service in which church members had tried to perform an exorcism on him. The most disturbing ethical issue to me is the intentional murder of autistic children. A frightening number die by filicide, especially maternal filicide, and often by parents who have previously been advocates of healing autism, as in the sadly popular case of Karen McCarron who killed her daughter Katie in 2006. Several lists of murdered autistics are being maintained online. In recent years, there've been at least three to four cases of filicide annually involving autistic children. Not that it would be an explanation, let alone a justification, but society's encouragement and underlying pressure to act on a cure, combined with a lack of support in order to manage every-day life, seems to be a fatal combination. It seems to me that a reversal of that fatal combination would help: To give families more support in their every-day life, and to alleviate expectations of cure.

All questions of ethics are obviously complex matters. While euthanasia and filicides are clearly painful to me, late-term abortions and alternative interventions are discomforting in a more subtle way. We are free to make decisions, or so we like to believe, but in reality it's quite possible that we only perceive ourselves as autonomous and free as long as we subject our life to the standards that society defines. A multi-disciplinary book on ethics titled *Life doesn't live* observed this curious connection between individual choice and national interest: "Self-determination doesn't want anything other than what society generally trends toward: One to two healthy children of qualitative value who fill our social security and health care reservoirs, and who are flexible enough to perform in the jobs of the new economy." At the same time, I'm convinced that no decision is made easily, whichever way it goes, and I respect every woman's right to choose. Due to the complexity of the matter and possibly also due to personal experiences, opinions about these issues inevitably remain flexible. Philosopher Martha Nussbaum has a nephew with Asperger's and Tourette syndrome. When I read some of her texts, it seemed to me that between her earlier works like *Human Functioning and Social Justice* in 1992 and later ones like *Frontiers of Justice* in 2006, she somewhat softened her opinion on what constitutes human life.

Walter Jens, former professor of Rhetorics at the German University of Tübingen, literary historian and prior president of the German P.E.N. Center and the German Academy of Fine Arts, was a publicly known supporter of medically assisted suicide in Germany. Then he was diagnosed with dementia, and while he had already lost his memory and most of his speech, he uttered repeatedly to his wife: "No killing, no killing." His wife Inge and his son Tilman decided not to execute his patient's provision. Inge Jens said in an interview that he had transitioned from intellectual to biological being, but that they still observed moments in which he clearly enjoyed life. He's apparently now especially fond of eating, which he had never been much interested in before. Did it matter whether he felt happy about an intellectual work of carefully crafted words, like he had done in the past, or about breadrolls with lunchmeat?

The flexibility and ambiguity inevitably connected with ethical questions didn't feel quite satisfying to me, and loving John I felt unable to come up with any kind of requirements to constitute a life worth living. Yet I realized that I don't have to find answers that are generally applicable as long as I can just acknowledge that I don't know what's right or wrong. It's most important that we have the freedom to live our life. A mother of a child in John's preschool once experienced problems manoeuvring her disabled son in a stroller in the streetcar, and held up traffic with that. A man said to her: "You know, today you don't have to have these kinds of children any more." Thankfully, she was able to tell him: "You're eighty years late to that kind of dictatorship."

12 Texel Island (The Netherlands) – Friendship

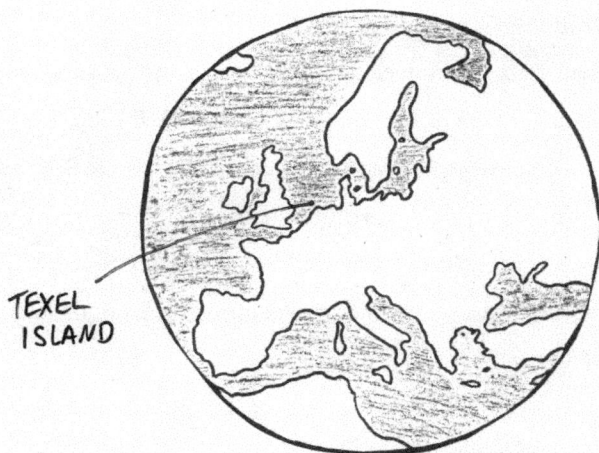

TEXEL
ISLAND

It is provided in the essence of things
that from any fruition of success, no matter what,
shall come forth something to make a greater struggle necessary.
(Walt Whitman)

After working in Prague and seeing that John was okay with it, I worked in Switzerland for ten days in the early summer of 2011. One evening, I stood in a phone booth close to the hotel and called home. I talked to Scott and heard John roam around loudly in the background. The contrast of that tumultuous life and the serene beauty of the gorgeous Alpine landscape I was standing in hung in the air. After ending the phone call, however, I noticed a disabled teenager on the other side of the street. He was with an adult, his father or caretaker. I thought that the teenager was probably autistic. I could see a meltdown building, and soon enough he was flailing his arms and making loud noises. I could see that the adult was under pressure trying to guide the teenager safely away from the street. I instantly felt like I was part of the situation. Only then did I realize how deeply I had come to identify with my different life. The meltdown belonged to me more than any serenity.

John handled my absence well, even though my Swiss trip was twice as long as Prague had been. He didn't cry in school. It seemed as if he had already gotten more used to the fact that I could be gone for a few days. At home, Scott didn't have any problems either. In fact, he said that it had even been easier at times. John knew well how to manipulate people into getting his way, and I was sometimes too responsive. John took advantage of that. Scott was less lenient.

When I returned from Switzerland and before we could start our own summer trip, we had to endure another appointment with medical services. They came every three months to see if John was well taken care of. It was part of the disability benefits and the whole thing usually didn't take long. It wasn't bad, but it slightly annoyed me because it was a mandatory control mechanism. Every two years, when the level of care had to be reevaluated, a doctor came for about two to three hours. He or she would ask all kinds of intimate questions, for example about the pregnancy and the birth. Full cooperation is expected, and that includes full disclosure of all disavowals, including financial and emotional ones. Since they sent a different person every time, we had to go through the painful process all over again every two years. Privacy was a luxury we couldn't afford if we wanted to get the help that we needed.

One doctor once wrote in his report: "The family lives in a small two-bedroom apartment." Maybe he lived in a house in the suburbs and therefore perceived it that way, but we enjoyed living in the city and liked our apartment. Why exactly was the size of our apartment of any importance to the evaluation of John's care in the first place? We were constantly being judged, it was inherent in the system. How many papers we had accumulated: Teachers, caretakers, doctors, they all wrote not only about John, but also about us parents. Granted that they were complimentary, it still felt a bit like trespassing.

When we had once gotten a new caretaker, the agency that he was employed with had requested that we address each other formally. The agency claimed that their policy ensured a certain professional distance between the family and the caretaker, but we perceived it differently. The social worker had keys to our apartment, because he would sometimes pick John up at school or from the bus and we wanted to give them the freedom to come and go as they pleased. The social worker also took John to playgrounds and John was prone to running away and couldn't estimate dangers properly. We selected our social workers carefully and naturally built a relationship with them. It would be ridiculous to contradict that with formal language. It had been an absurd situation and we were eventually allowed to make an exception. Were parents of non-disabled children ever told how to speak? I often had to think of Michel Foucault's *Discipline and Punish*. To me, the main difference in parenting a disabled child was that it was more demeaning – in subtle ways, but ways that wore you down over the years. All of the papers we signed, every month with the social worker, every appointment with the evening caretaker, and every meeting with medical services. All of the reports, binders, and files in so many places.

When I was frustrated, I imagined all of the paperwork piled up. I could throw in all of the papers that I had created myself: Seizure charts, ketogenic diet protocols, letters to doctors. If we all threw together our hard yet so often futile work, it could create a pretty good-sized bonfire. That'd be something John would enjoy.

Since the drive to Spain had pushed our limits the previous summer, we decided to go somewhere closer, less hot, but also on the ocean. We had heard only good things about family friendliness on the Dutch islands in the North Sea. My parents lived relatively close to the Dutch border and we could stay with them for a night or two en route. John knew them well, their house and garden, the neighbors and friends. Then the drive to Texel would only be about four hours from their house.

The Netherlands are a country frequently challenged by disastrous floods. Two-thirds of its land are prone to be affected. The 1953 North Sea flood led to the building of extensive dam works, dikes, and floodgates. On the Western coast, the impressive *Delta Works* had been built, while on the Northern coast, the Zuiderzee bay had already been dammed off since 1932, creating land by drainage and polders, and also creating the Ijsselmeer lake. A causeway, the *Afsluitdijk*, separates the Ijsselmeer from the North Sea. It leads right through the water for twenty miles. On the four-lane highway we pulled over to a viewing point mid-way. John stood in the strong wind, with his arms wide open like wings. With water on both sides, standing on top of the impressive dike was a treat for him.

We set out for the island by car ferry. We had rented a house in a complex of thirty-six vacation homes in De Koog, a coastal village mid-distance inland from the port. The house wasn't directly on the sea, but we could hear the waves a short distance away. The housing complex had a playground and the house was situated in a corner lot. It was spacious and had all the amenities we were looking for: Washing machine, dishwasher, and internet access. It was modernly furnished. Several flocks of seagulls were scouring over the village. Since we had some dried bread-rolls left over from the drive, Scott threw a few breadcrumbs out onto the lawn and within minutes, birds were flying in from all directions. John loved watching them in the sky, especially when they flew formations. Now they came so close. He watched them, thrilled. I was sitting inside reading the house's manual. One of the first items I happened upon was: "Please do not feed the birds."

Texel is an island of sixty-two square miles and about 13,600 inhabitants, the largest of the Dutch islands in the North Sea. Even though it is much bigger than Hiddensee in the Baltic, our experiences on Texel quickly resonated with those on Hiddensee. The island slowed life down. There was nothing much to do except to be in the nature. We took a ride in the car and our first stop was a sleepy village called De Waal. We took a walk and visited a small old church, but John didn't seem to like it, so we moved on and drove further up the East coast, enjoying the rural island scenery. A grass-covered dike ran along the entire coastline and sheep were grazing on it. We found a parking spot and took John up over the dike, which descended sharply down to the sea on the other side. He sat halfway down the slope, looking out to sea. A local fisherman was emerged waist deep in the sea, close to him several buckets with his catch. Walking by him, we asked about the jelly fish that were washed ashore. He said that they tended to come in with the tides more so on the East coast, and rather recommended the West coast for swimming. The water was cold anyway.

We continued our drive North, passing small farms and open fields lying inland. Intermittently, there were ponds with many species of birds and more sheep gathering around them. On the Northern tip, we came upon a tall lighthouse. The parking lot was packed with cars. John didn't like the idea of getting out until he saw a café with a large ice-cream sign by the front door. We were on our way, and with an ice-cream in his hand, John started steering us towards the sea. The sandy beach was wide, and we only got about halfway towards the shore when John got frustrated and wanted to return to the car. We decided to give him space and time to adjust to the vacation and drove back to the house.

We got a nice start to the next day by visiting the holiday park playground. John had the swings and the teeter-tauter all to himself. The sun was shining, it was warm and John giggled away while swinging. He still spoke mostly echolalic but he had advanced from somewhere around twenty words to about fifty. The school worked with a "first – then" approach of laminated symbol cards: First John was asked to do something that he'd consider work and then he could do something that he liked, like bringing out the garbage followed by time on the swing. Autistics cannot easily be manipulated, though, and John had come up with his own "first – then" idea, sitting on the swing in our holiday park shouting: "First ice-cream, then chocolate!" Good job defying conditioning.

We found two bike rentals close to our house. None of them had adaptive bikes, but they had regular tandems which we decided to rent. Years ago, we had inherited an adaptive tandem bike from a family whose autistic son had outgrown it. On the special tandem John was seated in front, enabling us to react quickly to what he was doing. Steering, pedaling and breaking were all controlled from the rear, but John had the option to help peddle. All he had to do was sit and hold on. Even so, it had taken him a while to get the hang of it. He jumped off several times at first and he moved to his left and right, making it difficult to balance the bike. He also tended to take his hands off the handlebar in order to flail his arms in the air. On the playground, he had once let go of the rope of a disc swing, a device one rides on a long cable from one end to another. He liked the ride so much that he felt like waving both arms in the air in excitement, which of course caused him to fall off at full speed. Next thing, we had found ourselves back in the emergency room and returned home with a broken arm in a cast.

Eventually, John had learned to ride the adaptive tandem but had recently outgrown its small children's frame in the front, and so we had passed it on to another family. Yet the experience with the specialized bike gave us hope that John was now ready to try a regular tandem. Because it was steered from the front, John would have to sit in the back. We figured that whoever wasn't riding with him would have to ride behind to watch what he was doing. John would also have to peddle along, because on a normal tandem the pedals synchronically function together. It was difficult at first, and we couldn't go fast. We had to make frequent stops, but it worked. We rode out alongside the beach where the first thing John discovered was a stand selling French fries, so we made our stop for lunch. The curious thing was that John wasn't interested in the sea, similar to the previous day at the lighthouse. We figured that it might still have to do with transitioning into the vacation, so we continued our bike ride on the cycling path alongside the beach. We passed a horse farm and green meadows, and John was in a great mood. Riding on the cement surface back at the bike rental, we hadn't noticed that the tires were low on air. The path's sandy surface along with John's jerking in the back made for quite a workout with the low air pressure, and the bikes hadn't come equipped with a pump, so we took turns several times.

Texel's West coast is made up of sandy dunes and split up into several national parks. *De Slufter* is a wide and sandy open salt marsh and dune valley. High tides bring in sea water, leaving behind small creeks and ponds, with one large body of standing water connecting to the North Sea, creating a perfect environment for birds and plant life. We parked our bikes on the far edge of the park. John wasn't too excited to get off, but agreeable enough. When we reached the top of the first dune, John saw what lay ahead of him and his mood soured. The wide open landscape at this point mainly signified "no opportunities," as in: No cafés, food stands, or convenience stores. John just laid out on top of that first dune. We had experienced this often. We would wait for a while, and at some point he'd get up and walk on. It took longer now, though. He wasn't budging. He looked as if he wanted to sleep, covering his eyes with his arms. He was calm, but decidedly intent on staying on the dune. Eventually we got him to move on, but his interest in nature seemed gone. He would have loved this site in the past, but not any more. John laid down again and started a low, momentum-building growl, which erupted into a loud roar. Lifting his hands in front of his face, twinkling his fingers in front of his eyes, watching his fingertips with gritted teeth, a howling sound emerged: "Eyyaarrrrooaaarrrrr." He bit into his hand and rolled on the ground. A major meltdown ensued and there was simply no way to continue. We waited for John to calm down before walking back to where our bikes were parked. He was already perfectly happy again by the time we mounted our bikes.

It was then, at that happy moment on the tandem, that we took one of the nicest photos of John, a hundred percent pure joy in his face. When I look at the photo, it's curious to me that a huge meltdown immediately preceded this image, and one cannot see a single trace of it. What the picture doesn't tell is far larger than what it does. It's an imbalance inherent in any portrait but never quite as strong as in this case. It exceptionally captures the disparity of our life, part of which is John's amazing diversity. (The photo is on the back cover of the book.)

My friend Claudia drove over from my hometown and visited us for a few days. We were able to explore the Northern tip of the island briefly, followed by a stopover at a beach restaurant, and then we returned to *De Slufter*. John cooperated this time, probably because of Claudia's presence. It was nice to have a visitor, as we spent so much time alone with John. Whenever we tried to do something together with other families, it was difficult. John's needs behavior were so specific. Even something simple like taking a walk together was difficult. John ran ahead, or he laid on the ground, and so we were often in a different place than everyone else, either way ahead or way behind. I met most of my friends when John was in school, or in the evenings when Scott stayed home with John. Even so, when John was in school I mostly had to work, and in the evenings I was often too exhausted to go out. Handling work and caretaking left little space. I found it increasingly hard to maintain friendships.

I lost one close friend after a misunderstanding revealed her unwillingness to meet with John. We had continuously failed in planning a get-together. I had explained that it would be best if she, her husband, and daughter came to our place. John could retreat into his room then whenever he wanted. Had we gone to their apartment, which is something I almost always did, John would have probably lasted all of ten minutes. We finally agreed on a day and time to meet for breakfast. Just to make sure, I asked: "Okay, so you're coming to our place, right?"

"No, you come to our place!" my friend said.

"But John's still home that day, his school only starts the following day," I explained. The day we had agreed upon was the last of his winter break.

"Oh, I didn't know that," she replied. "I thought that he was already back in school. We've made plans to meet another family at the museum at 12:30. We really can't come to your place beforehand, it's not enough time. I thought you were coming here by yourself."

She lived about a half hour away from us and why couldn't she get on the train at eight or nine in the morning, stay for a couple of hours and then go to the museum from our place? Especially because her daughter loved riding the train? She simply didn't want to do it and she had picked the date because she thought that John was back in school. Since there had been a history of such problems, this was the final straw for me. In our life, we just couldn't accommodate people who weren't willing to make any effort at all.

I tried not to loose too many friends and I hoped that we didn't get too isolated, but the older John got, the more difficult it became. He enjoyed company, as long as people took the time to get to know him. Not everyone seemed to have this kind of time and I guess it was easy for some to just stay away. Luckily, we did have some good friends.

At the same time, John was entering puberty and his behavior became more challenging. I had originally hoped that John himself wouldn't be so isolated, but we hadn't found a way to prevent that. Had John had a sibling who brought his or her friends into the house, I might have been able to at least occasionally persuade them into letting John be with them, but since John was our only child contact didn't come naturally. We had once tried a mixed sports group for disabled and non-disabled children, but apart from the long waiting list, the trial hour hadn't worked out. It was too loud and too confusing for John, he didn't like it. A noisy, reverberating large gym wasn't the right thing for his autistic perception.

On the playground, children hardly ever engaged with him, we were mostly on our own. The incidences in which children reacted positively to John are banner days in my memory. One time, we had been at a playground around the corner from us and John wanted to get on a multiple-person swing. Two Turkish-German girls were sitting on it and I asked them if John could join them. Normally, children then just jumped off and let John have the swing to himself, but these girls said: "Sure!" and made space for him in between them. They swung with him, John sitting in the middle with a big, happy smile on his face. I felt sad that something like that didn't happen more often, but how could we enforce it? Other children would have to want the contact.

One time, I had been shopping in a grocery store with John and he had been in a good mood, snapping his fingers at the packages on the shelves, as he frequently did in appreciation of their colors and shapes. Two young girls, maybe six years old, stood close to us. They observed John's interaction with the packages – his communication with things – and giggled at first, then one of them looked straight into John's eyes and said loudly: "You're disgusting!" I immediately addressed her, while the other one ran away. The girl tried to poorly justify herself by saying that her friend had laughed at John as well. I told her: "That doesn't matter to me right now. I'm standing here with you, and you said something to my son that was entirely inappropriate. There are many different kinds of people in the world, and you should know that they all have a right to be here, just like you." John started to cry in huge sobs. Whether he had understood her remark, or my remark, or just felt the tension, I didn't know. He was desolate, so I just put down our basket and we walked home. I remember feeling secure upon entering our apartment and closing the door behind us, and at the same time feeling irritated about that, because why would our apartment have to be a safe haven? It made me angry, sad and helpless at the same time. Not only did so much depend on John's disposition, but even happy moments like John enjoying packages in a grocery store could so easily be destroyed by influences from outside.

How could we help John connect to peers and feel accepted and loved by them? This was going to be our next focus. When John had been younger, the interaction with other children hadn't been as problematic. On the playground, they barely paid attention to him, and John himself roamed around contently on his own. More recently though, we had noticed that John increasingly watched other children. Once he sat on a swing and intently watched a group of children play soccer. Suddenly tears streamed down his cheeks. It looked as if he tried to understand what they were doing, but couldn't get it. He seemed painfully aware of his being different and the isolation that it caused. We offered him to go, but he didn't want to. He held on to the swing, determined not to let go, and continued to watch the other children. It reminded me of how courageous he had been about his epilepsy. I had tears in my eyes standing next to him, partly because I was sad about his isolation and struggle, but also because his resolve was truly moving. He did have to find a way to cope. He was different and always would be, and he was right: He had to face it. What a great kid.

I had initially thought that John's enthusiasm for the tandem might have kept him from wanting to walk on Texel. This guess proved wrong during the following days when his cycling enthusiasm wore off as well. It seemed as if he didn't want to do anything except hang around the house or ride in the car. Being on the move had been his primary way of being, but now things were different. The only thing he still seemed interested in was music. We had noticed that he liked to watch musicians perform, and so we watched a lot of youtube clips of NPR's "Tiny desk concerts," or bands playing on KEXP Seattle, or the French TV5 series *Acoustic*. We could also watch whole concerts, John for example liked to watch the *Old Friends* tour concert by Simon & Garfunkel.

We reverted to mainly exploring the island by car, listening to The Decemberists, Iron & Wine and Bon Iver. It was our luck that 2011 was a good year for music releases, so we had plenty to choose from. We discovered a quaint artist's village called Den Hoorn, which exhibited the art project *Klifhanger* while we were there. Among the installations were knitted hats – *Bloiende Bollen* – put on top of fence posts all around the village. It reminded me of guerilla knitting. In the evenings, we sometimes went to the beach like we had done on previous vacations after dinner, but John wasn't too interested. At eleven years old, he was entering a phase that might be rather typical for his age after all: Not knowing what he wanted, getting bored, yet being unhappy with any suggestion of activities.

Scott and I both enjoyed the island. I took lots of photos of sheep and thought that I could probably happily live somewhere on the North Sea photographing sheep for the rest of my life. Back in Berlin, John then no longer wanted to take excursions outside of the city any more, which we had often done during the weekend. Berlin is surrounded by the state of Brandenburg that belonged to East Germany between 1949 and 1990. There was an old Soviet military training ground that had been decontaminated after Germany's reunification, and turned into a nature reserve for the preservation of deer. John had always enjoyed going there, but even that was out now. We were moved suddenly from restlessness into the opposite extreme of immobility.

13 BERLIN (GERMANY) – AUTISM AS A METAPHOR

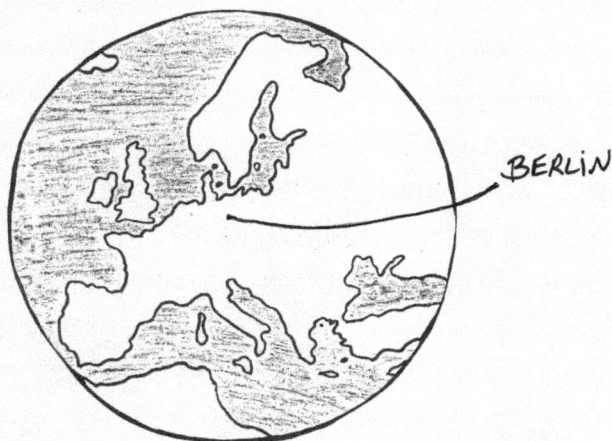

The prognosis is always, in principle, optimistic.
Society, by definition, never catches a fatal disease.

(Susan Sontag)

In October of 1997, I flew to Chicago for a three-months internship at the German Cultural Center *Goethe-Institut* while I was waiting for my master's thesis to be graded. I had booked myself into the downtown YMCA on Chicago Avenue, thinking that it would be somewhat similar to a youth hostel in Germany. I had a small room, toilets and showers were located in the hallway but didn't look very appealing. Someone kept banging on my door in the middle of the night. Quickly, I found an agency for roommates, looked at three apartments and then moved in with two roommates on North Avenue in the Goldcoast area. On the flea market, I bought a bike and within three days I had set myself up in Chicago, more than four thousand miles from home.

My relatives in Heidelberg connected me with someone they knew in the Chicago Suburbs, and so I ended up with an invitation for a Thanksgiving dinner where I met Scott. We talked and it felt as if we already knew each other. After dinner, Scott invited me to tag along to an after-Thanksgiving-dinner party. I extended my stay in Chicago, spent Christmas and New Year's. Scott and I spent happy months together, we went to concerts at the *Metro*, watched films at the *Music Box Theatre*, spent nights in the *Lounge Ax, Kingston Mines, Wild Hare, B.L.U.E.S.* Sometimes I find it hard to comprehend that those two young people were in fact us. Today, Scott and I often both don't feel like going out. John getting up so early makes for a difficult transition the next day. One evening, we went to a Great Lake Swimmers concert. Just before leaving, John had a bowel movement while I was giving him a bath and it was a tough clean-up job. Not even two hours later I looked around the *Festsaal Kreuzberg* and wondered if anyone else had just experienced anything similar. Yet when the music started, we eventually felt as if it were 1997 again on the balcony of the *Metro*. We experienced a moment in which we connected with the story of how it all began.

I read many books by parents of autistic or otherwise disabled children. I find in them a search familiar to me, for a way to not be swallowed by caretaking, while at the same time not letting the child down. Sometimes I think that it's a search for a middle ground where there is none, but when we experience moments like the one in *Festsaal Kreuzberg*, I know that perspective is too pessimistic. We're still the same people, with a shared history, and there's plenty of middle ground, it might just be harder to find at times.

An acquaintance recently told me about his wife's miscarriage. They had told everyone about the pregnancy as soon as they knew. They hadn't waited, as many couples do, for the first twelve weeks to pass. They didn't see any point in making a secret out of the matter, whatever was to happen. He told me that nobody then knew how to react. He and his wife naturally felt sorrow about the miscarriage, but they were accepting of what happened. They couldn't understand that people had such problems reacting to something that has always been part of life. He said that the next time around, they probably wouldn't tell anyone before the end of the first trimester – not because of their own attitude which hadn't changed, but because of those around them. It seems that our lives have become quite mainstreamed and polished. There are many things that we don't talk about publicly any more, because they don't fit into the desired image of a successful, happy life. When we talked about the miscarriage, it occurred to me again how important it is to accept the diversity of life. Our wishes are just that, idle wishes. Do we have to be happy all the time, and healthy, and successful? It's an illusion anyway. Life has never been like that. It's natural that one would want his or her child to be healthy. I don't want John to have seizures day and night either, but if and when he does, he's still John and a great kid. I don't think that our society, in its ever-present search for security, risk-minimizing and self-optimizing always realizes how these imperatives start to turn against us, making us less free and excluding individuals who don't fit into these logics.

Recent changes in DSM-5 have sparked new discussions about autism. In Berlin, there's a family with autistic triplets. The three children are very different from each other. One was able to attend a regular preschool, two were so severely affected that they attended specialized preschool with John, but even the two severely affected are different from each other in their compulsions, communication level, and social behavior. To me, these triplets don't only reflect the genetic basis of autism, but also speak strongly for the idea of an autism spectrum.

We enjoy living in Berlin. It's an international metropolis with a large English-speaking community of about 40,000. There's a monthly magazine for expats in English, the *Exberliner*, and we even have our own national public radio, NPR Berlin. We often drive through Berlin, John with his face glued to the window in the back seat, happily watching the streets, and when we don't listen to music we listen to the *Diane Rehm show* or *Fresh Air*. We have recently discovered a fountain on a square called Hausvogteiplatz in the city center. For some reason, John loves that place. We suspect it has to do with the soothing sound of the fountain water and the kiosk conveniently located across the street. Going to the square is one of the few things that he enjoys doing at the moment, outside of driving in the car, listening to music, or watching nature films. The highlight of many a recent Saturday has been counting how many times John runs around the fountain. Is it a Four-Rounds-Day, a Nine-Rounds-Day, or a Twelve-Rounds-Day?

Sometimes, staring is still an issue, but not as much as it used to be. In public, we continue to have both good and bad experiences. When we took a day trip to the city of Potsdam just outside of Berlin to visit the *Sanssouci* castle and gardens, the lady servicing the restrooms folded a paper ship for John and gave it to him. I told her: "He doesn't speak. Thank you," and she replied, smiling: "I know, but I'm sure he understands when someone gives him a gift." On the train going from Hannover back towards Berlin after visiting my parents, a waitress in the restaurant compartment asked me if John was allowed to eat ice-cream. I told her yes and thought for a second that she wanted to make sale, but she instantly pulled an ice-cream from behind her back where she had been hiding it, and gave it to John saying: "I was hoping so, because I would really like to make him smile." Which he did.

In March of 2013, a German journalist wrote in the weekly magazine *Der Spiegel* that we live in an ideology of egotism: "An ideology of coldness and autism. An ideology of psychopaths for psychopaths." Autism as a metaphor in fact seems to be everywhere in this early twenty-first century. In 2000, Bernard Guerrien founded the movement of *Post-Autistic Economics*. Autism is interpreted in lines of economic isolation which needs to be overcome. In 2012, geographer and architect Maria Kaika of the University of Manchester introduced the term *Autistic Architecture*. It signifies self-absorbed famous architects who aren't interested in their surroundings and whose iconic emblems no longer contribute to an organic cityscape. The autism metaphor can even be found in the *Colegio Andino* school in Bogotá, Colombia. "¿Eres autistico?" shouts one boy to another during recess: "Are you autistic?" My brother, who has been teaching in Colombia for the past three years, told me about the episode on the phone.

I subscribed to google alerts on autism many years ago in order to be informed about scientific developments, but instead thousands of examples of autism as a metaphor have jammed my email account since. For example one article claimed: "Computer games have driven hundreds of thousands into autism." Judging from the amount of autism metaphors used in connection with technology, almost anyone who has anything to do with computers seems suspicious of autism. Social media platforms enable constant contact with each other, but communication takes place virtually and so we ask ourselves whether we are truly connected. The autism metaphor serves as a reference point for a digitalized society in which everyone sits alone in front of their computer, caught between participation and isolation.

In the film *The Social Network,* Facebook founder Mark Zuckerberg appears as a nerd who doesn't maintain eye contact, has a hard time understanding ambiguity, takes everything literally, pedantically insisting on details even during innocuous conversations, and doesn't seem to realize how he offends others by his remarks. In short, writer Aaron Sorkin and director David Fincher portray Zuckerberg as autistic. Author Zadie Smith wrote about this in the *New York Review of Books* in November of 2010. She identified a new type easily recognizable today, the social autistic: "We know this guy. Overprogrammed, furious, lonely." In social networks, connection is the ultimate goal. The quality of relationships doesn't seem to be important. We portray ourselves "falsely jolly, fake-friendly, self-promoting, slickly disingenuous." The software doesn't make provisions for deeper dimensions: "Everything shrinks. Individual character. Friendships. Language. Sensibility. In a way it's a transcendent experience: We lose our bodies, our messy feelings, our desires, our fears," Smith writes. All of these developments are bundled up in her typology of the social autistic. She doesn't use autism as a diagnostic term, but to characterize a generation whose personality is shaped by superficial software formats.

Her text reminded me of an essay that sociologist Georg Simmel wrote as early as 1903: *The Metropolis and Mental Life.* In his text, Simmel dealt with the effect that living in ever larger cities has on our nerves. According to his argument, the way we lived increasingly asked for specialized performance and he claimed that this specialization would negatively impact the complexities of our personality. More than a hundred years later, we find a similar argument in Smith's text about the "social autistic." Simmel's argument can be read as a precursor to what we associate with autism today – specialized skills paired with an atrophied personality – at the time of course iterated without the name and concept of autism. Simmel called it atomization.

Journalist Nicholas Carr published an article in 2008 called *Is Google Making Us Stupid?* Carr interprets the internet as a turning point in evolutionary history and claims that it dangerously shortens our attention span. Since Carr's publication, we get bombarded with articles speculating on whether the internet causes information overkill or to the contrary improves the power of our brains. Sensory overload, a problem that autistics frequently struggle with, has become an issue that everyone can relate to. In a radiolab program in October of 2010, musician Sxip Shirey talked about the sense of being autistic when he first came to New York. There was so much stimulation that he couldn't filter or sort it. He felt like an autistic child, he said.

Researchers Nicholas Epley of the University of Chicago and Adam Waytz of Northwestern University published a study in October of 2011, according to which people with strong social bonds tend to dehumanize outsiders: "The most tightly knit groups — from military units to athletic teams — may also be the most likely to treat their adversaries as subhuman animals," they wrote. Participants of an experiment were divided into two groups. The first filled out a questionnaire while a friend was sitting in the same room, the other group did so in presence of someone they didn't know. Both groups were presented with eleven photos of alleged terrorists and were asked about their attitude towards torture techniques. The participants who filled out the questionnaire while a friend was present dehumanized the prisoners significantly more than the participants who answered the questions while someone unknown was sitting in the same room. "Being socially connected to close others has great benefits for one's own physical and mental health," the researchers concluded, "but it also satiates the motivation to connect with others." With our urge for connection satisfied, we're prone to not give enough time or thought to those outside our social sphere to fully grasp their humanity.

The autism metaphor today often signifies this kind of outsider realm. Searching for the term autism in the recorded protocols of parliamentary sessions in Germany, one encounters this phenomenon time and again, both on the state as well as on the federal level. For example, FDP-congressman Feldmann on one occasion asked: "Saying it clearly: The military plays with our existence, but claims that they have it all under control. Should we build our future on the grounds of such dangerous autism?" Deputy Hans of the CDU cautioned on another: "We have to distinguish between millions of muslims who are integrated in our society, and a few thousand fanatic autistics who globally threaten our culture." In political debates, autism is frequently put into place as the ultimate adversary of democracy. Adjectives like dangerous and fanatic increase that perception. The political metaphor mostly functions as an extreme variation of the good community versus the individual – autistic – renegade.

German child psychiatrist Reinhart Lempp wrote a book about parallels between autism and the fundamental characteristics of our time: *Autistic Society. Do We Loose Our Sense of Responsibility?* Lempp claims that we meet more people today, but that we don't get into psychological contact. According to his argument, people don't perceive each other any more, and as a result don't feel responsible for their community.

Similar observations were made in the magazine *Theater Heute* in a 2012 story about Belgrade, Serbia after the fall of communism: "On a daily basis, I hear how much better life was in times of socialism, in unified Yugoslavia. Democracy and capitalism didn't bring much good. A media scientist laconically said to me that people have become completely autistic, uninterested in their fellows. He's going to leave now." Next to diagnosing capitalism as autistic, the quote also hints at the autism of increasingly transitory existence. We've never moved around as much, world-wide, and changed our employments and partners as often, internationally. According to the idea of this autism metaphor, compassion, responsibility and a sense of community become harder to maintain in such a life. Everything's always in flux, and we could be somewhere else as early as tomorrow.

However, there also seems to be more to it. Negotiating autism as a metaphor also continues an artistic tradition of interplay between participation and isolation. The autism metaphor flirts with the idea of not constantly being accessible and in touch. It implies a temporary non-conformist behavior which, at least as an ephemeral experience, has a certain appeal in our time of connnectedness. Artists have celebrated "being removed" as an intriguing thought for a long time. French author Gustave Flaubert coined the term *impassibilité*, the cool detachment of a poet. Painter Paul Cézanne propagated life as a solitaire. Writer Paul Eluard wrote: "I dream of being completely disconnected. Unfortunately, there's hardly any chance that this dream will come true." How emblematic of a sentence this seems for our time.

Writer Susan Sontag has written famously about *Illness As Metaphor*. She observed how a syndrome can start to capture central fears of society. In the nineteenth century, this was the case for tuberculosis, in the twentieth century for cancer. According to research that Sontag cites, a syndrome develops a broader cultural significance when there's a high concordance between a syndrome's prevalence and widespread ailments of the time. For example, in the twentieth century a lot of people complained about pains similar to the pains related with cancer patients. When a syndrome or illness develops a cultural dominance, more and more people identify with it – and so it becomes a metaphor. This, I think, is true for autism today. In the nineteenth century, the "expression of the self" was symbolized by tuberculosis. Loosing a sense of individuality was symbolized by cancer in the twentieth century. Today, in the time of globalization, we struggle to maintain a sense of community and belonging – geographically, physically, emotionally – and this is symbolized by autism. While tuberculosis and cancer described the body being invaded, autism describes our increased dissociation from the body, and while death was the fundamental deterrent for tuberculosis and cancer, autism's fundamental deterrent is the social death.

Using a medical term in this way is highly problematic, though. In the process of making the metaphor fit, it's inevitable that it removes itself from the actual syndrome. In fact, the associations we have with the metaphor might eventually not have anything in common with the actual syndrome any more. This, too, is true for autism today. Contrary to the metaphorical autistic, the real autistic doesn't have an atrophied personality and he doesn't intentionally turn away from society. (In fact, it more often seems to be the other way around with society turning away from the autistic.) Autistics aren't necessarily isolated. In fact, they often live with their families longer than neurotypicals who usually move out after finishing high school. As far as our alleged loss of responsibility is concerned, dedicated relatives, therapists, teachers, doctors, and caretakers are prime examples of the high sense of responsibility that can be found in our society today.

How does the internet change the way we live, the way we work, and the way we feel? Does our technically dominated lifestyle and worklife drive us apart? Does the superficial software of social media platforms shape our personalities into being less complex? Will we be able to handle the constant information overload or does everyone eventually just disappear into their own life? Does the way we live today make us numb? All of these questions voice existential fears, and by using autism as a metaphor to express them, these fears have started to reflect back on the syndrome itself.

When Adam Lanza murdered twenty-seven people in Newtown, speculations about him having been autistic spread quickly and globally. Autism was used as a means to try and make sense of an irrational act. Autism's negative associations were fully carried out by mass media, naturally assuming a causal connection, not only in the U.S. but also in Germany, where we also had to suffer through grueling articles about autism in the aftermath of Newtown's catastrophe. Something similar happened a couple of months later when a German woman in Munich was murdered. Following up on their stereotyped thinking in the Lanza case, media reported that a neighbor of the victim thought that the murderer had been autistic. "Psychological Profile: This Is How The Alleged Murderer Thinks," read one headline.

Right around the same time, a study by the University of Western Australia in Perth was published. Researchers had done a whole-population study of Western Australians born between 1955 and 1969, more than a million-and-a-half people. They compared records of arrest with records of psychiatric diagnoses and came to the conclusion that there was no elevated risk of criminal acts due to psychiatric problems. While persons with a diagnosis of schizophrenia were arrested more often than persons with depression, the arrest numbers for persons with addictions were higher than for schizophrenia. Autistics in fact are more often victims than perpetrators, for example victims of mobbing and bullying. They often suffer from exclusion. Yet in the distorted way in which the media reports, autistics sometimes seem like outright psychopaths.

I feel that it's necessary to free autism from its negative misappropriation in terms of both the syndrome and the symbol, for even the symbolic usage is harmful. Whether we talk about *Post-autistic Economics*, *Autistic Architecture*, about the autism of our culture, politics, the internet: Autism is always made to define the distant, *the other*. The autistic embodies the dangers that are looming, he signifies where we don't want to be. By delegating fears that are within us to an outside that is allegedly different from us, we try to stabilize an idea of community. Both the deficits and the strengths of autism correspond with key questions of our time, but as concisely as we might be able to see contemporary concerns through the lens of autism, as urgently we have to ask ourselves about the consequences for actual autistics. Where can I see my family in a society that tries to negotiate its crises by metaphorically using the syndrome that we live? A society that assigns negative traits to my son's condition on a daily basis? To make matters worse, it even remains an open question how many of our allegedly new fears are not so new after all, but rather owed to age-old pessimism anyway.

Throughout the course of this book, I thought about many aspects that have to with the knowledge of autism and also its images. Symbol and syndrome often seem to melt in the way we look at autism. What remains a key issue for me after engaging with autism on various levels, is that to my feeling autism escapes us when it gets saturated with the knowledge and images that we have about it. Sometimes theories and images are in sync with my personal experiences, and sometimes they're not. For example, the concept of "Theory of Mind" – in short, the idea that autistics cannot put themselves into someone else's head – doesn't always seem to apply. John has rarely shown an understanding for the feelings of others, yet he has done so clearly noticeable on impressive occasions. While away on one of my business trips, John came down with the flu. During the night, Scott had to clean his entire bedding several times. He put John into the bathtub at four a.m., exhausted. He sat next to the tub, put his head in his hands and sighed. Suddenly he felt a hand patting his head and he looked up. John was watching him intently with a compassionate look on his face. He looked directly into Scott's eyes and then put his hand on Scott's shoulder as if to say: "I know this is difficult. Thank you for taking care of me." The magnitude if his gesture cannot be described.

John can also be sensitive towards music. On several occasions he has started to cry as sad songs played on the radio. In school, he cries whenever his best friend gets scolded. He doesn't react that way for any other child. These experiences speak against an all-encompassing mindblindness in autism.

Life is inexhaustible, and autism shows this to us by being inexhaustible in itself. It gets more and more complex the longer one lives with the syndrome. I recall an appointment with a specialist, during which I talked about the subtle changes that had taken place since our last meeting. At some point, the doctor put his pen down, looked at me, and said: "I couldn't tell you anything like this about my own children. I usually don't spend as much time with them and even when I do, I don't pay this kind of attention." It's only natural, because we normally rely heavily on language. It's only due to John being nonverbal that we have to pay that kind of attention. This also points to another seemingly counterintuitive notion: John cannot be left alone for a minute, we spend a lot of time together. We are deeply connected to him, and John to us. When we're not with him, teachers, social workers and caretakers are. For us, life with autism is a highly social affair.

We have a loose end to take care of. We would like to honor the memory of the boy whose picture and file we found in the Berlin Euthanasia exhibit and who reminded us so much of John. There's a project of cultural memorialization called *Stolpersteine*, Stumbling Stones. German artist Gunter Demnig creates cobble-stone sized concrete blocks with a sheet of engraved brass on top, commemorating the victims of the Nazi dictatorship by inscribing their name, birth date, and where and when they were murdered. Each stone is laid into the sidewalk in front of the victim's final address. These stumbling stones can be found all over Germany, as well as several other European countries. We've looked into sponsoring a stone for the boy who resembled John, and found out that he coincidentally even lived relatively close to where we live. Dedicating a stone for him to keep his memory alive hasn't turned out to be an easy endeavor, though. We've been transferred from one place to another and haven't been able to locate someone who can put our case on the waiting list. We'll continue to try.

Naturally still our biggest worry is the question of what happens with John when we are gone. One evening, I drove to the southwestern outskirts of Berlin where a disability organization hosted an evening with a female social justice judge. She has an adult daughter with an intellectual disability and has therefore known disability both professionally and privately for decades. She talked about awareness of biography. An intellectually disabled child, especially if nonverbal, mostly cannot transport his or her life throughout time on their own. The judge told of experiences from her professional life, of severely disabled adults who had lived with their parents their entire lives and then entered residential institutions with hardly any information about their past to be found. How do you connect to that adult then, and how can he or she remember? In the case of nonverbal children, parents are usually the key witnesses of their children's lives. What parents haven't written down or collected, all too easily dies with them. The judge recommended to create what she called a *life folder*, in which we recognize and preserve what has value for our child. It's our assignment as parents to leave a legacy – not our own, but our child's. We should record when we move house, change schools and therapists, any important shifts, highlights, travels of course, but also illnesses and stays in hospitals. Next to people, the judge recommended to include every-day photos of rooms, favorite things, and paths frequently taken. Views from a window or the picture of a loved toy might not seem important now, because they are *here* and therefore taken for granted, but they could invoke lots of memories decades later. We also don't necessarily have images of the most intimate family moments, yet they are so important and so she encouraged us to go home and think about which photos we're missing. What will my child enjoy looking at?

For visual thinkers, photos and videos are naturally of special importance. It reminded me of the documentary film *Her name is Sabine:* The touching moment when Sabine watches a video from many years before, of her trip to New York as a teenager, and she cries out of joy, sorrow, a mixture of feelings – and she wants to watch it over and over again because it means so much to her.

I saw in her the same courage that I've so often seen in John. Scott and I talked about how we think we'd be terrified if we were John. He has to put 100% trust into us and others who care for him, every day, every moment. Yet he has such energy and such a powerful will to live. Special education teacher Mariya Berkovich said in the 2012 Russian autism documentary *Anton's Right Here*: "What I'm going to say about the autistic world is, I believe, relevant to the world as a whole – except that it's more condensed in autism. For an autistic person, the most important thing is what you feel. All the fundamental questions are resolved with an amazing simplicity: By total absence of anything superficial and of conventionality.

It's a kind of life that has perhaps been taken to the absurd – or is in its purest form. Touching this world helps you discover what is already within yourself. It's as if you take a medicine, it's like you drink a whole cup of undiluted life. Life in its purest form. It's very potent. After something like this, it's very difficult to return to the normal, hidden, and closed state."

At the moment, John has completely stopped speaking, gone are even the echolalic exclamations and melody snippets. He sometimes uses a talker, a record-playback device assisting him in communication, but we don't get the impression that he's especially fond of it. John also uses some sign language, but he mainly employs the sign for candy for anything that he wants: Tipping on his cheek with one index finger. He developed his own way of emphasizing, twisting both of his index fingers around in his cheeks – sign language gone wild. John still likes to cuddle. When he plops down on us with his size of 5'6," it can turn into somewhat of a *combat cuddle*. He still goes through phases with disturbed sleep patterns and digestive problems. In terms of aggression, he's doing okay at the moment and only occasionally relapses into one of his full-force meltdowns. One of our biggest successes has been with toilet-training. During the day John is mostly without a diaper, with some accidents here and there. At night he needs a diaper, something we had overcome before, but he has too many accidents at the moment. We continue to navigate between developments and regressions.

Part of the mainland – Epilogue

No man is an island, this I know, but can't you see
that maybe you were the ocean when I was just a stone
(Ben Howard)

Looking back at our travels, I notice how many islands we've visited: Thassos, Hiddensee, Rhodes, Mallorca, Texel. John's great love is with water and he loves the seaside. Traveling with him throughout the islands, we could easily see how much more he is at ease with himself. There are reasons, but it's still a curious notion, as we had originally set out to *not* live on a desert island, as the mother in the parent group had told me about life with her adult autistic son when John had just been three-and-a-half years old.

Now he'll soon be thirteen. We don't know what will happen to us, so we have to think about alternatives in case the wind gets taken out of our sails. As part of Scott's German language courses, he completed two internships in residential homes for autistic adults to get a glimpse into our future. We're interested in a project where a few autistics live together with their parents, but where caretakers help in regular shifts. A kind of extended family life in which both the autistics and their parents have their own space, but also share. We dream of a new kind of community, something between a family home and residential placement. More likely, and we want to remain realistic, we will have to search for a good residential placement at some point.

We know a family whose adult autistic son has developed severe aggression in his residential placement. Since he's more than six feet tall and strong, this is dangerous. One time, he has thrown a female caretaker against a wall and she spent four days in the hospital with a concussion. The staff has called the police several times, and paramedics have taken him to a psychiatric ward, where his mother picked him up and took him home, which is also dangerous but understandable. The sad truth is that nobody is at fault. Not the autistic, not the parents, not the staff at the institutions, whether it be at the home or in the hospital. It's a situation where everyone involved reaches their limit, and so does society as a whole. The only thing we can do is to advocate for successful alternatives. It's possible, but it's staff-intensive and therefore expensive. The children and adults who won't ever fit in pose a fundamental challenge. To all the children and adults who have the courage and strength to live day-in and day-out with limited ability to communicate, limited means to express their needs, through isolation, frustration, and sorrow, we owe to find a better way.

Life alongside autism is an education of the heart. We hope that we can still live with John for a long time.

To mash up Fernand Deligny:

incurable
insufferable
impossible
that's what they call him
but society has everything planned
even places for the non-life

the symptom is highly visible

just because the unvarying

satisfies his needs

he will indulge in immobility and repetition

in ever the same

we are standing on the opposite pole

and in this boy

the key

to our existence is handed to us

but what to rely on

when language

is missing

tirelessly

it is not normal

not to get tired

like a wild child

a wolf child

one had to hold out

by day

and by night

despite of the impossible

the unbearable

and us

to tell the truth

quite stumped

but persevering

ACKNOWLEDGEMENTS

To autistic readers, I would like to acknowledge that an outside account, especially a parental one, could possibly be overbearing. I hope that my portrait doesn't feel patronizing. I respect autism and I hope that this is reflected accordingly in my text. Please do let me know if you find that I have misrepresented aspects that are important to you.

On a related issue, I am aware of the person-first debate and have thought about whether or not to use the term *autistic* or *person with autism*. I have read a lot of accounts by autistics and a majority seem to prefer not to use person-first language. Unlike other conditions such as epilepsy where one doesn't want to use the word *epileptic* any more because the person shouldn't be reduced to his or her illness, autism is often seen as encompassing and part of the personality. On this matter, I took the freedom to choose.

Many people have helped us and are still helping care for John. I am thankful to all of them and would like to mention a few. Dr. Michael Kohrmann at the University of Chicago Epilepsy Center and Dr. Christoph Korenke at the Children's Hospital of Oldenburg have made a difference in medical emergencies. John's child psychiatrist Dr. Michael Elpers has been of great help for many years now. Principal Susanne Rabe saved us by accepting John into her school. John's teachers Birgit Kirchner, Ralf Pöschke and their assistive staff are working wonderfully with John: Life has noticeably become less frustrating for him. His bus driver Sylvia

Wagner graciously deals with challenging behavior while driving John back and forth every day. Our caretakers David von Heynitz, Rainer Pätzke and Thomas Ackermann have been with us patiently, effectively and with compassion for many years.

I would like to thank everyone who supported this book project on Kickstarter. I thank Zoe Rosenblum for proofreading and Thomas Hölzl for trying to find a publishing company for this book's German version. I thank my aunt and uncle Johannes and Edeltraud Deeken who live in Berlin and have always helped us. I thank my parents, Ludger and Maria Scheele, for their tremendous support, always. I thank Scott for discussing this book with me it in its various stages, for editing the text and for cheering me on when I was doubtful.

NOTES

Being in the world - Prologue

1. It's still often wrongly cited that Hans Asperger introduced autism as a
    diagnostic term in 1944. That date refers to the publication of
    Asperger's habilitation treatise, but the term really stems from his
    lecture on October 3, 1938 at the University of Vienna hospital. This
    lecture was published in 1938 in vol. 51 of the *Wiener Klinische
    Wochenzeitung*. For more details see Brita Schirmer: "Autismus – Von
    der Außen- zur Innenperspektive" (2003). More information regarding
    the letter that Asperger sent to several colleagues in 1934, suggesting
    autism as a diagnostic term, can be found in Klaus-Jürgen
    Neumärker's book *...der Wirklichkeit abgewandt* (2010). It's also an
    excellent resource for tracing autism back to Kraepelin and Kahlbaum.
    In a book just published in spring of 2013, I happened upon an entry
    from 1945, in which a German doctor used the term autistic in a
    matter-of-fact way, as if it was entirely self-explanatory. In its usage as
    a symptom, "autistic" seems to have been quite popular in the
    German-speaking psychiatric context of the early twentieth century.
    The doctor had been assigned as temporary head of a Munich
    psychiatric ward and described patients that he encountered as
    follows: "They were primarily slow, indolent, autistic, and they had
    become apathetic and had lost any initiative due to lack of food." See
    Gerhard Schmidt: "Selektion in der Heilanstalt," cited in Götz Aly: *Die*

Belasteten (2013), page 273.

I think it would be highly interesting to further research the term autism's origins, as too many resources haven't been translated from German to English yet.

2. Regarding the understanding of other people's feelings, see for example Lisa Capps et al.: "Understanding of simple and complex emotions in non-retarded children with autism" (1992).

3. The quote by Dawn Eddings Prince is from her text "An Exceptional Path: An Ethnographic Narrative Reflecting on Autistic Parenthood from Evolutionary, Cultural, and Spiritual Perspectives" (2010), pages 56-68. I condensed her quote. The entire volume of *Ethos* was dedicated to autism.

4. Emily Perl Kingsley's parable "Welcome to Holland" can be found all over the internet, for example at: http://www.our-kids.org/Archives/Holland.html

5. The critical reply "Farewell to Holland" can be found at: http://www.angelfire.com/in4/farewelltoholland/

Chapter 1 – Thassos - Language

1. Michael Rutter's and Susan Folstein's study "Infantile Autism: A Genetic Study of 21 Twin Pairs" was first published in *Journal of Child Psychology and Psychiatry* (1977) and has been published online on December 7, 2006.

2. As of May 2012, Andrew Solomon mentions 279 gene mutations that have been identified, see Andrew Solomon: *Far from the Tree* (2012), page 759.

3. See Temple Grandin, *Thinking in Pictures* (1996).

4. For more information regarding PECS see Andrew Bondy and Lori Frost: *PECS. The Picture Exchange Communication System. Training Manual* (1994).

5. I translated the quote from Hugo von Hofmannsthal's Greek travelogue from the 2001 edition of *Augenblicke in Griechenland* [original: 1908]. The three-part account is made available online by the Gutenberg Project at: http://gutenberg.spiegel.de/buch/1008/1. Hofmannsthal's *Lord Chandos Letter* [1902] can be read at: http://gutenberg.spiegel.de/buch/997/1

Chapter 2 – Hiddensee – Parenting

1. The book *Foundations for Self-Awareness: An Exploration through Autism* (2006) by Peter Hobson et al. first alerted me to this idea. Uta Frith also considers the "absent self" a central problem, see for example her book *Autism. A very short introduction* (2008), page 101f.

2. Therapist Kristin Kaifas-Tennyson wrote about detachment strategies: "Most people think they will simply have the ability to detach when necessary. This is often not the case, however, because it is not natural to turn emotions off like the flip of a switch." Quoted from her text "Patience – The Least Important 'SuperPower'," published in *Embracing Autism* by Robert Parish & Friends (2008), page 35.

3. For more information on "Treatment and Education of Autistic and related Communication-handicapped Children" (TEACCH) see Gary Mesibov, Victoria Shea and Eric Schopler: *The TEACCH Approach to Autism Spectrum Disorders* (2004).

Chapter 3 – Rhodes – Epilepsy

1. One of my epilepsy references in English was Ilo E. Leppik: *Contemporary Diagnosis and Management of the Patient with Epilepsy* (2001). See more information on the ketogenic diet in John M. Freeman et al.: *The Ketogenic Diet. A Treatment for Epilepsy* (2000).

Chapter 4 – French Riviera – Deligny

1. *Autisme France* stated that 80% of autistic children are still unschooled in France, see PDF (in French) here:
   http://www.autisme-france.fr/offres/file_inline_src/577/577_A_14682_1.pdf
   In 2004, the *Committee of Ministers of the Council of Europe* published a decision by the European Committee of Social Rights, finding that France failed to fulfil its educational obligations to persons with autism under the European Social Charter. The decision upheld a collective complaint that *Autism Europe* had lodged against the French Government, see press release (in English) at:
   http://www.autismeurope.org/files/files/aevsfrance.pdf
   For more information on autism in France in English, see for example Liz Ditz: "A Culture of Abuse: Autism Care in France" (2012).
   http://www.thinkingautismguide.com/2012/01/culture-of-abuse-autism-care-in-france.html The article also has some information on the method "Le Packing" which has been criticized for years by *Autism Europe*.

2. I translated all quotes by Fernand Deligny from his book *Ein Floß in den Bergen* (1980), and I translated all quotes by Jacques Lin from his book *Das Leben mit dem Floß in der Gesellschaft autistischer Kinder* (2004). I took over the terminology of *wandering lines* and *customary lines* from a previous translation into English, quoted by Amit Pinchevski: "Bartleby's Autism. Wandering along Incommunicability" (2011).

I would just like to briefly mention that Deligny's thoughts on autism were important for the influential theories of philosopher Gilles Deleuze and psychiatrist Felix Guattari in *A Thousand Plateaus* (1980).

Chapter 5 – Mallorca – Prevalence

1. I translated Ernst Cassirer from *Versuch über den Menschen. Eine Einführung in eine Philosophie der Kultur* (1990), page 63.
2. The Fombonne estimate refers to his study "Autism and associated medical disorders in a French epidemiological survey" (1997).
3. The prevalence numbers published by the *American Center for Disease Control and Prevention* are on the CDC's website at:
   http://www.cdc.gov/ncbddd/autism/data.html
   For more on prevalence also see Michael Rutter: "Incidence of Autism Spectrum Disorder" (2005), and Lorna Wing and David Potter: "The Epidemiology of Autistic Spectrum Disorders: Is the Prevalence Rising?" (2002).
4. *The Hidden Epidemic* was a program on NBC:
   http://www.nbcnews.com/id/6844737/
5. *Autism: A New Frontier* was a program on CBS and can be viewed here:
   http://www.cbsnews.com/stories/2007/11/19/earlyshow/living/res ources/main3523363.shtml
6. Hilary Clinton calling autism a "national health crisis" is cited from the article "Clinton Would Boost Autism Funding" by Amy Lorentzen in the *Washington Post* on November 25, 2007.
7. With regard to retracted vaccination studies: Mark Geier and his son David had come out with a study in 2006 which was retracted in 2007. Andrew Wakefield had come out with a study in 1998 which was retracted in 2010. For more on vaccinations see for example Michael Fitzpatrick *Defeating Autism. A Damaging Delusion* (2008) and Seth

Mnookin: *The Panic Virus* (2011). For a good recent round-up of information on Andrew Wakefield see also Alex Hannaford: "Andrew Wakefield: Autism Inc." (2013).

In Michael Fitzpatrick's book, the California study revealing that autism numbers didn't decrease after Thimerosal's removal from vaccines can be found on page 27.

8. Tony Attwoods assumption that only 50% of persons with Asperger's are diagnosed today is quoted from bis book *Ein ganzes Leben mit dem Asperger-Syndrom*, page 58.

9. Many studies revealed how much prevalence depends upon the definition of criteria in the DSM, see for example Roy Richard Grinker: *Unstrange Minds* (2008), page 138. A study that looked at a group of 194 children associated with autism found that 51% of them were autistic according to the DSM's 1980 edition, but 91% were according to the 1987 edition. Researchers in Finland compared Kanner's diagnostic criteria of 1943 with the criteria of the *International Classification of Diseases* used in Europe. According to Kanner's criteria, there were 5.6 autistics per 10,000 people. According to the criteria of the *International Classification of Diseases*, that number rose to 12.2 per 10,000 – more than double the amount, see Grinker page 158.

10. The study by German researchers is cited from Michael Kusch and Franz Petermann: *Entwicklung autistischer Störungen (*1991), page 35.

11. The mistake that happened during the correction of the DSM galleys quoted by Grinker (page 140) can also be found in the article "Are you on it?" by Benjamin Wallace, *New York Magazine*, October 28, 2012. Wallace quotes the workgroup's chairman Fred Volkmar, head of child psychiatry at the Yale-New Haven Children's Hospital, to have said that "for the PDD-NOS diagnosis, a copy editor happened not to like an 'and' replaced it with 'or,' a seemingly tiny change that significantly expanded the diagnosis."

12. Comorbidity numbers are quoted from Liane Kaufman et al.: "The genetic basis of non-syndromic intellectual disability: a review" (2010).

13. Grinker's experiences with autism in various countries are quoted from his book *Unstrange Minds* (2008).

14. The increase by 43% of German children being admitted to the hospital due to psychological problems is quoted from the article "Die Not ist riesengroß" by Martin Spiewak in *Die Zeit*, November 5, 2010.

15. 6% of children have a special education need throughout Germany, 7% do so in Berlin. Numbers according to the Senate for Education: *Bildung in Berlin und Brandenburg 2008. Ein indikatorengestützter Bericht zur Bildung im Lebenslauf* (2008).

16. Stuart Murray's references towards the concept of normalcy can be found in his book *Representing Autism* (2008) on page 14.

17. Majia Holmer Nadeson's argument is quoted from her book *Constructing Autism* (2005).

18. The *Autism Matrix* (2010) chapter on deinstitutionalization starts on page 98. London psychiatrist Joanna Moncrieff also studied how psychiatric diagnosis became a political device; see her article "Psychiatric diagnosis as a political device" (2010).

Chapter 6 – Connemara – Therapies

1. John Bruer is quoted from *The Myth of the First Three Years: A New Understanding of Early Brain Development and Lifelong Learning* (1999).

2. For references to the autistic brain see for example: "Purkinje cell size is reduced in cerebellum of patients with autism" by S. Hossein Fatemi et al. (2002), "Neuropathology of Infantile Autism" by Thomas Kemper and Margaret Bauman (1998), and "The Neuropathology of Autism" by Manuel Casanova (2007).

For a while, the so-called *mirror neuron hypothesis* was popular, but it has largely been found to be deficient; see for example: "Interpersonal motor resonance in autism spectrum disorder: evidence against a global 'mirror system' deficit" by Peter Enticott et al. (2013).

The *altered-connectivity theory* (also known as *underconnectivity theory*) is still popular, see for example Marcel Adam Just and Timothy Keller: "Is 'underconnectivity' in autism specific to frontal cortex?" (2013).

For brain growth see for instance: "An MRI study of brain size in autism" by Joseph Piven et al. (1995) and "Head Circumference and Height in Autism: A Study by the Collaborative Program of Excellence in Autism" by Janet Lainhart et al. (2006).

3. Patrick Levitt and the Autism Genome Project are quoted from Michael Fitzpatrick: *Defeating Autism. A Damaging Delusion* (2009), page 80.

4. Diagnosing at age thirty months as opposed to twenty-four months is quoted from Uta Frith: *Autism. A very short introduction* (2008), page 18.

5. For biomedical interventions see for example Michael Fitzpatrick: *Defeating Autism. A Damaging Delusion* (2009). The increase in the number of chelations being performed between the years of 2000 and 2005 is quoted from his preface, page xv.

6. I translated Dirk Böttcher's quote from his article "Hoffnung in geringer Konzentration" (2008).

7. Implications of lab tests and biomedical interventions are quoted from Michael Fitzpatrick: *Autism. A Damaging Delusion* (2009), pages 21 and 125.

8. For the Northwestern University study by David Gal and Derek Rucker see: "When in Doubt, Shout! Paradoxical Influences of Doubt on Proselytizing" (2010).

9. With regard to Holding Therapy see Ute Benz: *Gewalt gegen Kinder* (2004).

10. Karsten Brensing et al.: "Can dolphins heal by ultrasound?" (2003). See also http://www.wal-und-mensch.de/wum2002/brensing.php

11. Information on the University of Würzburg study on Dolphin Therapy can be found at: http://www.i4.psychologie.uni-wuerzburg.de/mitarbeiter/dr_eva_stumpf/forschungsprojekt_delfinth erapie/

12. A critical report was published at http://www.wdcs-de.org/docs/Delfintherapie.pdf ("Kritische Betrachtung zum Abschlussbericht des Forschungsprojekts Delfintherapie der Uni Würzburg und des Nürnberger Delfinariums")

13. Michelle Dawson's suggestion of ethical evaluations is quoted from "An Autistic Victory: The True Meaning of the Auton Case" (2005). Published at: http://www.sentex.net/~nexus23/naa_vic.html

14. Jim Sinclair is quoted from his article "What does being different mean?" (2009) http://www.cjob.com/Blog/StationShared/Blog/OnTheEdge/bloge ntry.aspx?BlogEntryID=10024815

15. Angelika Empt is quoted from her text "Verpasster Anschluss" (1996).

Chapter 7 – South Tyrol – Neurodiversity

1. Jim Sinclair: "Don't mourn for us" (1993), http://www.autreat.com/dont_mourn.html

2. Regarding the term neurodiversity see also Singer's explanation: "For me, the significance of the Autistic Spectrum lies in its call for and anticipation of a Politics of Neurodiversity. The Neurologically Different represent a new addition to the familiar political categories of class/gender/race and will augment the insights of the Social Model of Disability. The rise of Neurodiversity takes postmodern

fragmentation one step further. Just as the postmodern era sees every once too solid belief melt into air, even our most taken-for granted assumptions: That we all more or less see, feel, touch, hear, smell, and sort information, in more or less the same way, are being dissolved." Judy Singer: "The Birth of Community Amongst People on the Autistic Spectrum: A personal exploration of a New Social Movement based on Neurological Diversity" (1998), pages 12-13.

3. Harvey Blume is quoted from "Neurodiversity. On the neurological underpinnings of geekdom" (1998).

4. The script for *Anderson Cooper 360 Degrees* can be found at: http://transcripts.cnn.com/TRANSCRIPTS/0711/19/acd.01.html

5. Ari Ne'eman: "An Urgent Call to Action: Tell NYU Child Study Center to Abandon Stereotypes Against People With Disabilities" (2007).

6. Joane Kaufman: "Ransom-Note Ads About Children's Health Are Canceled" (2007).

7. Robin Shulman: "Child Study Center Cancels Autism Ads" (2007)

8. Jacob Goldstein and Sarah Rubenstein: "NYU Bows to Critics and Pulls Ransom-Note Ads" (2007).

9. Gaynell Payne: "Communication Shutdown Day is answered with Autistics Speaking Day" (2010).

10. Nicole Schuster's quote is translated from her website at http://www.nicole-schuster.de/

11. The Tony Attwood citation is from the German edition of his book *A Complete Guide to Asperger's Syndrome* – Ein ganzes Leben mit dem Asperger-Syndrom (2008), page 394.

12. Susanne Schäfer's quote is cited from her talk "Mein Leben mit Autismus" (1998), page 49.

13. Gary Westfahl is quoted from his text "Homo Aspergerus: Evolution Stumbles Forward" (2006).

http://locusmag.com/2006/Features/Westfahl_HomoAspergerus.ht
ml

14. Marshall McLuhan: *Understanding Media* (1964), German edition *Die magischen Kanäle – Understanding Media* (1995). See also Oliver Lerone Schultz: "McLuhan, Pasteur des Medienzeitalters" (2004).

15. Dinah Murray, Mike Lesser and Wendy Lawson: "Attention, monotropism and the diagnostic criteria for autism." (2005).

16. Tweet:
https://twitter.com/#!/stoffelstab/status/135696214623662081
"Zwangsläufig ist, dass die Wikipedia-Seiten zum Asperger-Syndrom zu den detailliertesten und am besten sortierten gehören."

17. Specialisterne: http://specialisterne.com/

18. Autworker: http://autworker.de/

19. Auticon: http://auticon.de/

20. For SAP's announcement to hire hundreds of autistics see for example Martin Motzkau: "Untapped Talent: Autistic Workers a Worthwhile Challenge for SAP" (2013).
    I talked critically about the effects of such marketing campaigns on German NPR radio on May 27, 2013:
    http://www.dradio.de/dkultur/sendungen/thema/2121211/

21. More information on autistics and scientists joining forces in the AFK *Autism Research Cooperation* at: http://autismus-forschungs-kooperation.de/

22. Temple Grandin is quoted from Charlotte Moore: "Thoughts About the Autism Label: A Parental View" (2009).

23. Steve Silberman is quoted from: "The Geek Syndrome" (2001).
    http://www.wired.com/wired/archive/9.12/aspergers_pr.html

24. For Simon Baron-Cohen's hypotheses see for instance: *The Essential Difference: Male And Female Brains And The Truth About Autism* (2004).

25. For Christopher Badcock's and Bernard Crespi's takes on the issue see: "Imbalanced genomic imprinting in brain development: an evolutionary basis for the aetiology of autism." (2006).

26. Hans Asperger: "Die 'autistischen Psychopathen' im Kindesalter" (1944).

27. Theodor W. Adorno: *Minima Moralia* (1951), page 307.

28. With regard to Max Weber see for example Stephen Kalberg's chapter six of *Max Weber: Readings and Commentary on Modernity*: "The 'Specialist' and the 'Cultivated Man': Certificates and the Origin of Ideas in Science" (2008).

29. Michael Fitzpatrick summarized the worries as follows: "Normalizing autism may reduce stigma, but at the risk of trivializing the problems of those with more severe cognitive deficits and also of underestimating the extreme aloneness that results from the social impairment of autism, even in higher-functioning individuals." Michael Fitzpatrick: *Autism. A Damaging Delusion* (2009), page 36.

30. Majia Holmer Nadeson: *Constructing Autism* (2005), page 208f.

31. Donna Haraway's observations on AIDS are quoted from "The Promises of Monsters: A Regenerative Politics for Inappropriate/d Others" (1992).

Chapter 8 – Southern Sweden – Inclusion

1. The UN Convention on the Rights of Persons with Disabilities can be found at:
http://www.un.org/disabilities/convention/conventionfull.shtml
The German translation was executed almost without the involvement of disability representatives. Several disability rights groups tried to intervene and at least correct the most obvious mistakes, but to no avail. They did, however, create a translation of their own. Their

"shadow translation" can be found at:

http://www.netzwerk-artikel-
3.de/index.php?view=article&id=93:international-
schattenuebersetzung

Chapter 9 – Normandy and Alsace – History

1. Alois Scholz is quoted from Heinz Eberhard Gabriel and Wolfgang
   Neugebauer: *Vorreiter der Vernichtung? Eugenik, Rassenhygiene und
   Euthanasie in der österreichischen Diskussion vor 1938* (2005), page 59.
2. An excellent resource on the assumption that Hans Asperger was
   attempting to save the children from Nazi Eugenics is Brita Schirmer's
   text "Autismus – Von der Außen- zur Innenperspektive" (2003). It
   can be found on her website:
   http://www.dr-brita-schirmer.de/pdf/artikel112.pdf

Chapter 10 – Valencia – Culture

1. Gilles Trehin: *Urville* (2006).
2. George Widener currently has his first solo exhibition in a European
   museum at *Hamburger Bahnhof* in Berlin: January 25 to June 16, 2013.
   See:
   http://www.hamburgerbahnhof.de/exhibition.php?id=32941&lang=e
   n
3. Daniel Tammet: *Born on a Blue Day. Inside the Extraordinary Mind of an
   Autistic Savant* (2007).
4. Hans Asperger's dashes of autism are quoted from Michael John
   Carley: *Asperger's from the Inside Out* (2008), page 219.
5. Thomas Hobbes: *Leviathan* [1651].
   http://www.gutenberg.org/files/3207/3207-h/3207-h.htm

6. John Dryden: *The Conquest of Granada* [1672].
   http://www.gutenberg.org/files/15349/15349-h/15349-h.htm

7. With regard to the connection between autism and "Blessed Fools" see Uta Frith: *Autism: Explaining the Enigma* (2003).

8. The correspondence between François Truffaut and Fernand Deligny is available online. Truffaut wrote explicitly about Janmari becoming the model for *The Wild Child*: "Je suppose que votre garçon est trop fragile pour qu'il soit question d'envisager de le faire tourner et de lui faire jouer le rôle de 'l'enfant sauvage', mais la description que vous me donnez de son comportement est tellement proche de ce qu'Itard a décrit dans ses textes et de ce que nous voulons obtenir dans le film que je suis extrêmement troublé. Je crois, en tous cas, que votre garçon devrait nous servir de modèle à la fois pour choisir le garçon qui jouera effectivement le rôle et pour nous inspirer un style de comportement corporel."
   http://1895.revues.org/281#tocto2n15

9. Conrad Aiken's short story *Silent Snow, Secret Snow* [1934] is available online:
   http://www.scriptorpress.com/burningmanbooks/63_2009_aiken.pdf

10. Amit Pinchevski is quoted from his text "Bartleby's Autism. Wandering along Incommunicability" (2011). http://muse.jhu.edu

11. Stuart Murray is quoted from *Representing Autism* (2008), page 98.

12. Steve Silberman is cited through George Dvorsky: *How Autism is Changing the World for Everybody*, July 26, 2012.
    http://io9.com/5928135/how-autism-is-changing-the-world-for-everybody

13. Douglas Coupland: *microserfs* (1996).

14. Douglas Coupland: *jPod* (2007).

15. Stieg Larsson: *The Girl with the Dragon Tattoo* (2009).

16. Niall Ferguson: "America has Asperger's" (2004).

17. Mark Haddon: *The Curious Incident of the Dog in the Nighttime* (2004).

18. Ian Hacking: "How we have been learning to talk about autism" (2009).

Chapter 11 – Prague & Terezín – Ethics

1. "Racial biology was as international as today's biopolitics are," wrote JustIn Monday in "Eine Art von Verschwinden. Unter Umständen eine Verteidigung Foucaults gegenüber seinen LiebhaberInnen" in *Das Leben lebt nicht*, Die Röteln (2006), page 177.

2. The Hartheim statistic can be found online at:
   http://en.mauthausen-memorial.at/index_open.php

3. Historian Götz Aly just published a detailed book on the Nazi Euthanasia program: *Die Belasteten. Euthanasie 1939-1945. Eine Gesellschaftsgeschichte* (2013).

4. With regard to the *Remmelink Report* see for example Paul Van Der Maas et al.: "Euthanasia and other medical decisions concerning the end of life" (1991).
   http://www.ncbi.nlm.nih.gov/pubmed/1715962?dopt=Abstract

5. The development of Euthanasia practice in the Netherlands is quoted from Bregje Onwuteaka-Philipsen et al.: "Euthanasia and other end-of-life decisions in the Netherlands in 1990, 1995, and 2001" (2003), and Bregje Onwuteaka-Philipsen et al.: "Trends in end-of-life practices before and after the enactment of the euthanasia law in the Netherlands from 1990 to 2010: a repeated cross-sectional survey" (2012). http://press.thelancet.com/netherlands_euthanasia.pdf

6. For information on the *Groningen Protocol* see for example Eduard Verhagen et al.: "The Groningen Protocol – Euthanasia in Severely ill Newborns" (2005).

7. 90% of women terminating their pregnancy after a prenatal diagnosis of Down syndrome is quoted from Joan Morris and Anna Springett: *The National Down Syndrome Cytogenetic Register for England and Wales 2011 Annual Report* (2013).

   http://www.wolfson.qmul.ac.uk/ndscr/reports/NDSCRreport11.pdf

8. Michael Foucault: *Sexualität und Wahrheit* (1987), page 115.

9. Giorgio Agamben: *Homo Sacer* (2002), page 156.

10. Thomas Metzinger is quoted from the German version: *Der Ego-Tunnel* (2010), page 313.

11. For experimental stem cell therapy see for example:

    http://www.stemcellmexico.com/

12. For Matthew's story see for example Orac: "Stem cell quackery for autism, revisited" (2010).

    http://scienceblogs.com/insolence/2010/12/16/stem-cell-quackery-for-autism-revisited/

13. Bruce Dobkin is quoted from an NPR story by Louisa Lim: "Stem-Cell Therapy in China Draws Foreign Patients" (2008). It can be found at:

    http://www.npr.org/templates/story/story.php?storyId=88123868#88432812

14. Abu Bakar Tariq Nadama died from Disodium EDTA which some biomedical proponents were quick to assure was a confusion with Calcium EDTA, but the doctor said that he had always and exclusively used Disodium EDTA in his practice. For more information on Tariq Nadama see for instance Mike Stanton: "Kerry charged over Tariq's death" (2007).

15. The boy who died during an attempted exorcism was Terrance Cottrell. See for example Juliet Williams: "Minister charged in death of autistic boy at church healing" (2003).

    http://www.boston.com/news/daily/26/church_death.htm

16. Many bloggers have commented on Karen McCarron, her belief that vaccinations had caused her daughter Katie's autism and her journey with biomedical interventions. See for example Kevin Leitch: "Indefensible and Unprotested" (2006). See also the category "McCarron" at *Not Dead Yet*, a grassroots disability rights group: http://www.notdeadyet.org/category/mccarron

17. Kathleen Seidel's record of autistics who were murdered can be found at: http://www.neurodiversity.com/murder.html

18. Andrea Trumann: *Das Leben lebt nicht* (2006), page 30.

19. Martha Nussbaum: "Human Functioning and Social Justice: In Defense of Aristotelian Essentialism" (1992).

20. Martha Nussbaum: *Frontiers of Justice. Disability, Nationality, Species membership* (2006).

21. Arno Luik: "Ich sehe seinem Entschwinden zu" (2008). http://www.stern.de/lifestyle/leute/inge-jens-ich-sehe-seinem-entschwinden-zu-616970.html

Chapter 13 – Berlin – Autism as a Metaphor

1. Jakob Augstein: "Im Zweifel links: Ohne Zweifel links" (2013).

2. For information on *Post-Autistic Economics* see for example: http://www.paecon.net/HistoryPAE.htm

3. Maria Kaika: "Autistic architecture: the fall of the icon and the rise of the serial object of architecture" (2011).

4. Zadie Smith: "Generation Why?" (2010). http://www.nybooks.com/articles/archives/2010/nov/25/generation-why/

5. Georg Simmel: "Die Großstädte und das Geistesleben" (1903). http://gutenberg.spiegel.de/buch/6598/1

6. Nicholas Carr: "Is Google Making us Stupid?" (2011).
   http://www.theatlantic.com/magazine/archive/2008/07/is-google-making-us-stupid/306868/

7. Sxip Shirey is quoted from: "Do we make the city or does the city make us? How we become behaviourally enmeshed in cities and how they operate almost like independent organisms" (2010):
   http://www.radiolab.org/2010/oct/08/

8. Adam Waytz and Nicholas Epley: "Social Connection Enables Dehumanization" (2012). See also:
   http://www.kellogg.northwestern.edu/News_Articles/2011/connection-disconnection.aspx

9. MdB Rolf Feldmann: *Deutscher Bundestag. Plenarprotokoll 13/116* from June 27, 1996, page 10546.

10. Abg. Hans: *Landtag des Saarlandes, 12. Wahlperiode, 30. Sitzung am 26. September 2001, Gedenkworte und Erklärungen zu den Terroranschlägen in den USA am 11. September 2001*, page 1421.

11. Reinhart Lempp: *Die autistische Gesellschaft. Geht die Verantwortlichkeit für andere verloren?* (1996).

12. Branka Schaller-Fornoff: "Mehr Kampf, mehr Frust, mehr Intensität" (2012).

13. Paul Eluard: *Liebesbriefe an Gala* (1990), page 304.

14. Susan Sontag: *Illness as Metaphor* (1978).

15. With regard to the German coverage on Adam Lanza, see for example Cinthia Briseño: "Adam Lanza. Litt der Amokläufer von Newtown am Asperger-Syndrom?" (2012).
    http://www.spiegel.de/gesundheit/psychologie/adam-lanza-litt-der-amoklaeufer-von-newtown-am-asperger-syndrom-a-873088.html

16. Nina Job: "Mord an Katrin Michalk. Psychogramm: So tickt der mutmaßliche Sendling-Mörder" (2013).
    http://www.abendzeitung-muenchen.de/inhalt.mord-an-katrin-

michalk-psychogramm-so-tickt-der-mutmassliche-sendling-moerder.4e169bd0-c0c5-4a8f-98b5-b12eef016755.html

17. Vera Morgan et al.: "A whole-of-population study of the prevalence and patterns of criminal offending in people with schizophrenia and other mental illness" (2012).

18. Gunter Demnig's art project Stolpersteine can be found at: http://www.stolpersteine.com/index_EN.html

19. Mariya Berkovich is quoted from the 2012 Russian autism documentary *Anton's Right Here* by Lyubov Arkus.

20. Fernand Deligny: *Ein Floß in den Bergen* (1980), pages 12-21.

BIBLIOGRAPHY

Aarons, Maureen and Tessa Gittens. *The Handbook of Autism: A Guide for Parents and Professionals.* 2nd edition. New York: Routledge, 1999.

Adorno, Theodor. *Minima Moralia. Reflexionen aus dem beschädigten Leben.* Frankfurt a.M.: Suhrkamp, 1951.

Agamben, Giorgio. *Homo Sacer. Die souveräne Macht und das nackte Leben.* Frankfurt a.M.: Suhrkamp, 2002.

Ahrbeck, Bernd. *Der Umgang mit Behinderung.* Stuttgart: Kohlhammer, 2011.

Aiken, Conrad. *Silent Snow, Secret Snow* [1934].
http://www.scriptorpress.com/burningmanbooks/63_2009_aiken.pdf

Aly, Götz. *Die Belasteten. 'Euthanasie' 1939-1945. Eine Gesellschaftsgeschichte.* Frankfurt a.M.: S. Fischer, 2013.

American Psychiatric Association. *Diagnostic and Statistical Manual of Mental Disorders.* 2nd edition. Washington D.C.: American Psychiatric Association, 1968.

_____. *Diagnostic and Statistical Manual of Mental Disorders.* 3rd edition. Washington D.C.: American Psychiatric Association, 1980.

_____. *Diagnostic and Statistical Manual of Mental Disorders.* 3rd edition revised. Washington D.C.: American Psychiatric Association, 1987.

_____. *Diagnostic and Statistical Manual of Mental Disorders*. 4th edition. Washington D.C.: American Psychiatric Association, 1994.

_____. *Diagnostic and Statistical Manual of Mental Disorders*. 4th edition revised. Washington D.C.: American Psychiatric Association, 2000.

Arbeitsgruppe zur Erforschung der Geschichte der Karl-Bonhoeffer-Nervenklinik, eds. *totgeschwiegen 1933-1945. Zur Geschichte der Wittenauer Heilstätten seit 1957 Karl-Bonhoeffer-Nervenklinik.* 2nd extended edition. Berlin: Edition Heutrich, 1989.

Asperger, Hans. "Das psychisch abnorme Kind." *Wiener Klinische Wochenzeitschrift*, no. 51 (1938): 1314-1317.

_____. "Die 'autistischen Psychopathen' im Kindesalter." *Archiv für Psychiatrie und Nervenkrankheiten,* no. 117 (1944): 76-136.

Aspies e.V., eds. *Risse im Universum.* Berlin: Weidler, 2010.

Attwood, Tony. "Strategies for improving social integration of Children with Asperger Syndrome." *Autism*, no. 4 (2000): 85-100.

_____. *The Complete Guide to Asperger's Syndrome.* London: Jessica Kingsley Publishers, 2006.

_____. Ein ganzes Leben mit dem Asperger-Syndrom: Von Kindheit bis Erwachsensein - alles was weiterhilft. Stuttgart: Trias, 2008.

Badcock, Christopher and Bernard Crespi. "Imbalanced genomic imprinting in brain development: an evolutionary basis for the aetiology of autism." *Journal of Evolutionary Biology*, no. 4 (2006): 1007-1032.

Baird, Gillian, et al. "Prevalence of disorders of the autism spectrum." *Pediatrics*, no. 118 (2006): 139-150.

Baron-Cohen, Simon. *Mindblindness: An Essay on Autism and Theory of Mind.* Cambridge: A Bradford Book, 1995.

_____. "Psychological Markers in the Detection of Autism in Infancy in a Large Population." *British Journal of Psychiatry*, no. 168 (1996): 158-163.

_____. "Is Asperger syndrome/ high-functioning autism necessarily a disability?" *Development and Psychopathology*, no. 12 (2000): 489-500.

_____. *The Essential Difference: Male And Female Brains And The Truth About Autism.* New York: Basic Books, 2004.

Bauer, Joachim. *Warum ich fühle, was du fühlst. Intuitive Kommunikation und das Geheimnis der Spiegelneurone.* Hamburg: Hoffmann und Campe, 2005.

Benz, Ute. *Gewalt gegen Kinder. Traumatisierung durch Therapie?* Berlin: Metropol, 2004.

Bernard-Opitz, Vera. *Kinder mit Autismus-Spektrum-Störungen (ASS): ein Praxishandbuch für Therapeuten, Eltern und Lehrer.* Stuttgart: Kohlhammer, 2007.

Berney, Tom. "Autism – an evolving concept." *British Journal of Psychiatry*, no. 176 (2000): 20-25.

Bettelheim, Bruno. *The Empty Fortress: Infantile Autism and the Birth of the Self.* New York: Free Press, 1972.

Biklen, Douglas. *Autism and the Myth of the Person Alone.* New York NYU Press, 2005.

Binding, Karl and Alfred Hoche. *Die Freigabe der Vernichtung lebensunwerten Lebens. Ihr Maß und ihre Form.* Leipzig: Felix Meiner, 1920.

Bleuler, Ernst. "Dementia Praecox, oder die Gruppe der Schizophrenien." *Handbuch der Psychiatrie. Spezieller Teil, 1. Hälfte: 1-420.* Leipzig: Deuticke, 1911.

Blume, Harvey. "Neurodiversity. On the neurological underpinnings of geekdom." *The Atlantic*, September 30, 1998.

Bölte, Sven. *Autismus. Spektrum, Ursachen, Diagnostik, Intervention, Perspektiven.* Bern: Huber, 2009.

Bösl, Elsbeth, et al. *Disability history. Konstruktionen von Behinderung in der Geschichte.* Bielefeld: Transcript, 2010.

Böttcher, Dirk. "Hoffnung in geringer Konzentration." *Brand Eins,* no. 12 (2008). http://www.brandeins.de/magazin/glueck-rechnen-sie-damit/hoffnung-in-geringer-konzentration.html

Bondy, Andrew and Lori Frost. *PECS. The Picture Exchange Communication System. Training Manual.* Cherry Hill: Pyramid Educational Consultants, 1994.

Brauns, Axel. *Buntschatten und Fledermäuse. Mein Leben in einer anderen Welt.* Hamburg: Hoffmann und Campe, 2002.

Brensing, Karsten, et al. "Can dolphins heal by ultrasound?" *Journal of Theoretical Biology,* no. 225 (2003): 99-105.

_____. "Behavior of Dolphins Tursiops Truncatus towards adults and children during swim-with-dolphin programs and towards children with disabilities during therapy sessions." *Anthrozoös,* no.16 (2004): 315-330.

_____. "Impact of different kinds of humans in swim-with-dolphin programs in two settings." *Anthrozoös,* no. 18, 2005.

Briseño, Cinthia. "Adam Lanza: Litt der Amokläufer von Newtown am Asperger-Syndrom?" *Spiegel Online,* December 15, 2012. http://www.spiegel.de/gesundheit/psychologie/adam-lanza-litt-der-amoklaeufer-von-newtown-am-asperger-syndrom-a-873088.html

Brown, Ian: *The Boy in the Moon: A Father's Search for His Disabled Son.* Toronto: Random House Canada, 2009.

Bruer, John. *The Myth of the First Three Years: A New Understanding of Early Brain Development and Lifelong Learning.* New York: Free Press, 1999.

Byde Myers, Jennifer, et al. *The Thinking Person's Guide to Autism.* Redwood City: Deadwood City Publishing, 2011.

Capps, Lisa, et al. "Understanding of simple and complex emotions in non-retarded children with autism." *Journal of Child Psychology and Psychiatry*, no. 33 (1992): 1169-1182.

Carley, Michael John. *Asperger's from the Inside Out*. New York: Perigee Trade, 2008.

Carr, Nicholas. "Is Google Making us Stupid?" *The Atlantic*, July/ August 2011. http://www.theatlantic.com/magazine/archive/2008/07/is-google-making-us-stupid/306868/

Casanova, Manuel. "The Neuropathology of Autism." *Brain Pathology*, no. 4 (2007): 422-433.

Cassirer, Ernst. *Versuch über den Menschen. Eine Einführung in eine Philosophie der Kultur*. Frankfurt a.M.: S. Fischer, 1990.

Chew, Kristina. "Do we really need a cure for autism?" *The Guardian*, February 22, 2013.

Cohen, Jeffrey Jerome. *Monster Theory: Reading Culture*. Minneapolis: University of Minneapolis Press, 1996.

Coupland, Douglas. *microserfs*. London: HarperCollins, 1996.

_____. *jPod*. New York: Bloomsbury, 2007.

Courchesne, Eric. "Brainstem, cerebellar and limbic neuroanatomical abnormalities in autism." *Current Opinions in Neurobiology*, no. 7 (1997): 269-278.

Croen, Lisa, et al. "The changing prevalence of autism in California." *Journal of Autism and Developmental Disorders*, no. 32 (2002): 207-15.

Dath, Dietmar. "Der autistische Messias." *Frankfurter Allgemeine Zeitung*, March 13, 2006.

Dawson, Michelle. *An Autistic Victory: The True Meaning of the Auton Case*, 2005. http://www.sentex.net/~nexus23/naa_vic.html

Day, Nicholas. "No Big Deal, but This Researcher's Theory Explains Everything About How Americans Parent." *Slate Magazine*, April 10, 2013.

Deligny, Fernand. *Ein Floß in den Bergen.* Berlin: Merve, 1980.

Ditz, Liz. *A Culture of Abuse: Autism Care in France.* January 20, 2012.
http://www.thinkingautismguide.com/2012/01/culture-of-abuse-autism-care-in-france.html

Dryden, John. *The Conquest of Granada* [1672].
http://www.gutenberg.org/files/15349/15349-h/15349-h.htm

Dvorsky, George. *How Autism is Changing the World for Everybody*, July 26, 2012.

http://io9.com/5928135/how-autism-is-changing-the-world-for-everybody

Ehlers, Stefan and Christopher Gillberg. "The epidemiology of Asperger's Syndrome – a total population study." *Journal of Child Psychology and Psychiatry*, no. 34 (1993): 1327-1350.

Elkana, Yehuda. *Modernity and Barbarism. Reflections on the 20th Century and on the Future.* Holberg Prize Symposium, 2006.

Eluard, Paul. *Liebesbriefe an Gala.* München: dtv, 1990.

Empt, Angelika. "Verpasster Anschluss." *autismus,* no. 42 (1996): 20-23.

Enticott, Peter, et al. "Interpersonal motor resonance in autism spectrum disorder: evidence against a global 'mirror system' deficit." *Frontiers in Human Neuroscience*, May 23, 2013.
http://www.frontiersin.org/Human_Neuroscience/10.3389/fnhum.2013.00218/full

Essau, Cecilia and Judith Conradt. *Aggression bei Kindern und Jugendlichen.* München & Basel: Ernst Reinhardt, 2004.

Eyal, Gil, et al. *The Autism Matrix. The Social Origins of the Autism Epidemic.* Cambridge: Polity Press, 2010.

Fatemi, S. Hossein, et al. "Purkinje cell size is reduced in cerebellum of patients with autism." *Cellular and Molecular Neurobiology*, no. 22 (2002): 171-175.

Feinstein, Adam. *A History of Autism. Conversations with the Pioneers.* Chichester: Wiley-Blackwell, 2010.

Ferguson, Niall. "America has Asperger's." *Daily Telegraph*, May 25, 2004.

Fichte, Hubert. *Psyche. Glossen. Annäherung an die Geisteskanken in Afrika.* Frankfurt a.M.: S. Fischer, 1990.

Fitzpatrick, Michael. *Defeating Autism. A Damaging Delusion.* New York: Routledge, 2009.

Florance, Cheri. *A Boy Beyond Reach.* London: Simon & Schuster, 2004.

Fombonne, Eric. "Autism and associated medical disorders in a French epidemiological survey." *Journal of the American Academy of Child and Adolescent Psychiatry*, no. 36 (1997): 1561-1569.

_____. "Is there an epidemic of autism?" *Pediatrics*, no. 107 (2001): 411-412.

_____. "Epidemiological Surveys of Autism and Other Pervasive Developmental Disorders: An Update." *Journal of Autism and other developmental disorders*, no. 33 (2003): 365-382.

_____. "The Changing Epidemiology of Autism." *Journal of Applied Research in Intellectual Disabilities*, no. 18 (2005): 281-294.

Foucault, Michael. *Überwachen und Strafen* [1975]. Frankfurt a.M.: Suhrkamp, 1994.

_____. *Sexualität und Macht I. Der Wille zum Wissen.* [1976]. Frankfurt a.M.: Suhrkamp, 1987.

Frances, Allen. *Saving Normal: An Insider's Revolt Against Out-of-Control Psychiatric Diagnosis, DSM-5, Big Pharma, and the Medicalization of Ordinary Life.* New York: William Morrow, 2013.

Frankfurt, Harry. *The Importance of What We Care About*. Cambridge, MA: Cambridge University Press, 1988.

Freeman, John, et al. *The Ketogenic Diet. A Treatment for Epilepsy*. New York: Demos Medical Publishing, 2000.

Friedlander, Henry. *Der Weg zum NS-Genozid. Von der Euthanasie zur Endlösung*. Berlin: Berlin Verlag, 1997.

Frith, Uta, ed. *Autism and Asperger's Syndrome*. Cambridge: Cambridge University Press, 1991.

_____. *Autism: Explaining the Enigma*. Oxford: Blackwell, 2003.

_____. *Autism. A Very Short Introduction*. Oxford: Oxford University Press, 2008.

Fromm, Erich. *The Anatomy of Human Destructiveness*. New York: Holt Paperbacks, 1992.

Fuchs, Petra, et al. *Das Vergessen der Vernichtung ist Teil der Vernichtung selbst. Lebensgeschichten von Opfern der nationalsozialistischen ,Euthanasie.'* Göttingen: Wallstein, 2007.

Gabriel, Heinz Eberhard and Wolfgang Neugebauer: *Vorreiter der Vernichtung? Eugenik, Rassenhygiene und Euthanasie in der österreichischen Diskussion vor 1938*. Wien: Böhlau, 2005.

Gal, David and Derek Rucker. "When in Doubt, Shout! Paradoxical Influences of Doubt on Proselytizing." *Psychological Science Journal*, February 24, 2010. http://pss.sagepub.com/content/21/11/1701

Gallagher, Shaun. "The Practice of Mind: Theory, Simulation or Primary Interaction?" *Journal of Consciousness Studies*, no. 8 (2001): 83-108.

_____. "Understanding Interpersonal Problems in Autism: Interaction Theory as an Alternative to Theory of Mind." *Philosophy, Psychiatry, and Psychology*, no. 11 (2004): 199-217.

Gallardo, Maria and Miguel. *Maria und ich*. Berlin: Reprodukt, 2010.

Gardner, Daniel: *The Science of Fear. How the Culture of Fear Manipulates Your Brain*. New York: Plume, 2009.

Garland Thomson, Rosemarie: "The politics of staring: visual rhetorics of disability in popular photography." *Disability Studies: Enabling the Humanities*. Sharon Snyder, ed. New York: Modern Language Association, 2002.

_____. "Staring at the Other." *Disability Studies Quarterly*, no. 4 (2005). http://dsq-sds.org/article/view/610/787

Gillberg, Christopher and Mary Coleman. *The Biology of the Autistic Syndrome*. 2nd edition. London: Mac Keith Press, 1992.

_____, et al. "Autism and Asperger syndrome in seven-year-old children – a total population study." *Journal of Autism and Developmental Disorders*, no. 29 (1999): 327-331.

Glasberg, Beth. *Functional Behavior Assessment for People with Autism. Making Sense of Seemingly Senseless Behavior*. Bethesda: Woodbine House, 2006.

Goffman, Erving. *Stigma: Notes on the Management of Spoiled Identity*. London: Penguin, 1963.

Goldstein, Jacob and Sarah Rubenstein: "NYU Bows to Critics and Pulls Ransom-Note Ads." *Wall Street Journal Health Blog*, December 19, 2007.

Grandin, Temple. *Thinking in Pictures and Other Reports From My Life With Autism*. New York: Vintage Books, 1996.

_____. *Animals in Translation: Using the Mysteries of Autism to Decode Animal Behavior*. New York: Scribner, 2005.

Greenspan, Stanley and Serena Wieder. *The Child with Special Needs. Encouraging Intellectual and Emotional Growth*. Cambridge, MA: Perseus, 1998.

_____. *Engaging Autism: Helping Children Relate, Communicate and Think With the DIR Floortime Approach*. New York: Da Capo, 2006.

Grinker, Roy Richard. *Unstrange Minds. Remapping the World of Autism*. New York: Basic Books, 2007.

Häußler, Anne. *Der TEACCH Ansatz zur Förderung von Menschen mit Autismus*. Dortmund: Verlag Modernes Lernen, 2008.

Hacking, Ian. "How we have been learning to talk about autism." *Metaphilosophy*, no. 40 (2009): 499-516.

Haddon, Mark. *The Curious Incident of the Dog in the Nighttime*. New York: Vintage Books, 2004.

Hannaford, Alex. "Andrew Wakefield: Autism Inc." *The Guardian*, April 6, 2013.

Haraway, Donna. "The Promises of Monsters: A Regenerative Politics for Inappropriate/d Others." *Cultural Studies*. Lawrence Grossberg, Cary Nelson, Paula A. Treichler, eds. New York: Routledge (1992): 295-337.

_____. *Modest_Witness@Second_Millennium. FemaleMan_Meets_OncoMouse. Feminism and Technoscience*. New York and London: Routledge, 1997.

Hartmann, Hellmut. *Erweiterte Aufmerksamkeits-Interaktions-Therapie. Kleines Lehrbuch der modernen Autismus-Therapie mit dialogischem Schwerpunkt*. Tübingen: dgvt, 2011.

Hobbes, Thomas. *Leviathan* [1651]. http://www.gutenberg.org/files/3207/3207-h/3207-h.htm

Hobson, Peter, et al. *Foundations for Self-Awareness: An Exploration Through Autism*, Boston & Oxford: Wiley-Blackwell, 2006.

Hofmannsthal, Hugo von. *Der Brief des Lord Chandos: Schriften zur Literatur, Kunst und Geschichte*. Stuttgart: Reclam, 2000.

_____. *Augenblicke in Griechenland*. Frankfurt a.M.: Insel, 2001.

Honnefelder, Ludger and Dieter Sturma, eds. *Jahrbuch für Wissenschaft und Ethik*, no. 13. Berlin: De Gruyter, 2008.

Institut für Schulqualität in Berlin und Brandenburg. *Bildung in Berlin und Brandenburg 2008. Ein indikatorengestützter Bericht zur Bildung im Lebenslauf*. Im Auftrag der Senatsverwaltung für Bildung, Wissenschaft und Forschung Berlin und des Ministeriums für Bildung, Jugend und Sport Brandenburg, 2008.

Isaacson, Rupert. *The Horse Boy*. London: Little, Brown & Company, 2009.

Iversen, Portia. *Strange Son. Two M others, Two Sons, and the Quest to Unlock the Hidden World of Autism*. New York: Riverhead Books, 2006.

Job, Nina: "Mord an Katrin Michalk. Psychogramm: So tickt der mutmaßliche Sendling-Mörder." *Abendzeitung München*, January 26, 2013. http://www.abendzeitung-muenchen.de/inhalt.mord-an-katrin-michalk-psychogramm-so-tickt-der-mutmassliche-sendling-moerder.4e169bd0-c0c5-4a8f-98b5-b12eef016755.html

Jonas, Hans. *Das Prinzip Verantwortung. Versuch einer Ethik für die technologische Zivilisation*. Frankfurt a.M.: Suhrkamp, 2003.

Just, Marcel Adam and Timothy Keller. "Is 'underconnectivity' in autism specific to frontal cortex?" *Simons Foundation Autism Research Initiative*, March 22, 2013. http://sfari.org/news-and-opinion/specials/2013/connectivity/is-underconnectivity-in-autism-specific-to-frontal-cortex

Kaika Maria. "Autistic architecture: the fall of the icon and the rise of the serial object of architecture." *Environment and Planning*, no. 29 (2011): 968 – 992.

Kalberg, Stephen, ed. *Max Weber: Readings and Commentary on Modernity*. Oxford: Blackwell, 2005.

Kaluza, Martin. *Der Kitt der Gemeinschaft. Über die Funktion der Gerechtigkeit.* Paderborn: mentis, 2008.

Kanner, Leo. "Autistic Disturbances of Affective Contact." *The Nervous Child,* no. 3 (1943): 217-250.

Kamp-Becker, Inge. "Von der autistischen Psychopathie zum Asperger-Syndrom." *Autismus im Wandel - Übergänge sind Herausforderungen. Tagungsbericht,* Hamburg (2006): Autismus Deutschland, 220- 227.

Kaufman, Joanne: "Ransom-Note Ads About Children's Health Are Canceled." *New York Times,* December 12, 2007.

Kaufman, Liane, et al. "The genetic basis of non-syndromic intellectual disability: a review." *Journal of Neurodevelopmental Disorders,* no. 2 (2010): 182-209.

Kemper, Thomas and Margaret Bauman: "Neuropathology of Infantile Autism." *Journal of Neuropathology and Experimental Neurology,* no. 7 (1998): 645-656.

Kennedy, Robert Jr. "Deadly Immunity." *Rolling Stone,* no. 977/978 (2005): 57-66.

Kehrer, Hans. *Geistige Behinderung und Autismus.* Stuttgart: Trias, 1995.

Keulen, Konstantin and Kornelius. *Zu niemandem ein Wort.* München: Piper, 2003.

Kirby, David. *Evidence of Harm: Mercury in Vaccines and the Autism Epidemic. A Medical Controversy.* New York: St. Martin's, 2005.

Klee, Ernst. *'Euthanasie' im NS-Staat. Die Vernichtung unwerten Lebens.* Frankfurt a.M.: Fischer, 2009.

Kleinhubbert, Guido. "Depressive Stimmung." *Der Spiegel,* August 22, 2011.

Klin, Ami, et al. "Brief Report: Interrater reliability of clinical diagnosis and DSM-IV criteria for autistic disorder: Results of the DSM-IV autism field trial." *Journal of Autism and Developmental Disorders*, no. 30 (2000): 163-167.

Klicpera, Christian and Paul Innerhofer. *Die Welt des frühkindlichen Autismus.* München: Ernst Reinhardt, 1999.

Kuklys, Wiebke. *Amartya Sen's Capability Approach. Insights and Empirical Applications.* Berlin and Heidelberg: Springer, 2005.

Kusch, Michael and Franz Petermann. *Entwicklung autistischer Störungen.* 3rd and revised edition. Göttingen: Hogrefe, 2001.

Lainhart, Janet, et al. "Head Circumference and Height in Autism: A Study by the Collaborative Program of Excellence in Autism." *American Journal of Medical Genetics,* no. 140A (2006): 2257–2274.

Larsson, Stieg. *The Girl with the Dragon Tattoo.* New York: Vintage, 2009.

Leimbach, Marty. *Daniel Isn't Talking.* London: Fourth Estate, 2006.

Leitch, Kevin. "Indefensible and Unprotested." *Left Brain, Right Brain. Autism News, Science, and Opinion since 2003.* June 26, 2006. http://leftbrainrightbrain.co.uk/2006/06/26/indefensible-and-unprotested/

Lelord, Gilbert and Aribert Rothenberger. *Dem Autismus auf der Spur.* Göttingen: Vandenhoek & Ruprecht, 2000.

Lempp, Reinhart. *Vom Verlust der Fähigkeit, sich selbst zu betrachten.* Bern: Verlag Hans Huber, 1992.

_____. *Die autistische Gesellschaft. Geht die Verantwortlichkeit für andere verloren?* München: Kösel, 1996.

Leppik, Ilo. *Contemporary Diagnosis and Management of the Patient with Epilepsy.* Newton, PA: Handbooks in Healthcare, 2001.

Lerone Schultz, Oliver: "McLuhan, Pasteur des Medienzeitalters. Kausalität als Ansteckung." *Ansteckung – zur Körperlichkeit eines ästhetischen Prinzips*. Mirjam Schaub and Nicole Suthor, eds. München: Wilhelm Fink (2004): 331-350.

Lim, Louisa. "Stem-Cell Therapy in China Draws Foreign Patients." *National Public Radio Morning Edition*, March 18, 2008.
http://www.npr.org/templates/story/story.php?storyId=88123868#88432812

Lin, Jacques. *Das Leben mit dem Floss in der Gesellschaft autistischer Kinder*. Ostheim/Rhön: Peter Engstler, 2004.

Link, Jürgen. *Versuch über den Normalismus. Wie Normalität produziert wird*. Göttingen: Vandenhoek & Ruprecht, 2006.

Lorentzen, Amy. "Clinton would boost autism funding." *Washington Post*, November 25, 2007.

Lorenz, Konrad. *Das sogenannte Böse. Zur Naturgeschichte der Aggression*. 22nd edition. München: dtv, 2000.

Lovaas, Ivar. "Behavioral treatment and normal educational and intellectual functioning in young autistic children." *Journal of Consulting and Clinical Psychology*, no. 55 (1987): 3-9.

Arno Luik: "Ich sehe seinem Entschwinden zu." *Stern*, December 15, 2008.
http://www.stern.de/lifestyle/leute/inge-jens-ich-sehe-seinem-entschwinden-zu-616970.html

McLuhan, Marshall. *Die magischen Kanäle – Understanding Media*. Düsseldorf and Vienna: Econ, 1994.

Mecky Zaragoza, Gabrijela. *Meine andere Welt*. Göttingen: Vandenhoek & Ruprecht, 2012.

Mesibov, Gary, Victoria Shea and Eric Schopler. *The TEACCH Approach to Autism Spectrum Disorders. Issues in Clinical Child Psychology*. New York: Springer Science and Business Media, 2004.

Metzinger, Thomas. *The Ego Tunnel. The Science of the Mind and the Myth of the Self.* New York: Basic Books, 2010. (German: *Der Ego-Tunnel: Eine neue Philosophie des Selbst: Von der Hirnforschung zur Bewusstseinsethik.* Berlin: Berlin Verlag, 2010.)

Miller, Nancy. *Nobody's Perfect. Living and Growing with Children Who Have Special Needs.* Baltimore: Paul H. Brookes Publishing, 1997.

Mnookin, Seth. *The Panic Virus. A True Story of Medicine, Science, and Fear.* New York: Simon & Schuster, 2011.

Moncrieff, Joanna. "Psychiatric diagnosis as a political device." *Social Theory and Health*, no. 4 (2010): 370-382.

Moore, Charlotte. *George and Sam.* London: Penguin, 2005.

_____. "Thoughts About the Autism Label: A Parental View." *Journal of Philosophy of Education*, special issue no. 3&4 (2008): 493-498. http://onlinelibrary.wiley.com/doi/10.1111/j.1467-9752.2008.00652.x/full

Morgan, Vera, et al. "A whole-of-population study of the prevalence and patterns of criminal offending in people with schizophrenia and other mental illness." *Psychological Medicine*, no. 13 (2012): 1-12.

Morris, Joan and Anna Springett: *The National Down Syndrome Cytogenetic Register for England and Wales 2011 Annual Report.* London: Wolfson Institute of Preventive Medicine, February 2013. http://www.wolfson.qmul.ac.uk/ndscr/reports/NDSCRreport11.pdf

Motzkau, Martin. "Untapped Talent: Autistic Workers a Worthwhile Challenge for SAP." *Der Spiegel*, May 22, 2013.

Murray, Dinah et al. "Attention, monotropism and the diagnostic criteria for autism." *Autism*, National Autistic Society, May 2005. http://www.autismandcomputing.org.uk/139.pdf

Murray, Stuart. *Representing Autism: Culture, Narrative, Fascination.* Liverpool: Liverpool University Press, 2008.

Nadeson, Majia Holmer. *Constructing Autism. Unravelling the 'Truth' and Understanding the Social.* New York: Routledge, 2005.

Nature. *Special Issue Neuroscience: The Autism Enigma.* Vol. 479, no. 7371. Macmillan Publishers, November 3, 2011.

Nazeer, Kamran. *Send in the Idiots. Stories from the Other Side of Autism.* New York: Bloomsbury, 2007.

Ne'eman, Ari. "An Urgent Call to Action: Tell NYU Child Study Center to Abandon Stereotypes Against People With Disabilities." *Autistic Self-Advocacy Network*, December 8, 2007. http://autisticadvocacy.org/2007/12/tell-nyu-child-study-center-to-abandon-stereotypes/

Neumärker, Klaus-Jürgen. *...der Wirklichkeit abgewandt. Eine Wissenschafts- und Kulturgeschichte des Autismus.* Berlin: Weidler, 2010.

Nussbaum, Martha. "Human Functioning and Social Justice: In Defense of Aristotelian Essentialism." *Political Theory*, no. 20 (1992): 202-246.

_____. *Frontiers of Justice. Disability, Nationality, Species membership.* Cambridge, MA: Harvard University Publishing, 2006.

O'Neill, Jasmine Lee. *Through the Eyes of Aliens: A Book About Autistic People.* Philadelphia: Jessica Kingsley Publishers, 1998.

Offit, Paul. *Autism's False Prophets: Bad Science, Risky Medicine, and the Search for a Cure.* New York: Columbia University Press, 2010.

_____. *Deadly Choices: How the Anti-Vaccine Movement Threatens Us All.* New York: Basic Books, 2010.

Onwuteaka-Philipsen, Bregje, et al. "Euthanasia and other end-of-life decisions in the Netherlands in 1990, 1995 and 2001." *Lancet*, no. 362 (2003): 395-399.

_____. "Trends in end-of-life practices before and after the enactment of the euthanasia law in the Netherlands from 1990 to 2010: a repeated cross-sectional survey." http://press.thelancet.com/netherlands_euthanasia.pdf Published Online July 11, 2012 at: http://dx.doi.org/10.1016/S0140-6736(12)61034-4

Orac. "Stem cell quackery for autism, revisited." *Respectful Insolence*, December 16, 2010. http://scienceblogs.com/insolence/2010/12/16/stem-cell-quackery-for-autism-revisited/

Osteen, Mark. *Autism and Representation*. New York: Routledge, 2008.

_____. *One of Us. A Family's Life with Autism*. Columbia, MI: University of Missouri Press, 2010.

Parish, Robert & friends. *Embracing Autism. Connecting and Communicating with Children in the Autism Spectrum*. San Francisco: Jossey-Bass 2008.

Payne, Gaynell. "Communication Shutdown Day is answered with Autistics Speaking Day." *Examiner*, October 23, 2010. http://www.examiner.com/article/communication-shutdown-day-is-answered-with-autistics-speaking-day

Pinchevski, Amit. "Bartleby's Autism. Wandering along Incommunicability." *Cultural Critique*, no. 78 (2011): 27-59. Online access provided by the Hebrew University of Jerusalem on March 8, 2011 with *Project Muse. Today's Research. Tomorrow's Inspiration* at http://muse.jhu.edu.

Pinker, Steven. *The Blank Slate: The Modern Denial of Human Nature*. New York: Penguin, 2003.

Piven, Joseph, et al. "An MRI study of brain size in autism." *The American Journal of Psychiatry*, no. 152 (1995): 1145-1149.

Poustka, Fritz, et al. *Autistische Störungen*. 2nd revised edition. Göttingen: Hogrefe, 2008.

Prince, Dawn Eddings. "An Exceptional Path: An Ethnographic Narrative Reflecting on Autistic Parenthood from Evolutionary, Cultural, and Spiritual Perspectives." *Ethos. Journal of the Society for Psychological Anthropology*, no. 1 (2010), 56-68.

Rawls, John. *Justice as Fairness: A Restatement.* Cambridge, MA: Harvard University Press, 2001.

Remschmidt, Helmut and Inge Kamp-Becker. "Neuropsychologie autistischer Störungen." *Fortschritte in der Neurologischen Psychiatrie*, no. 73 (2005): 654-663.

_____. *Asperger-Syndrom.* Heidelberg: Springer Medizin Verlag, 2006.

Rizolatti, Giacomo and Corrado Sinigaglia. *Empathie und Spiegelneurone. Die biologische Basis des Mitgefühls.* Frankfurt a.M.: Suhrkamp, 2008.

Rödler, Peter. "Krise ist immer auch Bewegung – Autismus im Brennpunkt." Lecture in Osnabrück, Germany on November 20, 2004. http://userpages.uni-koblenz.de/~proedler/res/ktpub.pdf

Röteln, die. *Das Leben lebt nicht: Postmoderne Subjektivität und der Drang zur Biopolitik.* Berlin: Verbrecher Verlag, 2006.

Rohrbach, Günter. "Das Schmollen der Autisten." *Der Spiegel*, January 22, 2007.

Rutter, Michael and Susan Folstein. "Infantile Autism: A Genetic Study of 21 Twin Pairs." *Journal of Child Psychology and Psychiatry*, no. 4 (1977): 297-321.

_____. "Incidence of Autism Spectrum Disorder." *Acta Paediatrica*, no. 1 (2005): 2-15.

_____. *Genes and Behavior: Nature-Nurture Interplay Explained.* Oxford: Blackwell, 2006.

Sagan, Carl. *Demon-Haunted World: Science as a Candle in the Dark.* New York: Ballantine Books, 1996.

Schäfer, Susanne. *Sterne, Äpfel und rundes Glas. Mein Leben mit Autismus.* Stuttgart: Verlag Freies Geistesleben, 1996.

_____. "Mein Leben mit Autismus." *Mit Autismus leben – Kommunikation und Kooperation. Tagungsbericht.* Hamburg: Bundesverband Hilfe für das autistische Kind (1998): 45-54.

Schaller-Fornoff, Branka. "Mehr Kampf, mehr Frust, mehr Intensität." *Theater Heute,* January 2012.

Schaub, Mirja and Nicola Suthor. *Ansteckung. Zur Körperlichkeit eines ästhetischen Prinzips.* München: Wilhelm Fink, 2005.

Schirmer, Brita. "Autismus – Von der Außen- zur Innenperspektive." *Behinderte in Familie, Schule und Gesellschaft,* no. 3 (2003) Published also at: http://www.dr-brita-schirmer.de/pdf/artikel112.pdf

_____. *Elternleitfaden Autismus.* Stuttgart: Trias, 2006.

_____. *Psychotherapie und Autismus.* Tübingen: dgvt, 2006.

Scho, Petra. *Herausforderung Autismus: Authentische Einblicke in die 'andere Welt'.* Potsdam: Becker, 2008.

Schor, Bruno and Alfons Schweiggert. *Autismus, ein häufig verkanntes Problem.* Donauwörth: Auer, 1999.

Schreibman, Laura. *The Science and Fiction of Autism.* Cambridge: Harvard University Press, 2005.

Schuster, Nicole. *Ein guter Tag ist ein Tag mit Wirsing.* Berlin: Weidler, 2007.

Sellin, Birger. *ich will kein inmich mehr sein. botschaften aus einem autistischen kerker.* Köln: Kiepenheuer & Witsch, 1995.

_____. *ich deserteur einer artigen autistenrasse. neue botschaften an das volk der oberwelt.* Köln: Kiepenheuer & Witsch, 1997.

Senator, Susan. *Making Peace with Autism.* Boston & London: Trumpeter, 2006.

Sereny, Gitta. *Into the Darkness: From Mercy Killing to Mass Murder*. London: André Deutsch, 1974.

Showalter, Elaine. *Hystories: Hysterical Epidemics and Modern Media*. New York: Columbia University Press, 1998.

Shulman, Robin: "Child Study Center Cancels Autism Ads." *Washington Post*, December 12, 2007.

Silberman, Steve. "The Geek Syndrome." *Wired*, December 12, 2001.

Simmel, Georg. "Die Großstädte und das Geistesleben." *Vorträge und Aufsätze zur Städteausstellung. Jahrbuch der Gehe-Stiftung Dresden,* no. 9 (1903): 185-206. http://gutenberg.spiegel.de/buch/6598/1

Sinclair, Jim. "Don't mourn for us." *Our Voice*, no. 3 (1993). http://www.autreat.com/dont_mourn.html

———. "What does being different mean?" March 9, 2009. http://www.cjob.com/Blog/StationShared/Blog/OnTheEdge/blogentry.aspx?BlogEntryID=10024815

Singer, Judy. *The Birth of Community Amongst People on the Autistic Spectrum: A personal exploration of a New Social Movement based on Neurological Diversity*. Sydney: Faculty of Humanities and Social Science at the University of Technology, 1998.

———. "Why can't you be normal for once in your life?" *Disability Discourse*. Open University Press, February 1, 1999.

Smith, Zadie. "Generation Why?" *New York Review of Books*, November 25, 2010. http://www.nybooks.com/articles/archives/2010/nov/25/generation-why/

Solomon, Andrew. *Far from the Tree. Parents, Children, and the Search for Identity*. New York: Scribner, 2012.

Sontag, Susan. *Illness as Metaphor*. New York: Farrar, Straus and Giroux, 1978.

Spiewak, Martin. "Die Not ist riesengroß." *Die Zeit*, November 5, 2010.

Spork, Peter. *Der zweite Code: Epigenetik – oder Wie wir unser Erbgut steuern können*. Reinbek & Berlin: Rowohlt, 2009.

Stacey, Patricia. *The Boy Who Loved Windows. Opening the Heart and the Mind of a Child Threatened with Autism*. Cambridge: Da Capo Press, 2003.

Stanton, Mike. "Kerry charged over Tariq's death." *Action for Autism. Supporting Autistic People*. February 5, 2007. http://mikestanton.wordpress.com/tag/abu-bakar-tariq-nadama/

Stiegler, Bernard. *Die Logik der Sorge. Verlust der Aufklärung durch Technik und Medien*. Frankfurt a.M.: Suhrkamp, 2008.

Tammet, Daniel. *Born on a Blue Day. Inside the Extraordinary Mind of an Autistic Savant*. New York: Free Press Publishing, 2007.

Thomas, John. "Paranoia Strikes Deep: MMR Vaccine and Autism." *Psychiatric Times*, no.3 (2010). http://www.psychiatrictimes.com/autistic-disorder/content/article/10168/1531916

Thompson, Damian. *Counterknowledge: How We Surrendered to Conspiracy Theories, Quack Medicine, Bogus Science and Fake History*. London: Norton & Company, 2008.

Trehin, Gilles. *Urville*. London: Jessica Kingsley Publishers, 2006.

Van Der Maas, Paul, et al. "Euthanasia and other medical decisions concerning the end of life." *Lancet*, no. 338 (1991): 669-674. http://www.ncbi.nlm.nih.gov/pubmed/1715962?dopt=Abstract

Verhagen, Eduard, et al.: "The Groningen Protocol – Euthanasia in Severely ill Newborns." *The New England Journal of Medicine*, no. 359 (2005): 995-962.

Volkmar, Fred, et al. *Handbook of Autism and Pervasive Developmental Disorders*. 3rd edition. Hoboken, NJ: John Wiley and Sons, 2005.

Wallace, Benjamin. "Are You On It?" *New York Magazine*, October 28, 2012.

Watters, Ethan. *Crazy Like Us – The Globalization of the American Psyche*. New York: Free Press, 2010.

Waytz, Adam and Nicholas Epley. "Social Connection Enables Dehumanization." *Journal of Experimental Social Psychology*, no. 48 (2012): 70–76.

Wellenius, Kevin. *A Life Pretty Full of Love*. Photo Essay, 2010. http://www.kevinwellenius.com/foster_mm/index.html

Westfahl, Gary. "Homo Aspergerus: Evolution Stumbles Forward." *Locus Online*, March 6, 2006. http://locusmag.com/2006/Features/Westfahl_HomoAspergerus.html

Williams, Donna. *Nobody Nowhere. The Extraordinary Biography of an Autistic*. New York: Perennial, 1994.

Williams, Juliet: "Minister charged in death of autistic boy at church healing." *Associated Press*, August 26, 2003. http://www.boston.com/news/daily/26/church_death.htm

Wing, Lorna. *The Autistic Spectrum: A Guide for Parents and Professionals*. London: Constable, 1996.

_____, and David Potter. "The Epidemiology of Autistic Spectrum Disorders: Is the Prevalence Rising?" *Mental Retardation and Developmental Disabilities Research Reviews*, no. 3 (2002): 151-161.

Wunderlich, Christof. *Nimm mich an, so wie ich bin. Menschen mit geistiger Behinderung akzeptieren*. Holzgerlingen: Hänssler, 1999.

Zöller, Dietmar. *Wenn ich mit Euch reden könnte... Ein autistischer Junge beschreibt sein Leben*. München: dtv, 1992.

_____. *Ich gebe nicht auf. Aufzeichnungen und Briefe eines autistischen jungen Mannes, der versucht, sich die Welt zu öffnen*. München: dtv, 1995.

_____. *Autismus und Körpersprache. Störungen der Signalverarbeitung zwischen Kopf und Körper.* Berlin: Weidler, 2001.

Zwaigenbaum, Lonnie. "A Qualitative Investigation of Changes in the Belief Systems of Families with Autism or Down Syndrome." *Child: Care, Health and Development,* no. 32 (2006): 353-369.

FILMS

1969: Change of Habit | Run Wild Run Free

1971: Brother Carl | A Day in the Life of Joe Egg

1974: Silence

1977: A Circle of Children | Cube

1978: Lovey: A Circle of Children II

1979: Being There | Son-Rise: A Miracle of Love

1980: Touched by Love

1981: The Pit

1983: With Eyes Wide Open

1986: The Boy Who Could Fly | Child's Cry

1988: Rain Man | Summer

1989: Real Rainman | The Wizard

1990: Backstreet Dreams

1991: Little Man Tate

1993: AuPair | Family Pictures | House of Cards | What's Eating Gilbert Grape?

1994: Cries from the Heart | David's Mother | Forrest Gump | The Innocent | Nell | Relative Fear | Silent Fall | Touch of Truth | When the Bough Breaks

1995: Criminal | Silence of Adultery

1996: The Boys Next Door | George | Under the Piano

1997: Journey of the Heart | Mimic

1998: Down in the Delta | Little Voice | Mercury Rising | Spoonface
Steinberg

1998: Nightworld: Lost Souls | Perfect Prey | When the Bough Breaks II

1999: Molly | The Other Sister

2000: Bless the Child

2001: A Beautiful Mind | I am Sam

2002: Punch-Drunk Love

2003: Milwaukee, Minnesota

2004: Autism is a World | Miracle Run

2005: The Autism Puzzle | The Hope and Heartache of Autism | Marathon

2006: Autism Every Day | Normal People Scare Me | Snow Cake

2007: Autism: the Musical | Beautiful Son | Ben X | Her Name is Sabine |
Music Within| Mozart and the Whale

2008: The Black Balloon | Chocolate | Wrong Planet

2009: Adam | Dancing Trees | The Horse Boy | Mary and Max | Messages
of Hope from the Autistic Spectrum | One in a Million | Suzie

2010: Autisten | Burning Bright | Dad's in Heaven with Nixon | Loving
Lampposts | My name is Khan | Simple Simon | The Social Network |
Temple Grandin

2011: Fly Away| The Great Fight | Son of Stars | The Wall | Wretches &
Jabberers

2012: Anton's Right Here | Barfi! | Best Kept Secret | Louis Theroux:
Extreme Love – Autism | Shameful

About the author:

Monika Scheele Knight, born in 1972 in Oldenburg. Studied in Germany, France, and the U.S. and graduated from the Free University of Berlin with a master's degree in Comparative Literature. Works as a freelance translator, travel director, and patient representative in the Federal Joint Committee, Germany's highest political body for health care benefits. Lives with Scott and John in Berlin, Germany.

www.ingramcontent.com/pod-product-compliance
Lightning Source LLC
Chambersburg PA
CBHW051821040426
42447CB00006B/307